Venice
Against the Sea ~

ALSO BY JOHN KEAHEY

A Sweet and Glorious Land:
Revisiting the Ionian Sea

THOMAS DUNNE BOOKS

ST. MARTIN'S PRESS ✠ NEW YORK

JOHN KEAHEY

Venice
Against the Sea

A CITY BESIEGED

THOMAS DUNNE BOOKS.
An imprint of St. Martin's Press.

www.stmartins.com

Design by Kathryn Parise

LIBRARY OF CONGRESS CATALOGING-IN-PUBLICATION DATA
Keahey, John.
    Venice against the sea : a city besieged / John Keahey.—1. ed.
        p. cm.
    Includes bibliographical references and index.
    ISBN 0-312-26594-8
    1. Venice (Italy)—Threat of destruction. 2. Water levels—Italy—Venice, Lagoon of.
3. City planning—Italy—Venice. 4. Cultural property—Protection—Italy—Venice.
5. Flood control—Italy—Venice. I. Title.
DG672.5 .K43 2002
945'.31—dc21   2001051284

First Edition: March 2002

10 9 8 7 6 5 4 3 2 1

For Todd, Brad, and Jennifer

CONTENTS ~

CHRONOLOGY ~

1,000,000 YEARS B.P. (BEFORE PRESENT)—
The Adriatic had spread north and west, creating a huge bay across northern Italy, reaching nearly as far as present-day Turin. Eventually, over the millennia, that bay, where the Po Valley now lies, and the northern end of the Adriatic filled in with terra firma as far south as the site of modern Ancona, across to where Split, in Croatia, now sits.

21,000 YEARS B.P.—The waters of the Adriatic were once again reclaiming this land, dividing the Balkans from eastern Italy.

6,000–3,000 YEARS B.P.—The Venetian lagoon was created as the waters of the Adriatic moved northward following the end of the last ice age.

C.E.402—Alaric the Visigoth pillages Aquileia and the regions of Istria at the northern end of the Balkans, and Venetia in northeastern Italy. Some mainlanders begin their flight into the lagoons along the northeastern shores of modern Italy. Those lagoons were then home to only a handful of fishermen and salt collectors. The besieged mainlanders would return to their ravaged cities once the barbarians had left.

421—Friday, March 25, at twelve noon: the traditional founding of Venice. At this time the lagoons were still sparsely settled, and the date was probably created later for the convenience of Venetians eager to claim the earliest possible roots for their republic.

452—Attila the Hun begins his merciless scourging of northern Italy. The lagoons again become the sanctuary for mainlanders.

466—Representatives from the growing island communities within the various lagoons ringing northeastern Italy meet at Grado, an island in a lagoon south of Aquileia, some sixty miles north of where Venice was established. According to Norwich, this meeting was "the beginning of the slow constitutional process from which the Most Serene Republic [Venice] was ultimately to evolve."

568—The Germanic Lombards invade Italy.

568–639—As Lombard power spreads over northern Italy for seven decades, the people of Aquileia retreat to Grado, those of Concordia go to Carole, and those of Padua go to Malamocco, a barrier island between the Adriatic and the Venetian lagoon that centuries later is joined with other islands to create the Lido.

639—The Lombards capture Oderzo, the last imperial Byzantine foothold in mainland Italy. The struggling government of the once-great province of Venetia now moves to Heraclea. The Lombards eventually recognize a boundary line near Heraclea as the beginning of Venetian territory—still a province of Byzantium. Meanwhile, refugees from nearby Altinum (today the tiny village of Altino) escape to the island of Torcello.

726—Orso Ipato, the first doge, the lagoon communities' chief magistrate, elected.

742—The second doge, Teodato Ipato, Orso's son, moves his seat of government from imperial Heraclea to Malamocco.

809—Pépin, Frankish king of Italy and son of Holy Roman Emperor Charlemagne, attacks and captures Chioggia and Pellestrina, and assaults Malamocco from the sea, driving the residents and their government deeper into the lagoon, where historic Venice was then built. Pépin's oceangoing ships cannot unlock the mysteries of the Venetian channels, and the fleet departs.

828(or thereabouts)—Saint Mark's body is seized in Alexandria by Venetian merchants, who carry it to the doge's home next to the square that will later bear the saint's name.

1202—The Fourth Crusade, during which the doge enlists the Crusaders to subdue ports along the Dalmatian coast and to conquer Constantinople. This is the beginning of Venice's commercial supremacy in the eastern Mediterranean.

1373—Jews arrive in Venice and, by 1516, are quartered in the foundry area of the city.

1380—The Genoese from western Italy, the last of the serious early threats to Venetian supremacy, are defeated at Chioggia. The Venetians, now masters of the Adriatic, begin to look inland, eventually spreading their influence across northern Italy almost as far as Milan.

1403–5—The Venetian Republic assumes control of Bassano, Belluno, Padua, and Verona.

1453—The Turks take Constantinople. This is the beginning of the long, drawn-out end of the Venetian Republic's supremacy in the eastern Mediterranean.

1454—Venice acquires Treviso, Friuli, Bergamo, and Ravenna.

1498—The Portuguese seaman Vasco da Gama sails around the tip of Africa, opening sea routes from the West to the East.

1744—Construction of the *murazzi*, or defensive walls built along the barrier islands that protect the lagoon from the Adriatic, begins—a tasks that takes thirty-eight years to complete.

1797—Napoleon, a twenty-eight-year-old upstart just beginning his quest to conquer all of Europe, takes Venice, declaring *"Io sarò un Attila per lo Stato Veneto* (I will be an Attila for the Venetian state)."

1798—Napoleon gives Venice to Austria to govern in exchange for taking control of Lombardy. The French return to control in 1806, and the Austrians recover the city in 1814.

1846—The Austrians finish building the railroad causeway, forever tying the historic center to the mainland.

1848—The Venetians revolt against the Austrians and, though briefly victorious, eventually lose.

1866—Venice joins the recently unified kingdom of Italy.

About 1925—Industrial pumping of groundwater from beneath Venice begins on a major scale.

1931—The road causeway is built, parallel to the rail lines.

November 3–4, 1966—A disastrous storm-driven sea, on top of a high tide, causes the water in the Venetian lagoon to reach an exceptional height of 6.3 feet (1.94 meters) above relative sea level (the position and height of sea relative to land). The entire historic center is flooded for fifteen hours. The city is without electricity or telephone service for a full week. No deaths occur in the city's historic center because of this record high water, but ground-floor homes and businesses are devastated and historic buildings damaged.

1970—Italy's National Research Council, known by its initials as CNR for Consiglio Nazionale delle Ricerche, unveils projects for port mouths. This is the first official mention of building mobile gates. The government also begins a shutdown of industrial pumping of groundwater from beneath Venice, stopping the human-caused sinking of the historic city.

1973—Special Law 171 initiates legislation for Venice, intended to enable the interventions for the safeguarding of the city and its lagoon. The government creates the Consorzio di Credito per le Opere Pubbliche (CREDIOP) to seek an international loan of three hundred billion lire. The loan is made, but no money is ever released.

1974—UNESCO's General Convention urges the Italian state to guarantee the interventions lined up by the special law.

1975—The Public Works Ministry calls for international bids for works to defend the city from *acque alte* (high waters).

1978—A special adjudication panel decides that none of the proposed projects submitted in the international competition is suitable.

1980—The Public Works Ministry appropriates all plans submitted in the international competition and sets up a technical team to develop a project to protect the lagoon from flooding.

1981—The technical team comes up with a plan for a major flood-control project, known as the *Progettone* (big project).

1982—The Venice City Council approves the *Progettone* as long as it is part of a major push to restore hydrogeological and ecological balance to the lagoon.

The Venice Magistrato alle Acque (magistrate of the waters), under the supervision of the Public Works Ministry, draws up agreements for the Consorzio Venezia Nuova (CVN), or New Venice Consortium, to conduct studies, research, and trials and to undertake the construction of a fixed barrier at the Lido port mouth. The courts hold up completion of the agreements.

1984—The agreements between the Magistrate of the Waters and the Consorzio are signed after court objections are overcome. Nine months later the Italian parliament passes Special Law 798, earmarking 2.7 trillion lire to be spent between 1984 and 1992 on interventions to safeguard the lagoon and to raise the infrastructure within the lagoon's urban centers. It also creates an interministerial council, referred to as the *Comitatone* (big committee), made up of appropriate ministers, mayors, the regional president, and other officials.

1986—The Consorzio presents its general program of interventions. Its responsibilities are extended to cover the port mouths at Chioggia and Malamocco as well as the Lido, and the plan is approved.

1988—The Venice City Council seeks tighter controls on the Consorzio monopoly. Meanwhile the Consorzio rolls out its MOSE (Modulo Sperimentale Elettromeccanico, nicknamed Moses), an experimental model for the mobile-gates project. Twenty-two years to the day after the 1966 flood hit the city, the model is placed near the Lido entrance and is used for research.

1990—The Public Works Ministry, in an effort to appease the Port of Venice's opposition to the gates because of their impact on shipping, puts the gates project on hold so that the perimeters of the numerous small islands in the lagoon can be built up and reinforced to repel flooding. Also, the ministry declares that the gates project should be delayed until the lagoon can be environmentally cleaned up.

1991—The Organization for Economic Cooperation and Development (OECD) meeting in Venice appeals to the Italian government to stop political bickering and take immediate action to save Venice.

1992—MOSE, declared a success by the CVN, is removed. Meanwhile, officials begin a debate on building a subway beneath the lagoon—a project that does not go far.

1993—Massimo Cacciari, a lecturer in philosophy at the University of Venice, is elected mayor. He serves until early 2000.

1994—A decree provides for creation of an Agency for Venice, aimed at streamlining interventions for the city and the lagoon—but it is never set up. A Public Works Ministry council authorizes the mobile gates to enter the executive phase, calling for detailed design drawings that would precede actual construction. This never happens. The Venice City Council suggests a more thorough study.

1995—The Italian parliament passes a law that revokes the Consorzio's exclusive license to develop protection works for Venice. The interministerial council, or *Comitatone*, agrees to subject the mobile-gates project to an environmental impact study—in the Italian acronym, VIA, for *Valutazione d'Impatto Ambientale*—at the urging of the administration of the city of Venice. Meanwhile, a punctured pipeline near the lagoon spills oil into the water, and officials call for banning oil tankers and eliminating chemical activities at Porto Marghera.

1996—Some 185 billion lire ($115,625,000) is approved for Venice projects, to be spent over two years. The *Comitatone* meets in Venice and pledges "continuity" in the state's commitment to physically safeguard the city and to bolster its social and economic fabric.

1997—The environmental impact study is delivered to the national government. A panel of international experts is retained by the Consorzio to review the study. It finds that the Consorzio's interventions are sound and justified.

1998—Venice mayor Cacciari conducts his own review of the VIA and organizes debates between his panel of experts and the Consorzio. The *Comitatone* appoints its own experts as well. Government ministers involved with the lagoon and its problems endorse the gates with the exception of the Environment Ministry, which issues its own scathingly negative four-hundred-page report against the study.

1999—The European Parliament, of which Italy is a member, asks the Italian government to quickly make a definitive decision about the mobile gates. Promises to make a decision by the end of the year are not kept.

2000—Cacciari resigns as mayor to run for regional president and reverses his position on the gates, declaring his support. Paolo Costa, a mobile-gates supporter and University of Venice economist, who in the mid-1990s served a stint as Italy's public works minister, is elected mayor. The administrative regional court nullifies for technical reasons the Environment Ministry's December 1998 decree rejecting the Consorzio's VIA. The government must decide whether to appeal or call for a new VIA.

May 2001—Silvio Berlusconi is named prime minister following national elections in which his Center-Right coalition wins a significant majority.

December 6, 2001—Prime Minister Berlusconi's cabinet votes unanimously to proceed with the final design work, known as the Executive Project, for the mobile gates. Veneto Region President Giancarlo Galan predicts the gates will be operating by 2009.

[Venice is] a ghost upon the sands of the sea, so weak—so quiet—so bereft of all but her loveliness, that we might well doubt, as we watched her faint reflection in the mirage of the lagoon, which was the city, and which was the shadow.

I would endeavour to trace the lines of this image before it be for ever lost, and to record, as far as I may, the warning, which seems to me to be uttered by every one of the fast-gaining waves, that beat like passing bells, against the Stones of Venice.

—JOHN RUSKIN, *THE STONES OF VENICE*, 1853

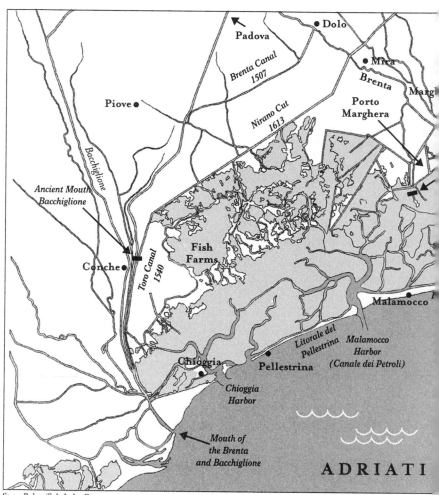

Steve Baker/Salt Lake City

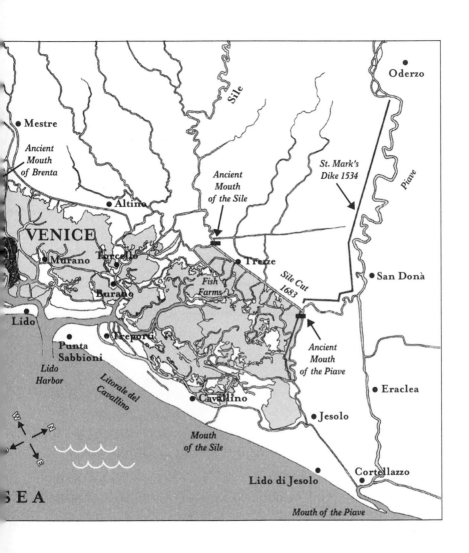

Oderzo

Sile

Mestre

Ancient Mouth of Brenta

Ancient Mouth of the Sile

St. Mark's Dike 1534

Piave

Altino

VENICE

Torcello

Treze

Murano

Burano

Fish Farms

Sile Cut 1683

San Donà

Lido

Treporti

Ancient Mouth of the Piave

Punta Sabbioni

Lido Harbor

Litorale del Cavallino

Eraclea

Cavallino

W N

E

Mouth of the Sile

Jesolo

Lido di Jesolo

Cortellazzo

SEA

Mouth of the Piave

Venice

Against the Sea ~

INTRODUCTION ~

My Venice, like Turner's, had been chiefly
created for us by Byron; but for me there was
also still the pure childish pleasure of seeing
boats float in clear water. The beginning of
everything was in seeing the gondola-beak
come actually inside the door at Danieli's,
when the tide was up, and the water two feet
deep at the foot of the stairs; and then, all
along the canal sides, actual marble walls rising out of the salt sea, with hosts of little
brown crabs on them, and Titians. . . . I
find a sentence in [my] diary of 8th May
[1841] which seems inconsistent with what I
have said of the centres of my life's work:

Thank God I am here; it is the Paradise
of cities.

—JOHN RUSKIN

The sound of thunder, the kind that starts
with a deep growl and then occasionally
snaps like a sheet on a clothesline caught in
sudden wind, came through my open window, so sharp that it rattled the window cas-
ings. The thunder seemed to be coming
from the east, beyond the Lido shoreline a
few hundred meters away from my small,

comfortable hotel room in the Villa Albertina. It was eleven o'clock, and my evening had been spent transcribing notes from audiotape. I was "typed out" and lying back, reading a new biography of Primo Levi, a post–World War II Italian Jewish writer who plunged either accidentally or intentionally down the stairwell of his house on April 11, 1987, decades after surviving the horrors of the Holocaust.

I was reading this book on April 5, 2000, a day after a full moon and at the beginning of what is called a spring tide, or the time when gravitationally pulled tides roll in at their highest. My visit to Venice was well after the end of the high-water season that generally hits the city from October through January—a combination of high tides plus winter storms that push the water even higher against the stones of this ancient city. The weather was warming, and I figured I had missed seeing the high water I had come here to learn about.

Deep into Levi's life as a chemist in fascist Italy, and ignoring the sound of thunder far out to sea, I was startled back to the present by the piercing sound of a siren warning residents of the Venetian lagoon of the approaching *acqua alta*, or high water. I checked the time. It was 11:15 P.M. I checked my tide chart—the kind an interested tourist (and few of them are) can purchase from a newsstand for a few dollars.

One of the great things about Venice and most other cosmopolitan cities is that a lot goes on in the late evening, and public transportation is plentiful through the earliest hours of the next day. I dressed, hurried down the stairs, and trotted a few hundred feet to the Lido bus stop, just in time to see one of the classic Italian orange buses approaching. Minutes later I was at the *vaporetto* stop in the Piazzetta Santa Maria Elisabetta, climbing aboard for the fifteen-minute ride to St. Mark's Square, a few miles west of the Lido.

The *vaporetto* passengers were mostly Venetians on their way to work the midnight shifts in hotels, in the historic center, or for the municipal water authority. Many carried plastic shopping bags with the tops of rubber boots peeking out. Keeping track of tide charts and paying attention to storm warnings has become a way of life for these residents going to work in one of the world's most waterlogged cities.

The scene at the San Marco stop was surreal. The docks—attached by walkways to the *fondamenta*, or pavement, bordering the Basin of St. Mark's—were riding high on the tide, the gangplanks sloping down and awash with water. The lagoon was invading the city inch by inch. Wavelet after wavelet was carrying the water closer and closer to the buildings. I stood in awe as Venetians pushed past to stop in the dock's boarding area long enough to yank their boots out of the bags and pull them on. City crews were working quickly to set out the *passarelle*, or duckboard walkways, that connected to the end of the boat-dock ramps and spread out along the *fondamenta* in both directions. I gingerly moved out on the temporary walkway and headed toward the Ponte della Paglia, the stone bridge on which millions of tourists have stood to snap photographs of the Ponte dei Sospiri—the Bridge of Sighs—that leads from the Doges' Palace to the ducal prisons across a narrow, dark canal.

At the front of the Danieli, a luxury five-star hotel, I stopped to watch an incredible scene: Green-coated porters, barefoot and with their black uniform pants rolled up to their knees, were scrambling to set up a shaky narrow walkway to lead from the main duckboard walkway to the hotel's front lobby. The door was wide open, and lagoon water had flowed inside, creating a giant puddle on the dazzling marble floor tiles between the door and the higher lobby farther back.

Stranded guests, dressed in evening gowns and tuxedos stood there in tight little groups, waiting patiently for their private walkway—barely wide enough for one person—to be set up.

I remembered the quote from nineteenth-century British art and architecture critic John Ruskin, who watched as a "gondola-beak" poked into the Danieli's foyer—right where these finely clad tourists were now waiting—during a particularly high tide more than 150 years ago. Now, in the last year of the twentieth century, I was watching the porters splashing around in water that for centuries had acted as Venice's sewer system. When, at low tide, this water pulled out of the lagoon and back into the Adriatic, it would carry with it about twelve hours' worth of Venice's accumulated waste.

I turned from the scene and walked over the bridge. At the top I heard a loud, tuneless voice singing some indistinguishable song. It was coming from an old, old man, sitting against the wall of the Doges' Palace. He was surrounded by his worldly possessions held flimsily against the water in plastic bags. He perched above the steadily rising tide on a stack of duckboards and aluminum frames. His feet were dangling just inches above the rising water, and tourists were taking his photograph. I had seen this old man here day after day. It was his spot and his life. He lived through every single *acqua alta* incident, since his abode is near the heart of St. Mark's Square a few hundred feet away—the lowest spot in the city and the first to be inundated by any tide that comes in at seventy centimeters above relative sea level (there are one hundred centimeters in a meter; a meter is roughly equal to three feet). These days that includes most of the tides that follow the full moon in each winter month.

I walked onto another series of wooden walkways set up on

their stubby aluminum stands. It was nearly midnight, and the high-tide peak was almost upon us. The walkway was jammed three abreast with possibly a few thousand tourists exclaiming at the surprise of high water—an almost daily event during winter for residents but unheard of among most visitors, who usually spend fewer than two days in this sublime city. The network of *passarelle* presented a clear path around the far edge of the piazzetta that borders the south facade of the Doges' Palace. They were strung past the yawning, bored waiters, who were smoking while leaning against the stone pillars that hold up the loggia of the Gran Caffè Chioggia in the ground-floor retail space below the Libreria Sansoviniana and Museo Archeologico. The waiters had seen all this before. With sardonic expressions, they watched the mostly college-age tourists splashing around in the water, the young people's pants, like the porters' at the Danieli, rolled up to their knees.

The water was full of trash, Styrofoam cups, and torn campaign posters touting candidates in the upcoming municipal elections. Here and there I spotted a pigeon, fluttering helplessly in the water, sure to become exhausted and drown. Soon the tide began to peak, and the water, slowly and almost imperceptibly, slipped back to the sea beyond the Lido. I walked back across the Ponte della Paglia with its most photographed view of the Bridge of Sighs darkly shadowed. I looked down at the old man, his thick winter cap with earflaps pulled down over his head. He had stopped singing and was muttering darkly to himself, still perched on his platform just inches above the retreating water.

Thirty-four years after the disastrous 1966 *acqua granda*—

which means "great flood" (the spelling *granda* reflects the Venetian dialect)—election candidates were still making promises to do something about flooding. The fight against high water had become so meaningless that the phrase *acqua alta* had taken on a derisive connotation. (In fact, in Venice, whenever something is confused or a big mess, someone will refer to it, with a laugh, as *acqua alta*, whether it has anything to do with high water or not.) One politician, the Center-Right mayoral candidate Renato Brunetta, made fun of the Center-Left's promises for Venice with the campaign slogan *A sinistra—Acqua Alta*, The Left—All Screwed Up. Nonetheless the Left, represented by Paolo Costa, won the 2000 election a few weeks after this real-life *acqua alta*.

Venice is in trouble.

The city—where tourists regularly chuckle as they accept rubber boots handed out by hotel concierges and then cross historic squares on elevated boardwalks placed where pigeons in drier moments scrabble for handfuls of corn—is dying, and the world is not ready to let it go. As its residents depart by the hundreds each year—frustrated at the increasing water level, the hordes of tourists, the loss of a sense of community, and the high cost of housing—Venice evolves into a crumbling museum.

Until November 1966 most visitors believed the city would last forever. For more than half a millennium its rulers had controlled "a quarter plus half a quarter" of the vast, disintegrating Western Roman Empire. Unlike Rome, which the republic replaced as the dominating force in the eastern Mediterranean, it did not strive to conquer lands and subjugate people simply for the sake of conquest or to satisfy the ego of a ruler. Instead it sought to control commerce in an ever-growing geographic circle that tied together East and West in a way that armies driven only by the sword had never succeeded in doing. Until the Portuguese, and then the Dutch—and even later the English—broke the Venetian monopoly on trade with the East, the Piazza San Marco really was the center of the world, where the peoples and languages of more than seventy nations could be seen and heard on any given day.

Since then, and particularly after Napoleon ended the republic in 1797—quietly and without a single shot being fired—it has been a dazzling, art-filled haven and architectural wonder for world travelers.

Some early visitors predicted its eventual demise. In fact, long before the city's plight became commonly known, in the late twentieth century, those with their fingers well placed on the city's delicate pulse also had premonitions, and Ruskin was not alone in recognizing that the steady beat of the Adriatic's waves against the stones of Venice would spell its doom. According to the historian Jan Morris, however, in her *World of Venice*, that might be regarded as a fitting end:

[Venice] sprang from the sea fifteen centuries ago, and to round her story off aesthetically, so many a writer and artist has felt, she only needs to sink into the salt again, with a gurgle and a moan. . . . Certainly the disappearance of Venice would give her history a wonderful symmetry of form—born out of the water, and returned at last into the womb. . . . Venice depends for her longevity upon the long line of islands, artificially buttressed, which separate the lagoon from the Adriatic, and keep the sea storms away from her delicate fabrics. She lives like a proud parchment dowager, guarded by the servants at the door.

How much longer can these "servants at the door" protect the city? Sixteen hundred years ago, around the time of Venice's founding, the Adriatic's standard sea level was sixteen feet below what it is today. A century ago, at about the time of Ruskin's death, St. Mark's Square was covered by water at extreme high tide only seven times a year. By 1989 such inundation occurred forty times a year. In 1996 water nearly as high as an average tourist's knee lapped ninety-nine times at piles of sandbags placed to guard the doorways of the Doges' Palace and St. Mark's Basilica.

Stephen Fay and Phillip Knightley, in their 1976 book *The Death of Venice*, put the numbers into perspective:

> In the 100 years before the great floods of 1966, there had been 54 *acque alte* (high waters) in Venice. In the first 50 of [those] 100 years, there were only 7 floods; in the last 35 years of the period there were 48 floods, and no fewer than 30 of these occurred in the final 10 years. Lesser flooding— water nevertheless high enough to cover the pavements—occurred 295 times in the period 1972–74, an increase of 80 per cent over 1962–64. That is the measure of acceleration. Nearly 15 per cent of the population of Venice now lives at— not above, or slightly above, but *at*—water level.

There are those who believe that this increasingly destructive pattern of flooding cannot be allowed to continue. Massive projects expected to cost billions of dollars—controversial since the day they were proposed—await government approval. Whether that approval ever comes, in Italy's ever-changing political environment—and whether mammoth gates to safeguard

Steve Baker/Salt Lake City

the city from the storm-driven tidal surges of the northern Adriatic are built—remains to be seen.

Increasingly high water is not all that batters and besieges the city, however. Venetians, who for centuries lived in a city that became a museum, turned Venice into a "living" museum. But as Venice's rate of crumbling accelerated in the twentieth century, many Venetians found that they could no longer live there.

Fay and Knightley tell us that in 1950 there were 184,447 people living in the historic center: "In each five-year period after that the number fell by approximately 20,000, until, by 1965, it was 123,733. In 1970, the population was only 105,656." In the year 2000, the population hovers around a mere 60,000 residents. The mayor of Venice in late 2000, Paolo Costa, challenges that lower number, saying he believes 70,000 live in the historic city, 100,000 live in the greater lagoon area, and 200,000 in the mainland area that in modern times is considered part of Venice proper.

Many of the city's leaders are no longer residents, if they ever were in the first place. They meet in a city hall in the historic center and then go to their mainland homes at the end of the day.

That is not all. Of the ten million visitors to this city each year, 80 percent are day-trippers who come for the day and leave by evening for cheaper quarters on the mainland. Only 20 percent stay in Venetian hotels, and then for an average of two nights. Once Venice had a high and low season, with some hotels closing down for the winter months. Today there is only a high season, year-round. Venetian hotels are 90 percent full nearly all year.

Rising waters, disintegrating services, and an exodus of its local inhabitants are turning Venice into an uninhabitable museum where only tourists prowl.

The world got an inkling of Venice's problems beginning at ten o'clock in the evening of November 3, 1966. A high tide had been predicted. What was not expected was its ultimate height or its duration. Such tides usually last six hours. Heavy and persistent rainfall over the Adriatic fueled this tide. The same storm drenched central and northern Italy as well, and the Tuscan city of Florence was inundated by the flooding Arno River. The storm tide, pushed by violent sirocco-driven wave motion (sirocco, spelled as in Venetian dialect, is a wind originating in North Africa) along the northwestern Adriatic coast, lasted an astonishing twenty-two hours.

The Venetian lagoon extends thirty-two miles from the Jesolo marshes in the north to just beyond Chioggia at the southern end. This indentation in the northeastern Italian coastline is protected from the Adriatic, as Morris wrote, by long, narrow, sandy islands known as *lidi*. The most famous, familiar to sun-worshiping tourists as the Lido, is the middle of three islands: Pellestrina on the south and Cavallino, which is really an extension of the coast, to the north.

These *lidi* are separated one from another by three narrow channels that open the lagoon to the sea and allow the tide to flow in and out twice a day, a process that "flushes" the Venetian canals and carries the city's accumulated sewage seaward.

In 1966 the seaward beaches of these *lidi* were devastated by the high, surging waves. Three thousand people were evacuated from the villages of San Pietro in Volta and Pellestrina on the island of Pellestrina.

In Venice itself this record storm surge pushed Adriatic tides through Venice's two hundred original channels, which form an urban network on both sides of the backward-S shaped two-mile-long Grand Canal. One hundred percent of the city was inundated. The salty seawater rose above the impermeable Istrian marble bases of the city's buildings and seeped into the fragile brickwork above, now a common occurrence during subsequent flooding, wreaking havoc on the

crumbling material. Centuries ago the builders of those structures never imagined that the sea would rise to such heights.

While subsequent storm surges have not yet equaled that
1966 ferocity, scientists believe it is only a matter of time. In
fact, high water nearly equal to the 1966 episode occurred in
November and December 1996, thirty years nearly to the day of
the monstrous record flood. On November 6, 2000, sirocco-
pushed water hit the city early in the evening, topping off at 1.44
meters, or nearly five feet, catching the city and its residents off
guard and flooding 93 percent of the historic center.

It is obvious to engineers, climatologists, government officials, archaeologists, and some Venetians that, if something
is not done soon, the city faces destruction.

If nothing is done to protect Venice from the irreversible,
global warming–driven rise in the Adriatic, scientists predict
that by the year 2055, many of Venice's walkways, piazzas, and
its buildings' ground floors will be under high water every day.

This, then, is the story of the struggle to save Venice.

The issue is global in scope, because Venice is truly an
international city that has had significant impact on the history
of the world since the Middle Ages. The city grew out of the
mud and muck to dominate the Mediterranean world for centuries and then declined, but in its decline produced some of
the greatest art the world has ever seen and began to show off
the remnants of its once-glorious days to pleasure-seeking
travelers.

Scientists, Italians, and Venetians all disagree on how Venice should be saved, but one thing is certain: It will cost billions of dollars, and few people beyond those who would build
the various proposed structures and benefit financially are sure

the fix will last more than a few decades and blunt the impact of nature's forces on the city.

Eventually, of course, the earth's surface will change and, over geological rather than human time, mountain ranges and deserts, and certainly cities, will come and go as land and sea shift and intermix. But humans who want to try to keep Venice alive for a few more generations are convinced technology will provide a solution.

To understand why Venice is in peril and what can be done to hold back its inevitable reclamation by the sea, it is helpful to know why and how this lagoon was settled. Just how did a city of stone and shimmering domes—a city-state that became known as *La Serenissima*, the Most Serene Republic—rise above low, marshy islands, beginning in the early fifth century C.E., just as the Western world was about to descend into what is generally known as the Dark Ages?

CHAPTER ONE ~

The Beginning

A large fraction of the study area does not exceed an elevation of 2 [meters above mean sea level] and therefore is quite sensitive even to minor modifications of both sea level and coast morphology.

—GIUSEPPE GAMBOLATI ET AL.,
"COASTAL EVOLUTION OF THE UPPER
ADRIATIC SEA . . ."

Who knows when the first prehistoric people, standing on the edge of the Italian mainland and scanning the horizon toward the rising sun, first ventured out into the lagoons that had formed along the coastline of the northwestern Adriatic?

What geologists and archaeologists *can* tell us is that the crescent-shaped lagoon we moderns call Venice—a 255-square-mile combination of land and sea thirty miles long and eight and a half miles wide—was formed perhaps between three thousand and six thousand years ago. This is well in time for crude human habitation, however fleeting, of the reedy, grassy islands created by silt carried from the mainland, down numerous rivers and streams into the coastal waters of the Adriatic. As the fresh river water slowed and then fanned out into the sea, it dropped its cargo onto the lagoon floor that once was dry land. These were not rocky islands formed by volcanic action, but low-lying mudbanks that, with the rise and fall of the sea's tides, were repeatedly submerged and exposed in an ages-old cycle of burial and resurrection. This cycle produced salt and nurtured birds and marine animals coveted by the people who eventually, millennia later, settled along the coastal mainland.

A bird's-eye view of the lagoon's ancient landforms would, of course, differ greatly from the same view of those landforms today. For example, the two long islands—Lido and Pellestrina—that make up the barriers between the lagoon and the Adriatic began as a cluster of nine or more islands separated by natural channels. Through those channels the tides shoved and sucked their way, the currents curling in odd patterns across the shallow mudflats. By the 1700s six of those nine channels were filled in so that the tides, directed through fewer openings, would scour out the channels of the remaining three openings and allow for more easily maintained shipping lanes.

We do know that if humans had not tampered with this lagoon now called Venice—particularly through the Middle Ages, when they diverted many rivers and streams from the lagoon to pour directly into the Adriatic—it would have filled in, become dry land, and eventually become part of mainland Italy. One scientist says dry land would have taken over some five hundred years ago.

This is the same process of sea becoming land that happened in the fifteenth century to another great European port, Bruges, in Belgium. At about the same time, Venetians were diverting their rivers from the lagoon. In Bruges no such massive undertaking was launched to stop the river Zwijn's dumping of silt into the sea inlet that connected the city to the coast. Within a few decades, merchant ships could not reach Bruges' piers, and its domination of North Sea shipping was taken over by Antwerp. Venetians, with a massive series of public works involving tens of thousands of laborers, did not allow that to happen in their lagoon. They created an artificial body of water that bought them centuries of time to ply their trade and live in their safe, watery world.

What geologists and hydrologists have always known—and early Venetians never accepted—is that a lagoon is theoretically a transitional phase in the building up, or breaking down, of things terrestrial. If left undisturbed over a relatively short period of time, a lagoon becomes either land or sea, depending on the direction of each geologic cycle. The artificial restraints early Venetians built into their lagoon have fought this natural cycle until this very day.

The tiny islands, which must have numbered in the high hundreds within those lagoon boundaries, were crisscrossed by streams and cut through by narrow rivers. The waters were never deep. Even today the lagoon's depth averages only around two feet. This is deceptive, especially at high tide when the entire lagoon takes on the appearance of a deep, massive body of water. At extremely low tides the mud layers are exposed, and the visitor can see just how dangerously close the lagoon has come over the centuries to filling up with land.

The layers of silt that now cover the lagoon bottom ranged from ten feet deep in ancient times to fifteen feet deep today. Archaeologists know this because they have discovered that the early lagoon dwellers who sunk their alder poles into the muck to support their houses of wood and later stone, cut those long, flexible poles five feet shorter than they did toward the late eighteenth century.

The deep ancient channels, natural and human made, were the only way people could navigate from place to place, especially at low tide and even with flat-bottom boats that evolved in this specialized environment. Because the routes of those channels were known only to the island dwellers and not to the piratical seafarers of the ancient world, the islands developed into ideal places for those early humans to be out of harm's way as they harvested salt from the sea and captured the abundant marine and bird life.

In the beginning there likely were huts, probably built on wooden stilts sunk by hand into the soft, yielding silt that had collected, layer by layer, on the lagoon bottom. These temporary dwellings were places in which mainlanders could wait out a storm, store their gathered goods, or spend a night or two while on a hunting-gathering expedition. Perhaps there were some residents who spent entire lives in these primitive shelters, but there is no record that anyone ever attempted to establish a city among these islands until near the decline of the Roman period in the fifth century.

Only recently, archaeological work at Isola di San Francesco del Deserto, located northeast of historic Venice, has uncovered evidence of a Roman-era port. Here the Romans received trade goods directly from the Adriatic, when it was more of a clear shot from the sea into the lagoon than it is today. Those goods were then probably ferried to the mainland, perhaps three to four miles to the west.

But major habitation of the lagoon islands themselves, where people took up permanent residence and began to build communities, had to wait until the sixth or seventh centuries C.E. That is when the unabated threat of the Germanic Lombards eventually forced the coastal inhabitants at Altinum, for example, to abandon their mainland city and head due south into the lagoon. There, on a muddy spit of land close to the mainland, they built a city at what we know today as Torcello, site of the oldest lagoon structure still standing, the former cathedral of Santa Maria Assunta. Those frightened and beleaguered Romans dismantled Altinum stone by stone, including most of the paving stones from their Roman roads and city streets, and moved them by boat across the shallow waters to Torcello to create a city in the late 630s that by the twelfth century would support a population of thirty thousand souls.

Torcello was the first-known permanent settlement of the Venetian lagoon and the closest to the mainland. Its citizens were not yet ready to commit to life far out into the lagoon's outer reaches. Eventually Torcello was abandoned because the inevitable buildup of silt dumped by the nearby Sile and other rivers created marshlands that bred mosquitoes and malaria. The people looked farther out into the lagoon toward other islands and moved seaward, away from the dangerous mainland.

Today Torcello is an abandoned, overgrown paradise, with only a church that dates back to the sixth century and a tourist restaurant or two. The city is gone, like Altinum from which it was born, dismantled stone by stone.

But I am getting ahead of my story.

Scientists learned the approximate age of the Venetian lagoon by dating samples of plant fibers found embedded in what used to be the dry land of the original coastline. They have discovered a rock formation, called "beachrock," ten meters below the Adriatic's current surface just east of the Venetian lagoon. According to Professor Giuseppe Gambolati of the University of Padua, this beachrock is a fossil remnant of a 3,900-year-old shoreline that "provides documentary evidence of both the retreat of the beach and the settlement process undergone by the upper Adriatic coast in historical times as well."

It is all part of an ongoing cycle, brief when measured in geological time but staggering for mere humans to contemplate.

To get a better understanding of this process, I visited Professor Gambolati in his office. He is a stocky but fit, exuberant middle-aged man, wearing a well-tailored suit more appropriate for a corporate boardroom than for the small, standard-issue Italian university office. His space is piled high with the usual papers found in such offices, competing for room on his desktop, equipped with only the most essential items: a pen here, a small bowl of paper clips there, the ubiquitous pad of colorful Post-its. He sits back in his chair, passes a hand over the tanned, shiny dome of his distinguished-looking bald spot, and takes on the easy demeanor of someone happy with his surroundings and the people around him.

Gambolati develops numerical methods to help civil engineers understand what will happen, over time, to landforms in the course of normal subsidence, or sinking caused by natural forces of compression, and that other subsidence caused by human interference. His small, computer-filled lab is just down the hall. It bustles with graduate students and colleagues analyzing, for example, just how much the sea bottom off Venice, or even under the city itself, will sink if the government allows a drilling company to tap the undersea natural gas reserves discovered there.

In late 1999 his findings persuaded the Italian Ministry of the Environment to forbid drilling in a gas field located just three miles east of the Venetian lagoon's southern end and nine miles from the historic Venetian center. The gas pocket is 7.2 miles long and three miles wide. It sits 4,265 feet beneath the Adriatic Sea bottom, which itself is under thirty-three to sixty-six feet of water.

"In twenty-five years, our model predicted that drilling would cause one centimeter of subsidence at Chioggia," a fishing port at the lagoon's south end. That, Gambolati says, was unacceptable to the environment minister and to members of Italy's Green movement. After all, who needs to speed up Venice's sinking problem during times when it is already sinking naturally and billions of dollars have been proposed to protect the city from an ever-rising sea?

Later, with two or three graduate students in tow and his arm linked in mine in the typical fashion of two Italian gentlemen strolling side by side, we head off to a popular university-area trattoria for a late lunch. Gambolati, steering me past deep puddles left over from a heavy rain just a few hours earlier, talks about how today's Venetian lagoon had once been deep sea and, hundreds of thousands of years later, high-and-dry land before becoming part of the sea again as we know it today.

Our conversation was revealing. Between one and two million years B.P. (before present), the Adriatic Sea pushed most of the way across northern Italy, east to west. It formed

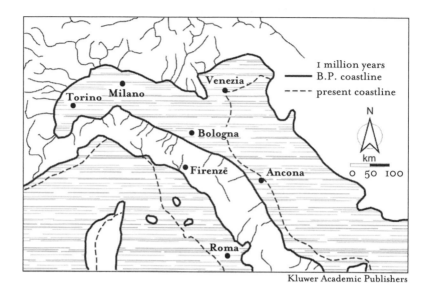

Kluwer Academic Publishers

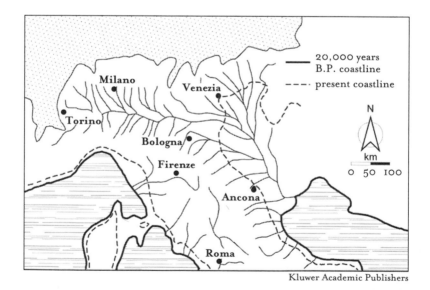

Kluwer Academic Publishers

a wide gulf filling what we know today as the Po Valley, with the sea contained in the north by the Alps and in the south by the Apennines. The deep, roiling waters ran from where Venice is now, on the northeast coast, to well beyond Turin and on toward the northwest coast, near the border where today Italy meets France—a distance from Venice by *autostrada* of about 250 miles. With this giant gulf in place, all that connected the Italian Peninsula to the European continent was a narrow sliver of land, now making up the low-lying coastal mountains that link southeastern France with northwestern Italy.

At that time the Ligurian and Tyrrhenian Seas on Italy's west coast, and the Adriatic to the east, invaded most of the coastal lands of the Italian Peninsula, leaving only the narrow spine of modern Italy—the Apennine range—exposed above the level of the sea. The sites of present-day Rome, Ancona, Bologna, Venice, Milan, and Turin all would have been well under water. Florence, now deep within the Italian interior northeast of Rome, would almost have been a coastal city had it existed then.

But everything cycles continually and, in human terms, imperceptibly. Eventually the Alpine and Apennine ranges degraded into the massive east-west basin of today's Po Valley, gradually filling in the depression and forcing the sea out, to the east.

"These sediments are very small particles, very fine," Gambolati says, spearing a piece of tubular pasta with his fork. Under Venice the sediments that filled in the Adriatic Gulf and created the Po Valley are thicker, by nearly a thousand feet, than those underlying Turin at the "top" end.

"The thickness of the sediments increases west to east, north to south. So the area of maximum sediment is from Venice to Ravenna, the farthest extension of this process from the mountains," he says.

Ancients built Ravenna in the direct path of the sediment-dumping Po River delta so they could use the marshy, water-soaked lands as a defensive barrier, much as the early Venetians used their lagoon. Under the city the sediments are nearly double what they are under Venice, or almost two thousand feet thick.

"So all of this area is in a very precarious setting, naturally speaking, because it is unstable," the professor says. In the west end of the prehistoric gulf, the shallower sediments finished compacting long ago. In the east at Venice and Ravenna, "the deeper sediments continue to compact; they go down progressively. In Venice we see natural subsidence of 0.5 millimeter per year, but in Ravenna we have 2.5 millimeters per year." Ravenna is sinking naturally at a faster rate simply because the sediments are deeper and compression has farther to go.

Gambolati is saying that while Venice is sinking, it is not alone. All of that portion of the Adriatic coastline—from Ravenna northeast to Trieste, all the once wide-open sea making up the prehistoric gulf—is sinking as well. It has ports, people, homes, and buildings that are just as susceptible to long-range flooding destruction as Venice and Ravenna. But there seems to be little concern about Ravenna or the coastal lagoonal areas north and northeast of Venice. The focus has always been on Venice and its buildings and art treasures.

But in prehistoric times no one was around to care or to form a committee to discuss the problem endlessly. Over most of those million years that the huge west-east gulf lapped across northern Italy, the Po River and its sisters continued to drain this basin as the sea level of the Adriatic declined a phenomenal 393 feet (120 meters). Eventually, by twenty thousand years ago this river-borne sediment filled up what we know today as the Gulfs of Venice and Trieste with new land. It continued filling in and pushing out the sea well to the south of Ravenna and Ancona on the Adriatic's west side and about as far south as Split, in Croatia, on the east coast.

This was the time on Italy's west side, which was also rising out of the sea and creating vast new stretches of real estate, when a land bridge connected Corsica with the then-much-wider Italian Peninsula.

"So what happened twenty thousand years ago to stop this 'filling up' trend?" Gambolati asks me, as a professor might ask a student who doesn't have the foggiest notion of an answer. He smiles that professorial smile and then lets me off the hook.

"Glaciers high in the Alps started to melt and the sea level progressively began to rise," reclaiming the new land that covered today's northern Adriatic and turning it once again into sea. It took, then, fourteen thousand years for the rising water of the Adriatic to recapture the landmass from Ancona back to modern northeastern Italy.

"The Venetian lagoon began forming approximately around six thousand years ago. Of course, we can only guess. And we can only guess at the shape of the lagoon then as well," Gambolati says. "As the sea continues to rise, the area underneath is still unstable. While the sea level increases, the sediments below are still progressively going down. The sediments are still compacting, and the sea is rising—partly from natural events and partly from human events. Now the sea is going back," he says with an ironic smile, possibly "to the way it was a million years ago," when it nearly severed northern Italy from the rest of Europe.

What we have seen in human time concerning the northern Adriatic and the lagoon of Venice represents only a brief, flickering moment—a moment quicker than the click of a camera's shutter, faster than the blink of an eye—of geological time. Eventually, in tens of thousands of years, the high-water problem of Venice will have solved itself—geologically speaking. Humans, in the end, will have nothing to say in the matter.

CHAPTER TWO ~

"Frightened Men"

It is the historians of Venice, just as much as
her architects, who have sunk their foundations into shifting sands.
—JOHN JULIUS NORWICH,
  A HISTORY OF VENICE

The cold chill sweeping down from beyond
the north of Italy—in the form of wild barbarian armies—began gradually, in the earliest days of the fifth century C.E. Over the
next two centuries this rampage by peoples
from the fringes of the Roman world
pushed deep into the heart of Italy, eventually all the way to Rome and beyond.
These barbarians—the word translated in
those days to mean "non-Romans"—moved
to fill the growing vacuum spurred by the
gradual disintegration of the empire in the
West. A similar kind of movement took
place nearly a thousand years earlier, when
the fledgling Roman Republic and the Car-
thaginians scrambled to fill the vacuum of

power left by the sudden, inexplicable death of Alexander the Great. Now, nearly a millennium later, Rome, which had kept the Mediterranean Sea from becoming a Carthaginian lake, was teetering. This created an opening for the peoples on the boundaries, who for centuries had coveted recognition as Roman citizens, to flood Italy, demanding their due.

How all this affected the Venetian lagoon and the northeastern crescent of Italy is shrouded in the mists of legend, which have endured because not much was written down about the early inhabitants of these lagoons. The ancient Roman and Greek historians wrote about the earliest lagoon residents only in passing—almost as an afterthought.

Careful reading of the first century Roman historian Livy and the Greek/Roman geographer Strabo shows that they spoke of Venetia only as an entire region around the head of the Adriatic. Venetia then was one of the eleven provinces established by the first Roman emperor, Augustus.

The Roman province of Venetia reached from Ravenna to Aquileia in the north, just west of modern Trieste. The principal cities between those two points were Padua, on the Brenta River, and Oderzo, with smaller settlements such as Altinum (today's Altino) in between. Livy had special familiarity with the area; he came from Padua, which started as an early Roman city and is located near modern Venice.

These early writers refer to people of the lagoons, and they could have been talking about the lagoon dwellers near present-day Grado, south of the mainland Roman city of Aquileia, or those in any of the smaller lagoons between Grado and what became Venice. Strabo was the only one to mention tides. He observed, for example, that the Mediterranean itself had small tides, but that large tides were known in the northern Adriatic.

So the task for modern historians is difficult. They are forced to examine the accounts created by the medieval "historians" whom the wealthy Venetian state paid to glamorize its founding and the lineage of its patricians. It is difficult to cut deep into the truth when there is a paucity of written documentation of these earliest years near the beginning of the European Dark Ages.

For example, the "myth of Venice" would have us believe that when the people from the mainland came into the lagoon to escape from the various barbarian armies, the lagoon was an empty paradise awaiting the touch of their divine hands. Early paintings chronicling this arrival show jewel-bedecked people of high station, outfitted in glorious golden clothing, stepping from flat-bottomed boats onto the first untouched, empty islands and staking their claim much as Columbus is portrayed planting the flag of Spain on the shores of North America.

While such glamorous representations may be unrealistic, I can still imagine these landlubbers moving onto the water with trepidation yet determination. Their lives and way of life, after all, were in jeopardy. I often think of the words by the unknown storyteller who penned *Beowulf*, an ancient tale about a people in a place far, far away from Italy. Those words, as translated by Seamus Heaney, sing out: "You waded in, embracing water, / taking its measure, mastering its currents, / riding on the swell." It is a noble image, one the early Venetians would have hastened to embrace had that stanza been written about them. However, that kind of description could have suited the people who were probably already there when the mainlanders arrived, people who had made a life for centuries—before, during, and after the Romans—in and around the lagoon harvesting salt and marine animals for sustenance and trade.

Colgate University archaeologist Albert Ammerman, a long-time Venetian scholar, likens the Roman mainlanders to the New York City bankers who, during the early twentieth century, moved to Maine and pushed out the long-entrenched locals, taking over the running of day-to-day community life. "The Maine lobster guy was there for years with his boat, scraping by year after year, and this New York banker—type comes in and buys up all the beautiful real estate," Ammerman relates, his delightful upper Midwestern twang accenting his description. It was not much different throughout the Adriatic lagoons in these earliest days after the fifth-century fall of the Roman Empire, he says. The islands "were not united politically. It is like this little archipelago; it isn't even all connected" from Grado to Venice. In those earliest centuries, it was just a ragtag cluster, here and there along the Adriatic coastline, of tiny island dwellings, their populations swelling with the influx of terrified Roman gentry.

Eventually, as the former mainlanders who had been forced by marauding barbarians to wade onto these islands took root, they came to believe that *they* were the ones who had really established these wondrous places. The original lagoon dwellers, much like the Native Americans in North America, faded in the collective memory. Official Venetian histories of the time paint the picture of an empty lagoon, placed there by God as a refuge to save his "chosen people" from the unholy northern hordes.

During the centuries of the Roman Empire, the Po River was the southern border of the province of Venetia. The city of

Ravenna is located on the coast, where the Po formed a massive delta. In imperial times Ravenna was a major naval base. Later it would become the seat of the Western Empire, supplanting Rome, and it would eventually become the home of the barbarian kings of Italy, who replaced the emperors and catered to Byzantium, which had its headquarters in Constantinople, now called Istanbul.

In contrast to what happened in Venice, when Ravenna's builders came along, the Po River delta had replaced that prehistoric lagoon, and the city could be built on relatively stable soil. Venetians, on the other hand, wanted to remain a city of people "embracing water." So the Venetians, unlike what happened naturally farther south, over the centuries stopped nature in its tracks, diverting the rivers around from one section of the lagoon to the other and, eventually, directly to the Adriatic, halting the lagoon's natural progress toward becoming dry land.

In his book *Civic Ritual in Renaissance Venice*, the American historian Edward Muir writes:

> Francesco Lanzoni, the Italian folklorist, pointed out the common practice among medieval peoples of fabricating pseudo-histories of themselves. . . . Many of the early legends thus invented slipped from collective memory. . . . In many cases local legends became official dogma, and to criticize them was to compromise the state. In the seventeenth century in Switzerland any book that questioned the authenticity of the legend of William Tell was publicly burned, and in Venice a tract that controverted the alleged antiquity of Venetian independence from Byzantium suffered a similar fate.

It is no different, say, than Americans creating the myth of George Washington cutting down his father's cherry tree and admitting to it because he could never tell a lie. This American myth gave the "father of our country" a life steeped in honor and virtue. It creates an allegory for schoolchildren about the virtues of honesty, but in all probability it is historically inaccurate.

Muir points beyond Venice to the mythological underpinnings of other Italian cities. He shows that in the early fifteenth century it became more convenient for Florentines, who had long believed that the imperial soldiers of Julius Caesar had founded their city, to take their city's origins back a bit further, to the armies of the Roman Republic. Still later it became fashionable for Florentines to portray the Romans as mere interlopers, and avow that their city was originally Etruscan, established long before the Romans swept down the slopes of Rome's Palatine Hill in search of empire.

So why shouldn't the Venetians compose their own myths about the earliest beginnings of their city? It makes sense that it was the transitory terror of the early-fifth-century Visigoths, Ostrogoths, and Huns, led by Attila, and later in the sixth century, the sustained terror of the Lombards, that led to the foundation of permanent cities on islands in the lagoons. If it is a myth that these invasions were the major catalyst for landlubbers to move onto the water, then the logic of it could account for its endurance.

What is more difficult to accept is the myth that the Italian people who left the mainland and entered the lagoons were descendants of Trojan warriors—the same mythological warriors who are variously credited with building all the cities from Hungary in eastern Europe to Lake Como in northwestern Italy. But why early Venetians selected the Trojans as forebears is also easy for modern historians to comprehend. Muir writes:

> The Trojans were widely interpreted as a people who never paid tribute to anyone and who had been willing to abandon even their city [Troy, located just west of modern Istanbul] in order to preserve their freedom. Trojan roots gave the Venetians a claim both to great antiquity, therefore primacy, and to the purest noble blood, untainted by intermarriage with barbarians.

Who would *not* want to be linked to such a fine people, even if the Trojan story is a myth in its own right? Muir points out that every other major city of the era, including Rome, at one time or another made the same claim of Trojan lineage.

Venetians commonly referred to the Attila story therefore—with some embellishment, one supposes—as the reason their forebears began to stay in their lagoons permanently. Reputable modern historians agree that the invasions of the barbarian hordes are at least part of the reason for the Venetian genesis. And the subsequent grandeur that became the thousand-year Venetian Republic could only mean to early Venetians that Venice was the appropriate heir to Rome.

Rome, the city, had been abandoned as the seat of empire in the early fifth century. The throne of its Western emperor was in Ravenna, situated farther north along the Adriatic coast, and a poor second to once-glamorous Rome. The Eastern emperor was more securely ensconced on the Byzantine throne in Constantinople.

As the fifth century opened, no one could guess that the

Western Empire had only seven more decades of life remaining. In 401 one of the earliest barbarian armies, this one led by Alaric the Visigoth, first blew out of eastern Europe. By this time the Western Empire possessed only a flicker of its past greatness. The once-invincible Roman army was a mere shell of its former self, weak and absent. It provided no military comfort to the inhabitants along the northern and northwestern Adriatic shores, and Rome insisted on taxing the people repeatedly while providing Roman citizens no protection from the barbarian hordes.

Before their gradual exodus seaward, the people lived substantial lives along the mainland. But, with the arrival of Alaric, their comfortable, settled existence began first to tremble and then to crumble. It would take successive invasions over decades before these brief escapes into the lagoon would become longer lasting and then permanent.

At least initially, once Alaric's and succeeding barbarian armies passed, the beleaguered Italians would creep out of their damp hiding places, leave them to the more permanent lagoon dwellers, and return to sort out their lives within the smoldering ruins of their cities.

The invaders were to have significant impact on the future of this troubled Western world. If Attila the Hun, nearly a half century after Alaric, had not acted on whim, for example, islands in the Venetian lagoon might never have contained more than a few clusters of rickety wooden houses on stilts.

According to tradition, in 452 Attila was about to give in to the stubbornness of the defenders and lift his siege of the northeastern Italian city of Aquileia, located a few miles to the west of Trieste and just a few miles north of the Grado lagoon.

But as he mounted his horse to make ready his army's departure, so the story goes, he noticed a flock of storks, with their
young, flying out of Aquileia. He took this as a sign that the
city was about to fall, and Attila renewed his attack, eventually
leveling the city and driving its inhabitants once again into the
lagoon.

This kind of random violence all along the Adriatic's
northwestern crescent surely contributed to the creation of
Venice as a permanent city. Attila, who in reality was just passing through, was followed by the more determined Lombards,
or Langobardi—a Germanic group that in the mid-sixth century, more than a hundred years after Attila's departure, established an independent kingdom and duchies across
northern Italy that lasted for two centuries. It was their more
sustained presence that finally drove the mainland Romans—
characterized by historian Norwich as "frightened men"—into
the lagoon for good. Its islands moved from being a temporary
refuge to form the nucleus of a city-state that would eventually
dominate for nearly one thousand years "one quarter plus
one-half of one quarter" of the Western Roman world.

From Alaric to Attila to the Lombards, most modern historians believe that it took many decades, if not a few hundred
years, for the various lagoons to become populated and established with permanent settlements.

The traditional founding of Venice is conveniently set in a
year that is very early in this process—C.E. 421, two decades
after Alaric's invasions and thirty years before Attila followed
in his footsteps. And the traditional time and date for Venice's
founding is uncannily precise: high noon on March 25. This
genesis, too, is cloaked in myth. Also conveniently, March 25

is the day of celebration for Venice's patron saint, Saint Mark, giving the founding a foothold in Christianity. The historian Patricia Fortini Brown writes: "Such dating, of course, affords the city impeccable Christian credentials from the beginning." Ironically, the saint's remains, as we shall see later, did not arrive in the city for another four centuries.

But the date is based on a document that describes the arrival, at the mudbanks that now comprise the city of Venice, of three consuls from Padua. Their hope to establish a trading post there "is a good deal more plausible than it is authentic," according to historian John Julius Norwich. He agrees that such a mission may have landed on those islands, and they may even have built a church there to commemorate the event. But, Norwich concludes, this is all unlikely. The Paduans did little to follow up on their plans for an outpost, and people who may have lived there were scattered throughout that particular cluster of islands. It is not likely that these "residents" had made the decision to remain permanently. That decision came decades later—after Attila and the Lombards and, even later, the Franks.

But who can argue with tradition? Legend also has it just forty-five years later—in 466—that representatives from the various island communities throughout the lagoons met together at Grado, sixty miles to the north of modern Venice. They formed a loose association of government that established, says Norwich, "the slow constitutional process from which the Most Serene Republic was ultimately to evolve."

What we do know is that twenty-five years after Attila, in 476, the Western Empire, soon to be ruled by barbarian kings, was without an emperor—either in Rome or in Ravenna—and it relied for its governance on the Eastern ruler in distant Constantinople. Italy had ceased to be the home of the emperors and was ruled by a long succession of foreign kings drawn from the ranks of the Vandals, Lombards, Saracens, and Normans.

Through all this, and nearly untouched by the politics of the declining empire, the lagoon communities in the faraway former Roman province of Venetia began their lives.

Norwich writes: "[T]he geographical isolation of these early Venetians did enable them to hold themselves politically aloof from the successive upheavals by which Italy was being shaken." When the Western Empire finally did fall in 476—with a soft thud and a sigh, rather than a crash—the event "caused few ripples out in the lagoons."

In the late fifth century, the barbarian kings, like their immediate Roman predecessors, were ensconced in Ravenna. Whether these rulers felt they controlled the Venetians is left to conjecture. But it is certainly known that there was significant business conducted between the inhabitants of the lagoons—who had begun their commercial ventures trading salt and fish during Roman times—and the rest of Italy.

In a perspicuous letter to lagoon dwellers written in 523 by Cassiodorus, a government official of the Ostrogoth king Theodoric, we get a glimpse of what life on the islands in the various lagoons was like—and a hint of their mercantile leanings—only seventy-one years after Attila left the scene:

> For you live like sea birds, with your homes dispersed, like the Cyclades, across the surface of the water. The solidity of the earth on which they rest is secured only by osier and wattle [willow branches interwoven among wooden poles]. . . . Your people have one great wealth—the fish which suffices for them all. Among you there is no difference between rich and poor;

your food is the same, your houses are all alike. Envy, which
rules the rest of the world, is unknown to you. . . . Be dili-
gent, therefore, to repair your boats—which, like horses, you
keep tied up to the doors of your dwellings—and make haste
to depart.

This letter is often cited by guide books and others as
an example of the simple but democratic life lived by the
lagoon dwellers more than half a millennium before the
Venetian Republic began its rise with the sack of Constantinople during the Fourth Crusade in 1204. But rather than
an accurate description of lagoon life (Cassiodorus, ensconced in palatial comfort in Ravenna, far to the south,
probably never even visited the lagoons), it was more likely a
"buttering up" by the scribe on behalf of his king, Theodoric. The barbarian king, allowed to rule Italy in the West by
the true emperor in Constantinople, wanted the lagoon
dwellers to use their boats, sail across the northern Adriatic
to the Istrian Peninsula in what today is Croatia, and carry
back for trade the olive oil, wine, and wheat that were grown
and manufactured there. Interestingly, in the letter Cassiodorus never mentions the Venetians, who have yet to place
any significant settlement on the Rialto islands that now
make up the historic city. According to Michela Sediari of
the Venice Music Conservatory, the first chronicler to use
the name "Venice" for a town was Paul the Deacon, who
wrote at the end of the eighth century. Cassiodorus was simply writing to lagoon dwellers in the northern Adriatic—and
they could have been anywhere, from the Grado lagoon near
Trieste to the fishing port of Chioggia at the southern end
of what is now known as the Venetian lagoon.

The Venetians, of course, have claimed for centuries that

Cassiodorus was referring to them, which is another example of the primacy they claimed for themselves in the Adriatic and, later, the Mediterranean world. But from his letter and the lagoon dwellers' probable agreement to use their boats to sail across the northern Adriatic, we see the continuation of a fledgling mercantile activity that began in earnest in the fifth century—the one before Cassiodorus's letter—and that may well have been connected to Roman Altinum, just inland from what today is known as the ancient port area around Torcello.

Cassiodorus's letter offers a description of peacefulness and equality among the people that would not stand up to modern historic challenge, for historians today know that the lagoons were contentious and rife with overambitious peoples struggling for supremacy in their little corner of the Adriatic.

So, through this clutter of myth and reality, when did Venice become Venice?

For a few hundred years after Alaric made his first appearance in the early 400s—the period encompassing the times described by Cassiodorus in the letter quoted above—the area was made up of perhaps twelve small villages dispersed throughout tiny islands scattered between modern Chioggia south of Venice to Grado in the farthest lagoon to the northeast.

One of the early settlements that rose to prominence during the time of the barbarians and Lombards was on the island of Torcello. People fled there in 638 to seek refuge from the excesses of the Lombards, but they likely were met by a handful of descendants of people who had landed on the barren island to escape from Attila in 452. By the seventh century—still only about two hundred years after Alaric the Visigoth kicked off the barbarian rampage—the island was described as a "miniature city with a miniature cathedral."

Its early population of—one guesses—about one hundred contained the refugees from the mainland cities of Altinum and Heraclea. Torcello's cityscape was soon dominated by a cathedral with its characteristic red-brick tower, which today is part of the oldest building in the lagoon. It would seem that this island community was the dominant center in the inhabited lagoon's earliest days, as Grado was in its lagoon, farther to the north. It was centuries before more than a handful of hardy souls inhabited the cluster of islands, centered around what became known as the Rialto, that support today's Venice.

By the twelfth century Torcello's population would eventually top thirty thousand, historians say; in the spring of 2000 it was said to be a mere twenty-seven year-round residents. None of the city's original buildings remains, save for its cathedral and the adjacent chapel. Those and only a handful of tourist structures are all that greet the visitor. Venice, out in the middle of the lagoon and farther from the mainland—thus more secure than Torcello—started to grow during Torcello's glory days. Jan Morris in *The World of Venice* tells why Torcello declined and Venice arose from the mudbanks of what became known as the islands of the Rivo Alto, or Rialto, which translates to "high embankment":

> [After the twelfth century, Torcello's] canals were clogged up with silt from the rivers, not yet diverted from the lagoon, and her people were decimated by malaria and pestilent fevers. Her trade was killed at last by the rising energy of the Rialto islands, better placed in the center of the lagoon, near

the mouth of the Brenta. Torcello fell into lethargy and despondence. Her most vigorous citizens moved to Venice, her merchant houses folded and were forgotten. Presently the island was so deserted and disused that the Venetian builders, when they were short of materials, used to come to Torcello and load the remains of palaces into their barges, scrabbling among the rubble for the right size of staircase or a suitably sculpted cornice. Through the centuries poor Torcello rotted, crumbling and subsiding and declining into marshland again . . . [leaving visitors with] a positive ecstasy of melancholia.

So, gradually, Venice rose to dominate all the settlements within the two major lagoons that line the Adriatic's northeast crescent. Ironically, the location of the island city we know today as Venice was the fourth choice for the seat of government. The first power rested on the mainland at Oderzo, now a little village. When that city fell in 639 under the unrelenting pressure of the Lombards, the provincial capital was moved to Heraclea at the northern end of the Venetian lagoon. There, one of the first doges was elected.

In 742 the capital was relocated to Malamocco, then one of the handful of separate islands that centuries later would be combined into what we know as the Lido. And when Pépin, son of Charlemagne and named king of Italy while his father was the Holy Roman emperor, tried to subdue the lagoon dwellers in the early ninth century, he attacked Malamocco. Its citizens escaped across six miles of intricate channels and mudbanks to the more secure Rialto islands that became Venice, protected by a labyrinth of hidden channels. When the Frankish leader tried to take his ships into the lagoon in pursuit— the myths dutifully report—the vessels ran onto the shoals, where they were attacked by lagoon dwellers, who, unlike the Franks, intimately knew the lagoon's channels.

Pépin's withdrawal prompted his father to recognize that the Venetians, now firmly established on the Rialto islands, were subjects of Constantinople, not Rome. The historian Horatio Brown, in his late-nineteenth-century work *The Venetian Republic*, says:

> This concentration [in 811] at Rialto marks the beginning of the history of Venice as a full-grown state. . . . The site chosen, the midmost islands of the lagoon, was a compromise between the danger from the mainland and the danger from the sea. Attila and [the Lombards] had proven the former, Pépin's attack had demonstrated the latter. . . . The place and the people had made one another. With the emergence of Rialto, we have to speak no longer of Heraclea, Jesolo, Malamocco, as separate lagoon-communities; we are face to face with the united Venice of modern history.

The American author Mary McCarthy, describing the power struggles among the peoples of the various islands and towns of the lagoons, makes the observation that the historic city we know today is ringed by a series of "dead cities, each representing a Venetian possibility that aborted."

While the rest of Western Europe was locked in the Dark Ages, Venice evolved into a city-state as a client of the Byzantine Empire, successor to what had once been the glory of Rome. That empire in the East was based in Byzantium, or Constantinople (today Istanbul). Morris, in her book *The Venetian Empire* (1990), writes:

Venetians had organized their affairs within the fold of Byzantine power. Sometimes they availed themselves of Byzantine
protection, sometimes they acted as mercenaries for Byzantium, and so loyal had they been . . . that one of the more
fulsome of the emperors had called Venice "Byzantium's fa-
vourite daughter."

Early Venetians, writing their own history, liked to convey
the idea that the city had never been under the thumb of the
Byzantines. In fact, the myth that the city was born free was
perpetuated by John Locke, who in the seventeenth century
wrote that Venice, along with Rome, had been developed by
"the uniting together of several men free and independent one
of another, amongst whom there was no natural superiority or
subjection." In reality Venice achieved independence because
the Byzantine Empire itself was in decline and in no position
to rigorously control the Venetian merchants.

In the eighth century, for example, the Byzantine rulers in
Constantinople first accepted the Venetian leaders, known as
doges, who were not appointed by these overseers, but elected
by local will alone. (The Latin word *dux*, or leader, became
doge in the Venetian dialect and *duce* or *duca* elsewhere in Italy.)
This was the beginning of Venice's gradual move toward independence.

It started with a bold, daring stroke. In 827 or 828 Venetian
merchants—one was reputedly from Torcello, giving rise to the
idea that the Venetian islands were now united in a single cause—
stole from the city of Alexandria in Egypt, which was under Arab
rule, what were reputed to be the remains of Saint Mark the
Evangelist. McCarthy, in her classic travel narrative *Venice Observed*, looks at this event with well-honed sarcastic wit: "The
capture of St. Mark's body from the heathens in Alexandria by

two Venetian merchants . . . was almost the last action of Venetian merchants that could be considered 'holy.' "

Whether it was the true body of the saint is incidental to
the story. Tradition says the merchants slipped it past the Mus-
lim customs officials by covering it with pork, repugnant to
Arabs. And myth has it that Saint Mark saved the merchants
from storms en route to the northern Adriatic. When the body
was deposited in the Doges' palace, it caused miracles there as
well. All this tied in to an earlier, more believable myth that,
while he was living centuries before, Saint Mark had actually
visited the Roman cities along Italy's northwest crescent. Then
the myth loses credibility when it goes on to say that Saint
Mark stopped to spend the night on the mudbank of the Rialto, where Venice would be built centuries later—a convenient
coincidence.

Of course, there is no hard documentation that Saint Mark
ever went there in his lifetime, just as there is scant evidence,
other than that based on faith, that Saint Peter ever visited
Rome. But the tradition was enough for early Venetians, who
viewed the return of Saint Mark's bones as further evidence
of his bond with them.

Saint Mark became the city's patron saint, much as Saint
Peter belongs to Rome. Muir quotes colleagues who believe
that the presence of Saint Mark's bones in Venice enabled the
Venetian doges to establish spiritual sovereignty over Grado to
the north, which often challenged residents of the Venetian
lagoon for temporal and spiritual dominance. Muir writes,
quoting a colleague: "The myth of Venice" was born on the
very day the Evangelist's body was accepted. "Just as the Pope
had inherited the authority of Peter, so had the Venetians
inherited that of Mark. The popes were autonomous;
therefore so should be the Venetian state."

The theft of Saint Mark's body began a long chain of similar appropriations by Venetians. Venice became, through these years, the repository of "stolen" relics and goods—all designed to give the city recognition as a major commercial power and as the center of the Mediterranean universe. As Mary McCarthy details, Venetians in 1100 conspired to loot a monastery in Myra in southern Asia Minor (modern Turkey) and steal the body of Saint Nicholas. They were beaten to the theft by seamen from Bari, in southern Italy. A few years later, Venetians attempted to steal the bones of other saints from various Christian centers. They lifted granite pillars from Syria and carted them home, where they became displays in Venetian buildings that can still be seen today. They stole an Assyrian bronze chimera—a mythological fire-breathing she-monster with a lion's head, a goat's body, and a serpent's tail—that later was modified to become Saint Mark's bronze lion, and they looted so many sacred relics throughout these years that the booty piled up where ships' crews dumped them on the Riva degli Schiavoni, the walkway along the city's edge in front of the Doges' Palace.

"Booty and trade concessions were extorted by the Venetians impartially from Christian and heathen," McCarthy writes. "This impartiality, in the end, was what caused them to be hated, as sometimes the Jews have been, for being 'outside' the compact." Later in her story she adds:

> Venice, unlike Rome or Ravenna or nearby Verona, had nothing of its own to start with. Venice, as a city, was a foundling, floating upon the waters like Moses in his basket among the bulrushes. It was therefore obligated to be inventive, to steal and improvise. . . . [T]he get-up-and-go of the early Venetian businessmen was typical of a self-made society.

However controversial its methods, the city was coming into its own by creating myths to shore up and justify its right to its place in the eastern Mediterranean.

Since the tenth century, Venice had had the naval strength to clear the northern Adriatic of pirates. By 1000, growing Venetian sea power dominated the entire northern Adriatic along both the Italian and Dalmatian coasts. The sea between these landmasses dividing East from West was identified on some maps of the period as the "Gulf of Venice." Then, in 1054, Venice and Constantinople were separated theologically when the Great Schism divided the Latin Church, based in Rome, from the Greek Orthodox, headquartered in Constantinople; Venice had stayed with the papacy on a spiritual plane, but continued to trade in both directions on a more temporal one. In 1095 Pope Urban II called for the First Crusade, and the Venetians began their long practice of contributing ships and supplies to the cause against the Turks.

In 1202, with Venice already in existence for nearly five hundred years and its domination of the northern Adriatic assured, an event occurred that propelled the Venetian city-state into a maritime empire: The pope, Innocent III, launched the Fourth Crusade—this one to Muslim-occupied Alexandria.

The Church once again needed help transporting Crusaders. The decisions made by the city's forty-first doge, Enrico Dandolo, would, according to Jan Morris in her book *The Venetian Empire*, "make him and all his seventy-nine successors, at least in name, Lords of a Quarter and a Half-Quarter of [what had been] the Roman Empire."

The city was ready for such a step. Dandolo's Venice contained some eighty thousand souls and was one of Europe's largest cities. Morris writes that Venice "was organized by parishes, each with its own strong character, its own social hierarchy, so that there was no rich quarter of town, and no poor. It was mostly built of wood."

The city of stone that visitors have seen in recent centuries had not yet fully emerged. In 1202 much of the city, Morris says, was new. Wooden bridges were being replaced by stone ones, and *campi*, those open squares that dominate each neighborhood, were just beginning to be paved. Venetians at this time were master shipbuilders, hence the need of the armies of the Fourth Crusade for their services.

In late 1201 Crusaders arrived in Venice to be boarded on Venetian ships. The knights and soldiers were encamped on the Lido. The first problem they faced was that their leaders were short of cash. The Crusaders borrowed money so that the ships could be built in Venice's Arsenal, one of Europe's busiest shipbuilding centers, which in its heyday could turn out a ship every twenty-four hours. The warriors for Christ had to give many of their precious possessions to the Venetians for payment as well, which the ever-sensible Venetians melted down to make coins.

Then there steps into the scene a character largely unknown to history and bearing the name Young Alexius. He was a pretender to the Byzantine throne in Constantinople, in exile because of his pretensions. He let it be known to the Venetians that if he were made emperor, he would help bring the Greek Orthodox Church in the East back into the fold of Rome, now the well-established center of Christianity in the West.

That was all Doge Dandolo needed. He struck a deal with the Crusaders, who were still short of the cash they needed to make the journey to Alexandria on Venetian ships. Dandolo— some say he was in his nineties and blind, others that he was in his eighties and had poor vision—proposed that the Cru-

saders wipe out their debt by stopping at ports such as Trieste,
Muggia, and Zara along the eastern Adriatic—the Dalmatian
coast—to help the Venetians consolidate their control along
the Adriatic's length. And by the way, the doge added, help
us [the Venetians] install the Byzantine pretender on the
throne at Constantinople. Dandolo worked out the plan with
conspirators from the Crusaders' top ranks, and so knew
the "soldiers of Christ" were not going to make it to Alexandria. Rank-and-file Crusaders did not realize the ruse until the ships were well on their way to Constantinople. The
riches they pillaged there, the Greek women they raped, and
the wholesale destruction they wrought were more than
enough to make them forget their original "holy" mission to
Alexandria.

Constantinople was taken, Young Alexius was seated and
then overthrown. ("You stupid youth," Morris, in *The Venetian
Empire*, says Dandolo reportedly called the young pretender:
"We pulled you out of the dung, and we'll soon put you back
there." And Dandolo eventually did just that.) After some
more sparring around, the Crusaders became masters of the
empire, gratefully splitting it with the helpful Venetians, who
ended up with numerous coastal cities and the island of Crete,
another of its island stepping-stones along what were to become Venetian-dominated trade routes to the Holy Land.

Constantinople was stripped of its treasures and relics,
which found their way to places all over Europe. Says Morris:
"The Venetians, though, were the most organized looters.
They alone maintained the discipline of their forces, and
looted methodically, under orders, for the glory of their
nation."

The riches—marble columns, the quartet of little porphyry

knights, the four golden horses that Venetians believe represent Venice's independence from Byzantium—can all be seen
today by tourists marveling at what once resided in Constantinople and other eastern cities that fell under the republic's
control.

Getting what they wanted, the Venetians withdrew to the
sidelines and quietly built up the trade routes that would serve
them well for hundreds of years, creating their *Venezia Domi-
nante*. They did this amid the death throes of the Eastern
Empire, which died the same kind of slow death that the Western Empire had experienced more than half a millennium
earlier.

With the sack of Constantinople, Venice—a commerce-based
city-state—acquired instant empire. Dandolo's approach after
the capture kept Venice from following the mold of the war-
like, territory-grabbing Roman Empire it replaced. All Dandolo and his immediate successors wanted was unfettered trade
between Venice in the northwestern Adriatic, south along the
eastern Italian and western Dalmatian coasts, and east
throughout the islands of the Aegean and through Cyprus and
Crete across the Levant—the lands bordering the eastern Mediterranean—and from there to the spice-rich Far East.

It was here that trade goods brought overland by caravans—
the silks, teas, and spices of China and beyond—were gathered
for transport in Venetian ships, back to Venice, and then sent
throughout Europe. Everything, whether it went east or west,
had to be transported that way. The landlocked Far Eastern
merchants were bound to Venetian shipping because Venice
controlled all the ports between East and West. The republic's

power was monopoly based, and its warships fought off all pretenders for more than two centuries, keeping those vital ports in Venetian hands.

All these territorial gains from the sack of Constantinople onward were designed not to bring huge landmasses of newly conquered territory and peoples under the Venetian flag, as the Romans aspired to do centuries earlier, but only to protect and expand Venetian shipping.

Most of all, the people who gave the Venetians control of their harbors and ports often welcomed the republic's protection. Venetians, while owing spiritual allegiance to Rome, were more independent than Christians elsewhere. This led them to be more tolerant of other religious traditions and cultures, particularly when those peoples could provide useful services to the republic. In Corfu, for example, under Venetian control Jews were the principal bankers, and their financial systems served the republic well. There they grew and prospered under their grateful overlords.

Venice itself became a relatively safe place for Jews, who often sought refuge in the lagoon from pogroms and other atrocities inflicted on them elsewhere in Europe. The Venetians, after a costly war with Genoa, invited Jewish moneylenders from the mainland to move into the waterborne city so Venetians could use the Jews' financial acumen to help kickstart the Venetian economy. Their job done, the Jews were expelled but later reinvited. But even in racially tolerant and culturally diverse Venice—tolerant perhaps as long as Venetian self-interests were being served—Jews were segregated from the sixteenth century on.

In 1516 the Venetian leadership ordered that the Jews con-

gregate on a small island in what is known today as the Cannaregio section of Venice, located to the north of the
modern train station. The Jews were settled on a parcel of
land once the site of a foundry or some type of metal-
fabrication plant. The word in Venetian dialect for "foundry"
is *getto,* the origin of today's word *ghetto.* There the Jews conducted their business; they could move throughout the city by
day but were confined within the walls of their tiny enclave by
night, guarded by Christians whom they were forced to pay
out of their own pockets.

The Venetian Jews of this period were limited to dealing
in textiles, moneylending, and medicine and were forced to
wear caps and badges, at various times colored yellow or red.
Were the Venetians protecting these much maligned and
abused people from the brutal outside world, or did they per-
ceive—their thinking controlled by the prevalent racist fears of
gentiles that Jews were a threat—that they were somehow protecting their own interests?

This ghetto existed until Napoleon—who occupied Venice
in 1797 and ended the Venetian Republic—pulled down the
gates. Later, when the Austrians ruled over the city, the Jews
were once again confined. In 1866, under the newly created
Italian nation, they were finally granted their freedom. One
guidebook says that six hundred Jews live in Venice today, and
only five Jewish families live within the actual boundaries of
the old ghetto.

The power of the Venetian Republic, which began its rise to
glory on the sheer guts and determination of Doge Dandolo
in 1202, slowly, almost imperceptibly, began to dissipate by
the late fifteenth century.

The somber decline began in 1499, when news of two events drifted into Venice: The Turks had defeated the Venetian fleet off Sapienza, on the southwest corner of the Greek Peloponnese. That same year, the Portuguese seaman Vasco da Gama rounded Cape Horn and made it all the way to Calicut in search of spices. He found them, and he founded new deep-sea lanes from west to east that gradually began to undercut what had been a Venetian monopoly in the Mediterranean.

The combination of land and shallow sea routes, pioneered by the Venetians in their boats designed expressly for Mediterranean waters, no longer dominated the European marketplace.

All Venetians immediately understood the significance of da Gama's feat. Stephen Fay and Phillip Knightley summarize the Venetian reaction to this event succinctly: "Once the decline began, the Venetians were incapable of stopping it; perhaps for that reason they determined to enjoy it." And so began Venice's long, slow decline, marked, as Jan Morris tells us, by "the carnivals of the Venetian decadence," which she says characterized the beginning, in the sixteenth century, of Venice as a tourist attraction. "The more decadent they became, the more people flocked to them."

The Turks, battle after battle, century after century, had started to wear down Venetian resistance. Venice's great ally to the east, Constantinople, eventually fell into unfriendly hands. Over the next few hundred years, their fear of the now-neutered Venetian navy rapidly lessening, pirates once again returned to the Adriatic.

In the sixteenth century, for example, a group of pirates known as the Uskoks could take plundered Venetian goods north to an international market in Trieste. Under the protection of the Austrian Hapsburgs, the pirates could sell their ill-gotten wares, essentially under the very noses of the Venetians themselves, who were fortified on their islands fewer than one hundred miles away.

Pirates were so bold along the once-Venetian-dominated Dalmatian coastline of the eastern Adriatic that, for a time, the Venetian leadership docked its ships in the few remaining friendly ports in what is now Albania to take its merchandise in overland caravans to modern-day Turkey. In the sixteenth century Venetians created a route from Split, which was parallel to that Albanian pathway. Because it was located much farther to the north, it enabled them to bypass most of the Adriatic altogether.

The Venetian Republic's glory years were well in the past. Following that decisive late-fifteenth-century naval defeat by the Turks at Sapienza, says Muir,

> The Venetians lost their claims to many Greek and Albanian cities vital to the eastern trade of *La Serenissima*. . . . [And] Although it was a century more before Venice experienced a permanent loss as a result of the Portuguese adventure, the startling news that it had been outflanked [by da Gama] in the campaign to secure the lucrative pepper traffic eroded domestic confidence in Venice's traditional domination of the Levant [Holy Land] trade.

So came the end of the end. It had taken the Venetian patricians five hundred years to spend the capital accumulated during the "glorious" period; "when it was finally dissipated, there was nothing left to live for," McCarthy writes.

This finale coincided with the arrival of Napoleon in the Veneto in 1797. The conquering French general ended *La Serenissima* forever, dismissing the final doge, Lodovico Manin, and announcing that he, Napoleon, would become the city's new Attila. The following year he turned the city over to the Austrians in exchange for the old Lombard territories across the north of Italy, beginning a seesaw exchange of ruling powers until 1866, when Venice became part of the new Italian nation.

It was under the Austrians that Venice, in the middle of a vast lagoon, became physically connected to the world. In 1841, at Venetian expense and much to Venetian disgust, the Austrians began the railroad bridge that connects the city to the Italian mainland.

J. G. Links, in *Venice for Pleasure*, writes:

> [Venetians] never really wanted a railway bridge and even less did they want a road bridge. . . . Before the railway bridge was built, the traveler entered his gondola or post boat at Mestre or at Fusina, leaving his carriage, if he had one, at the inn before embarking.

So Venice was no longer secure in the midst of its vast moat. It had lost control of its destiny and sat like a tired, old grande dame at the end of a long, long dinner party, waiting for someone to take her home. This is much the way Venetians feel today—that their destiny and that of their city are being decided by outsiders.

Interestingly it was the Venice of this post-Napoleonic period that was described by famous world travelers and writers who gave most tourists the enduring picture of the city that we have today. The city of the doges is lost to us forever.

Here is how McCarthy sums up the Venice seen by modern tourists—those who slip into the city for a day or a day and a night and then depart:

> No stones are so trite as those of Venice, that is, precisely, so well worn. It has been part museum, part amusement park, living off the entrance fees of tourists, ever since the early eighteenth century, when its former sources of revenue ran dry. The carnival that lasted half a year was not just a spontaneous expression of Venetian license; it was a calculated tourist attraction. . . . In the Venetian preserve, a thick bitter-sweet marmalade, tourism itself became a spicy ingredient, suited to the foreign taste. . . . Venice is a folding picture-postcard of itself.

We have Jan Morris's corroborating—but more generous—description in *The World of Venice* as well:

> Today her money is in tourism. Her chief function in the world is to be a kind of residential museum, a Tintoretto holiday camp, just as Coventry makes cars and Cedar Rapids corn flakes: and though the city in summer can be hideously crowded and sweaty, the mobs of tourists unsightly, and the Venetians disagreeably predatory, nevertheless there is a functional feeling to it all, as of an instrument accurately recording revolutions per minute, or a water-pump efficiently irrigating.

CHAPTER THREE ~

The Lagoon and the City

Where you goin' to go someday, kid, when there ain't no Nature to put you in your place when you think you're smarter than God?

—IDAHO FARMER, C. 1952

There is nothing natural about the Venetian lagoon. It is a delicately balanced living organism that has been artificially controlled for the last thousand years. If people had not interfered with the natural forces of this lagoon's environment, it would have filled up over the centuries and become Italian coastline, just as at one time millennia ago it was dry land that became sea.

Sometimes in their stewardship humans have been attentive; more often they have been negligent and shortsighted. The historic city that was created on islands within the lagoon's center was placed there because terrified newcomers needed it for defense. The horse-riding barbarians who repeatedly pushed these Roman citizens from their comfortable coastal cities onto the islands did not have boats, and the coastal inhabitants could go out into the marshes knowing they likely would not be followed.

When they were threatened in the early days by major naval powers, such as Pépin's Franks, the enemy had no idea where the lagoon's deeper channels were located—knowledge possessed only by the inscrutable Venetians. The invaders quickly discovered that their large ships could not navigate the shallow lagoon and frequently became mired on mudbanks hiding just beneath the lagoon surface. It was a safe haven for the lagoon dwellers and, for the times, unable to be breached.

Today, of course, the city is no longer in danger from roving bands of maritime bandits. But the lagoon and this ancient need to maintain its watery integrity are so deeply ingrained in the Venetian psyche that the city's communication with the sea through the three lagoon entrances must, by modern Italian law, remain inviolate.

Night after night during a two-month stay in Venice in early 2000, I would quit the tedious work of transcribing notes and leave my small hotel room on the Lido to venture out into the blackness of the lagoon aboard a *vaporetto*, or municipal waterbus. It was especially pleasing late at night when the day-trippers, who jam Venice during daylight hours and leave in the later afternoon for less expensive lodgings farther inland, are long gone. These are *morde e fugge*, or snack-and-run, visitors. This late-evening waterbus carries few tourists. They sit slumped in their seats, heads on each other's shoulders after a night of bar-hopping, dancing, or listening to the music of

Vivaldi deep in the recesses of some ornate church near the Rialto. Most passengers on such late-night boats, however, are locals returning to their homes after dinner, a concert, or more likely their evening jobs.

I never sat inside the shelter of the boat's cabins as Venetians do, unfolding their daily newspapers and burying their noses deep in the vagaries of Italian politics and soccer; these closed-in, stuffy cabins seemed too confining. Instead I always stood at a position usually to starboard and just aft of the operator's tiny wheelhouse. There, between the Lido and the Santa Elena stop near the historic center, I could experience the darkness of the lagoon and feel the boat glide as its bow cut through the gently rolling water, black and occasionally silver in the moonlight. Sometimes I would ride all the way up the Grand Canal and back again; other times I would get off at one of the two stops for St. Mark's Square so I could wander within the expanse of this world's "greatest drawing room" when it was free of the estimated 120,000 pigeons that frequent the city—more than 3,000 per square kilometer—and camera-toting tourists. At that late hour I could "feel" the wide-open space, and wonder how I could be in the heart of one of the world's greatest cities and experience such solitude and, often, overwhelming loneliness.

Once, during a restless night, I left my Lido hotel at three in the morning, climbed aboard one of the hourly *vaporetti*, rode across the lagoon with only three other passengers, and glided on jet-black water along the edge of the Basin of St. Mark's, the area of the ancient port of Venice that locals still refer to as the *Molo*, or wharf. This is where the Grand Canal begins its serpentine, backward-S route to the city's train station a few kilometers away.

The moon was only half full, the tide was low, and the

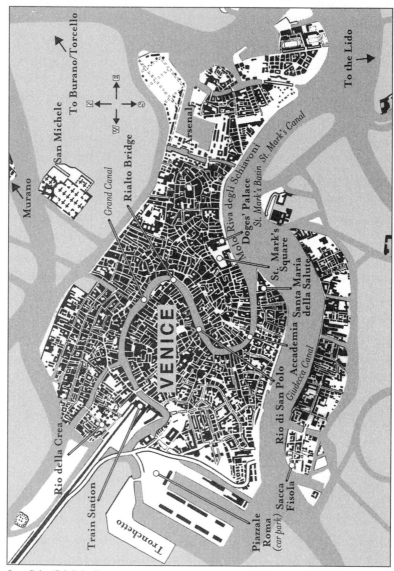

To Burano/Torcello

San Michele

Murano

Grand Canal

Rialto Bridge

Arsenale

Riva degli Schiavoni

Doges' Palace

St. Mark's Canal

St. Mark's Basin

Molo

St. Mark's Square

Santa Maria della Salute

Accademia

Giudecca Canal

Rio di San Polo

VENICE

Rio della Crea

Train Station

Tronchetto

Piazzale Roma (car park)

Sacca Fisola

To the Lido

N
E
S
W

Steve Baker/Salt Lake City

palazzi, like elderly gentlemen dozing in deep, plush chairs, seemed to be slumped dark against the canal. The only buildings with illumination, it seemed, were those that served as hotels. If it were not for the white "street" lights along the few short *fondamente*, or sidewalk-like pavements, infrequently placed along the Grand Canal, it would be like going along a dark country road in a car with its lights turned off. The *vaporetto* has no headlights, and between stops it glides through black ink, the water's surface tension rarely breaking because there are no motorboats about at this time of night.

At three o'clock in the morning, Venice is a dark, silent world, devoid of the clatter and clack of water taxis and commercial boats delivering frozen goods, vegetables, and, yes, FedEx packages. At three A.M., even the waterbus motor seemed muffled. And it was a quick trip: forty minutes from one end of the Grand Canal to the other, instead of the nearly hour-long journey the packed daytime waterbus usually takes. The *vaporetto* would brush up against the bobbing dock and then quickly move away again as it became obvious to the operator that no one was getting on or off.

It was during these late-night, early-morning excursions around the silent, dark city that I was able to talk to boatmen. During the day, they must push their way through sardine-like packs of people to get from the operator's cabin to the *vaporetto*'s side to tie the waterbus fast against the pier and lift the metal gate from its slots, slide it back, and then jump out of the way as passengers jostle one another for position in the scramble to get off. Late at night I could question the boatmen about their jobs, and—either to relieve the boredom of what is a painfully repetitive job or just to pass the time—they would talk about interesting things. From one of them I learned that the word for the boat cleats that hold the mooring

lines, the frayed manila ropes, in place is *bitta*. I liked the
word. It reminded me of the "bite" made by a calf roper in
an American rodeo, who holds the rope tightly between
clenched teeth, keeping it ready to whip around three of the
struggling calf's flailing legs. The obliging boatman, tolerantly
smiling at my attempts to ask questions in faltering Italian,
said the mooring line holding the waterbus to the dock is
nearly an inch (two centimeters) in diameter and must be
replaced every fifteen days or so. It depends on the weather,
he said. A period of heavy rain might break down the fiber of
the manila rope within a week, or even in half a week. And
its life might even be shorter from the repeated pressure on
it when a waterbus jerks too violently because of a hand's slip
on the throttle or a sudden rolling wave that sends people
standing on deck grabbing for handholds—or each other. This
rope that creaks so melodically sings the same song as ropes
holding canvas sails on large seagoing sailing ships, a song that
has sung to sailors for millennia. Occasionally, during daytime
rides, I see a bus-company service boat pull up to a pier, where
a man in coveralls leaps off the deck and onto the dock, scoop-
ing up an arm-filling wad of these used-up, stretched-out,
frayed ropes tossed behind the pier's *bitta* by passing boat han-
dlers.

The only way to truly see Venice is from the water, as people
have done for centuries. It puts the city in proper perspective,
in both space and time. The late-night/early-morning journey
should be an important part of a serious tourist's itinerary.

　　Once, in evening twilight, just before the few electric lights
twinkled on in buildings lining the canals, I experienced a
feeling of the "old" Venice. An archaeologist friend had

invited me aboard his small Venetian-style boat, modeled after what the locals call a *topo*. We were sitting in the middle of the Grand Canal, and he reached down and shut off the tiny outboard motor, set his long wooden oar into a hand-carved oarlock unique to Venice, and, standing, soundlessly rowed his way along a stretch that, for a few magical moments, was empty of waterbuses, motorized taxis, or any other machine-propelled craft. It was just the two of us in this nearly empty stretch of water, and two gondolas, each with two silent tourists aboard. I traded glances with the people in the gondolas, and they appeared as awestruck as I by the silence and by the evening light on the pastel-colored buildings.

"You are experiencing the Venice of more than one hundred years ago—Venice before motors," my friend said softly, as if the sound of his voice would destroy the moment. I nodded, knowing that in this time and space we were among the luckiest of people. I absorbed the sensation, feeling it in every pore. A few minutes later a *vaporetto*, jammed to the railings with chatting, laughing passengers, poked around the Grand Canal's gentle curve just ahead, heading our way. My brief, nearly private moment of Venetian magic ended.

The buildings seem to float in this watery world, but of course they are eventually anchored to solid land deep below the lagoon's mud. But anchored to what?

It does seem inconceivable that a great stone city sits in this spot. There is no other place like it: a single piazza—the largest in all of Italy; innumerable, smaller *campi*, plopped down amid multistoried stone buildings lining stone-sided canals.

One of the finest books describing how the ancient Venetians built their city on this motley collection of mudflats is *Venice: The Golden Age, 697–1797*. In remarkable drawings and vivid detail, its author, Alvise Zorzi, describes the layout of the original islands, where the historic center now sits, and shows how the islands were expanded from the early ninth century after the Venetians escaped there when Charlemagne's son Pépin conquered the seat of the lagoon's government at Malamocco.

According to Zorzi: "Venice's existence is due to an accident of geography, the presence of the *Realtine* islands, which are more sand banks than solid ground at the center of the waters, reeds and mud that make up the changing face of the lagoon. . . . By [the twelfth century] Venice had assumed more or less its present shape."

We know that Venice's commercial center has, since the ninth century, been in the Rialto, which then had the only bridge, an early wooden one, across the Grand Canal. Here were the stalls of the moneychangers, where today sit hundreds of stalls where trinkets and characteristically Venetian *Carnevale* masks are sold to tourists. It is ironic that this highly commercial, overmarketed, tourist-jammed area is where western capitalism, and the banking industry, was born.

And we know that the government center has always been where St. Mark's Square, with its basilica and the Doges' Palace, sits. The large square is the one Napoleon called "the greatest drawing room in Europe," and is the only open space in Venice known as a piazza. The other, smaller squares are known as *campi*, or in the case of the other square adjoining the Doges' Palace, the Piazzetta San Marco. Zorzi says that the Piazzetta was originally a watery arm of the lagoon that was long ago filled in. The piazza, which once abounded with fruit trees, was in earliest times bisected by a river, or *rio*, that coursed between two small islands. It was filled in during the republic's early centuries so that the government could create the massive square of St. Mark's that has become Venice's signature.

So, just how did Venetians build huge stone palaces on such unstable mudflats and filled-in channels? Zorzi says that Venice's natural environment led to several unusual features in its building methods. "Constructions had to be light and flexible in order to survive on the unstable floor of the lagoon." Flexible they are, even today. John Millerchip, who has lived in Venice for more than thirty years, said that when earthquakes wreak havoc on the nearby Italian mainland, "We sort of feel within our buildings a gentle to-and-fro rocking. It is quite pleasant, really."

Venetian building techniques represent a remarkable feat. In modern construction, we pour concrete foundations on top of concrete footings along a building's perimeter to support the bulk of a structure. Venetians created foundations by sinking into the lagoon's mud row after row of long, slender poles of alder trees harvested from the Italian mainland and from the Istrian Peninsula on the Adriatic's eastern shore.

The poles, sharpened at one end, were light enough to be set into place by two workers. They would push each pole straight down into the mud, and when it became too hard to be pushed by four hands, the workers used a crude pile driver, or drop hammer, that they could slide up and down at the pole's top end. Venetian folklore tells how these workers kept rhythm with a chanted song as they implanted, over the centuries, millions of these poles. They were like American gandy dancers singing in rhythm as they set rails to a series of beats and carefully choreographed steps. For the Venetians the renewed force of this pile driver/drop hammer pushed the sharpened poles ten to fifteen feet through the lagoon's sediments until the poles hit the clay-and-sand bottom, known as *caranto*. This more stable earth in prehistoric, geologic times had been dry land long before the rising sea once again invaded the coastline.

"The piles were either arranged in several rows about the edge of the building," says Zorzi, as a modern concrete foundation is laid out, "or [the poles] covered the entire surface area [beneath the building] if the building was to be very heavy."

Across the tops of the closely packed wooden piles were laid sawn planks, mostly made of oak from Dalmatia, across the Adriatic, and on top of these wooden planks were laid several courses of Istrian marble, also brought across the northern Adriatic from the Istrian Peninsula. It is this impermeable stone, which then protruded well above the high-water line, that most resembles a modern foundation.

Eight or more rows of Istrian stone made up the secondary foundation, the wooden piles now fully submerged in the lagoon's mud serving as the first. It was across this stone foundation, from edge to edge of the proposed building, that wooden beams were placed to distribute the weight of the structure itself. And on these stone foundations were laid, one on top of the other, rows of brick that created the building's exterior walls.

Many see Venice as a city of stone: John Ruskin, for example, titled his 1853 definitive study of the city *The Stones of Venice*. In reality most of Venice above the Istrian stone foundations is made of brick, faced with stucco. Throughout the city today visitors can see where this stucco has fallen off many buildings, exposing the moldering, damp, and crumbling brick beneath. Also, wood was used in large quantities, with Venetians—ever the consummate boat people—employing shipbuilding techniques to tie their structures together.

This is how these separate islands, clustered together in the midst of a watery lagoon, were united into a single city. Each of the islands was gradually expanded, and this process created narrower and narrower rivers and streams between them. In the local vernacular a river is a *rio*; the plural is *rii*. As the buildings were constructed to the very edge of these *rii*, the shrinking waterways became the canals we see today. Often a smaller canal was filled in to make a pathway for pedestrians. The remnants of such filled-in canals are identified in today's street names, often preceded by the words *rio terra*, or, literally, "land river." Sometimes portions of buildings were constructed over these filled-in *rii*. Because the fill was not as compact as the more stable land of an adjacent island, the portion of the building that sits over the former canal, or *rio*, often settled at a faster rate than did the rest of the building, erected on more solid island ground. Visitors today can see the effects of this imbalance in leaning towers (never in competition with Pisa's), such as the one on the island of Burano, or in a few somewhat skewed buildings along the Grand Canal.

The most frenetic period of filling in canals took place in the nineteenth century, after the dissolution of the republic. Canal filling then ceased for the most part; the last filling in of a waterway took place in the 1950s. Since then, despite the efforts of some Venetians to restore many waterways and move people to the *fondamente* along the sides, as they were centuries ago, very few "land rivers" have been reversed. A recent—and rare—exception involves a portion of the Rio della Crea, which had been filled in decades ago where it entered the Canale di Cannaregio north of the train station. It was dug out during the mid-1990s to improve water flow.

The idea that wooden poles—ranging in length from ten to fifteen feet and buried for centuries deep in the lagoon's mud—are holding up massive stone palaces boggles the imagination. But they do. In their airless, oxygen-free (anaerobic) environment deep within the mud of the now-hidden islands, the alder poles are preserved and actually became stronger—almost petrified—with each passing century. If left undisturbed and never again exposed to air, they can probably last for centuries more.

What threatens the city today is the rising waters and the impact of tide-borne seawater repeatedly dousing the fragile brick walls. When the buildings were constructed, the brick courses sitting on the impervious Istrian stone were well above regular high-tide level and, historically, were almost never touched by the seawater as it ebbed and flowed throughout the lagoon twice daily. As twentieth century seas have risen much faster, due largely to modern human impact on nature, the brick facades are increasingly unable to withstand this incessant battering by the waves of the Adriatic.

Ancient Venetians dealt with rising water simply by raising the pavements around the buildings, or they demolished the buildings, built up the ground and constructed new structures—a process that today's preservationists would find unthinkable.

The pillars of the Doges' Palace were much taller than they are today. Archaeologists have found five levels of older pavements in St. Mark's Square beneath the one on which today's tourists tread.

Often over the centuries, particularly in the Middle Ages, when Venice was at the height of its empire, terra firma was gaining on the city as well. The lagoon, as such environments are wont to do when they progress from water to dry land, began to fill up with the sediments carried down by the rivers. Left unhindered, these soils would create marshes, and the marshes would evolve into dry land, filling the spaces between the mainland and the barrier islands of the Lido, Pellestrina, and Cavallino. We only have to remember what happened to Torcello in the seventh century, the first permanent lagoon settlement to understand what the later lagoon dwellers on the islands that make up historic Venice would eventually face. Torcello was abandoned because the mouth of the Sile River began to silt up close to the settlement, producing mosquitoes and malaria that has killed hundreds of thousands in Italy over the centuries. The salt marshes that resisted mosquitoes, and gave the residents of Torcello distance from their enemies, began to disappear because of the river-borne silt.

Many rivers traversed the fertile lands north and west of the lagoon. Over time, as the mainland foothills were deforested, probably to provide some of the timbers that propped up Venetian buildings during these decades of frenzied building, inordinate amounts of silt flowed into the lagoon, turning its edges into marshes and threatening a kind of buildup similar to the one that led to Torcello's demise.

Venice, sitting in a former lagoon filled in with earth, would be as susceptible as any other coastal city to marauding armies. To reverse this natural evolution from lagoon to dry land required bold moves by the republic's leaders, and, beginning in the fourteenth century, they were up to the task. The Adige, Bacchiglione, Brenta, Sile, and Piave Rivers all flowed naturally into the basin. For a while, through the republic's earliest days, this provided brackish water, but by the Middle Ages the Venetians realized that if nothing was done, the lagoon would become marshland and silt up.

In 1324 a canal was dug that diverted the water from the mouth of the Brenta. This mighty river, which began in the Dolomites and flowed south almost to Padua before turning east, dropped its waters into the lagoon at Fusina on the mainland, just opposite the south end of Venice's Giudecca Canal. This was the first of several canal extensions that moved the Brenta's waters progressively farther away from Venice itself, giving the Venetians the ability to direct them at will to a variety of locations within the large lagoon's southern end.

By 1613 a new cut, which completely redirected the Brenta's waters, plus those of several other rivers, was completed around the lagoon's southern edge, diverting the rivers' combined mouths directly into the Adriatic at a point south of Chioggia, the tiny mainland fishing village opposite Pellestrina.

Meanwhile, in the sixteenth and seventeenth centuries, major canals were constructed northeast of Venice, diverting the waters of several other rivers, including the Torcello-defeating Sile, into the old bed of the mighty Piave, whose waters had already been diverted elsewhere. In 1534 a massive structure known as St. Mark's Dike was completed between the lagoon and the Piave's traditional course to protect the former from the periodic floods of the Piave, which now carried the waters of the Sile and other lesser streams.

Eventually, with the rivers diverted and the lagoon protected from filling up with waterborne earth, the Venetians turned their attention to protecting the barrier islands of Lido and Pellestrina. This was accomplished late in the republic's life—less than one hundred years before Napoleon's invasion and subjugation of the city in 1797. Seawalls were built along the Adriatic side of the long, narrow islands that had stood guard at the lagoon's eastern edge for millennia, protecting the fragile environment within.

Then, in the twentieth century, builders went too far. As described in *The Lagoon of Venice: Environment, Problems, Remedial Measures*, written for scientists attending a 1997 water conference in Venice:

> During the last century man modified the lagoon system much more intensively: he dug new deep canals for navigation, extended the intertidal flats to provide the necessary areas for a new industrial and urban center, and extended the fish breeding areas, which he protected from the precarious equilibrium of the basin water by dykes. Furthermore, in the last decades a rash exploitation of the groundwater caused a land subsidence much heavier than the natural process, whose effects are very serious for Venice because of its precarious land elevation with respect to mean sea level.

The river diversions and seawall constructions were incredible engineering feats—as incredible in their time as the modern proposal to put giant hydraulic steel gates at the lagoon's three mouths to protect Venice from widespread flooding. But, just as the modern proposals are considered by many to be Venice's only hope of survival in the twenty-first century, the work accomplished over four hundred years starting in the Middle Ages was vital to safeguarding Venice then.

To learn how the Venetians moved whole rivers and di-verted unfathomable amounts of water from the lagoon into the sea, I met with Giovanni Caniato, an archivist for the Archivio di Stato di Venezia (Venetian State Archives). Over the course of several meetings, I discovered that he is also a writer of early Venetian history and a leader in Venice's boat-restoration movement.

"In the sixteenth century, when they started the major works of diverting rivers, the Venetians did not have the financial security we have today and certainly not the technical systems we have today," says Caniato. He is seated at the end of a long, gleaming wooden table inside the state archives building lo-cated in a former convent adjacent to the church of Santa Maria Gloriosa dei Frari. An earnest and youthful-appearing man in his early forties, he has a deep tan that makes it obvious he spends a great deal of time in his oar-powered boat, known since ancient times as a *batela*, plying the waters of his native city.

"It was not easy for the state, as rich and powerful as it was then, to find the money for such huge hydraulic works, be-cause maybe they were at war with the Turkish Empire and so they had to finance their army or their navy as well. But they managed to do certain huge works that today nobody would think to do. Diverting a river for twenty, thirty, or fifty miles is not something that is so simple.

"It was done by hand, naturally—digging by hand and then taking away the earth." Unlike the Romans and the Greeks, whose empires were built on the backs of conquered peoples, the Venetians used the local people who lived in numerous villages along the mainland.

"The workers were paid," Caniato says. "A good system Venice had was to have these works done especially in the wintertime. They did this first because the tide was usually lower in January and February. And, second, they used winter because the peasants from the hinterland worked in agriculture in the summer and had no work in the winter. So there was a ready work force. They were paid a fair wage, and the Venetians had thousands of peasants, or country workers, who were brought from places like Brescia, from Treviso, from Padua, from Belluno—and they did this excavation by hand."

All this, he says—"centuries and centuries of works"—was designed to maintain the delicate balance between sea and land. "The goal was to maintain the lagoon wide and maintain the lagoon salty, because without this the republic would have crashed." Without the saltwater and freshwater balance, mosquitoes would breed and Venetians would have died by the tens of thousands. "The republic, without the protection of the lagoon militarily, would have found herself in a bad position."

But in these works as in many others, the Venetians were never in a hurry, and Caniato suggests that the push to build multibillion-dollar gates today could benefit from this take-it-slow approach. The thirty years during which Venetians, other Italians, and the international community have been debating gates is nothing in the grand scheme of time, the archivist-writer suggests.

"For diverting the Piave, they took about 150 years from the first discussion to the decision. They started discussing it in the first half of the sixteenth century, and they did the diversion in the second half of the seventeenth century. They would start a certain diversion, see that it would not work, and they would then change it until the actual course of the Piave was changed."

I could not help but wonder, as we honor the great artists of Renaissance Italy, why we have so little knowledge about the practical civil engineering skills of a dedicated collection of people who centuries ago created Venice and kept it afloat far beyond what its natural life would have allowed.

CHAPTER FOUR ~

Tides, Winds, and Global Warming

Sun-girt City, thou hast been
Ocean's child, and then his queen;
Now is come a darker day,
And thou soon must be his prey.
—SHELLEY, "LINES WRITTEN AMONG
  THE EUGANEAN HILLS"

Located near the top of the Adriatic, a distance of five hundred miles from the main body of the Mediterranean, Venice is in the middle of a giant moat surrounding the republic's historic center. The city's geographic location is so unique that it was allowed to survive for centuries, despite successive challenges, until 1797. The Adriatic's average width is only about one hundred miles, which makes the sea more defendable than, say, the wide-open Mediterranean. And the short distances between Venetian-controlled ports along the Italian and Balkan Peninsulas made it possible for large flat-bottomed Venetian boats, designed specifically for the shallow Mediterranean coastline, to hug friendly shores and spend each night in a safe port.

Ultimately, if the Adriatic was ever breached by a foe, Venice's main defense was the giant lagoon, which surrounded the city's center. Venetian boats made their way across the vast mudflats and along hidden channels whose mysterious routes and locations, then unmarked (in contrast to today's giant wooden pilings and amber lights), were known only to the tight-lipped Venetian boatmen.

But while this position is enviable with regard to holding back invaders, it makes Venice and its lagoon vulnerable to the region's climate and tidal action. And this position, near the Adriatic's rounded north end—often likened to the rounded end of a giant bathtub—is where conflicting winds like the northbound sirocco and the southbound *bora* collide over Italy's shallow eastern shoreline. This conjunction of wind and tide contributes much to the lagoon's climatic grief in today's world of rising sea levels.

One side of the Adriatic is different from the other. Along the Italian coastline south of Venice to the southern edge of the peninsula's heel, where the Adriatic meets the Ionian Sea, the coast is relatively straight, with few islands. To the east, along the Balkan Peninsula, there are numerous steep mountainous islands with shorelines that plunge deep into the sea. In a sense these islands and their multitude of inlets resemble Norwegian fjords.

To the west the relatively tame nature of the Italian coast also means the waters there are shallow, particularly between Venice and Ravenna, where the mighty Po River spills out into the Adriatic.

Throughout the Mediterranean it is often difficult to determine where one sea begins and another ends. By contrast, the Adriatic's configuration makes it a definitive body physically separate from the rest of the Mediterranean's subsets of seas, often indistinguishable from one another by any landform. It is this separation—and the physical layout of the two shorelines running north and south—that creates tides not found elsewhere in the greater Mediterranean.

Adriatic tides, linked with those of the Ionian Sea, sweep up along the Italian and Balkan coasts from the south. The tidal range—the distance between low and high tide—averages three feet. Elsewhere in the Mediterranean that range is less than a foot. Strabo was one of the earliest of the ancient writers who noted that the narrower Adriatic experienced higher tides than the rest of the Mediterranean.

Tides, of course, are caused by the gravitational effects on the earth by the moon and the sun and, to a lesser degree, the other planets. When the moon is overhead, its gravitational pull forces water beneath it to rise up. Then the force of this heavenly body pulls the water across the seas' surfaces as the moon moves around the earth.

Generally there are two high tides and two low tides each day. The sun and other heavenly bodies also enter into this equation, and the effects of their combined gravitational pull on the earth's surface as the earth rotates on its axis and moves around the sun compound the moon's effects. These astronomical impacts by themselves can be figured precisely. Calendars that predict the precise times for high and low tides and their relationship to relative sea level in every location worldwide are drawn up years in advance.

But the mere presence of the moon and the sun and their relative positions to Earth do not fully explain tidal phenomena. Bulges of water pulled up by heavenly gravitational forces are affected, as they move around and across the earth's seas, by the continents they bump into, by the inertia of the water itself, and by the depth of the water at any given moment.

This explains why all tides are not equal around the world, and, more specifically, why the Adriatic's tides are different from those found in the rest of the Mediterranean: the narrowness of the Adriatic itself, and the nature of the relatively shallow Italian coastline versus deeper water off coasts elsewhere.

For ships far out to sea, this tide bubble floating above relative sea level in a pattern dictated by the moon and the sun is not noticeable. Tides are most easily observed along seacoasts, where they move up and down beaches and into and out of river estuaries. As these tides run into the shallow waters along the edges of continents, their rate of advance is reduced, and their rise and fall are amplified. It is along such landmasses—with their variety of coastal depths, gulfs, channels, and estuaries—that tidal differences occur from place to place around the globe. And it also depends on where the moon is between being full or slack, and on its position relative to Earth, and on Earth's location with respect to the sun.

It is all these variables, plus the exceptional variable of what weather may be doing to the waters of the seas at any given moment at any given point, that make the prediction of actual tides so difficult. As many as forty components are often used to calculate tidal predictions at any one location on the earth's surface at any one time.

The tides at Venice that so dramatically affect the city and cause repeated flooding are no higher than they have traditionally been during human occupation of the Italian Peninsula. The problem there and elsewhere is that ocean levels are higher than they were when the medieval city was built. Of course the regular tides then ride in on these higher seas, routinely pushing water higher and higher against the city's defenses.

Added to this is the fact that the land underneath the Venetian lagoon is sinking—both naturally, as soils that were deposited by ancient rivers continue to compress, and because humans in the twentieth century began removing groundwater from the aquifer beneath the city for industrial uses along the lagoon's coastal periphery. This was stopped in the early 1970s, and subsidence has slowed considerably. However, the seas continue to rise.

The higher sea level exaggerates the effect storms have on the tides and what they do to the land when the laws of probability win out and certain storm conditions collide with the rise of regular tides.

For example, a high-pressure weather system pushes down on the water in the sea; a low-pressure system pulls it up into a dome. This happens worldwide but most dramatically, for our purposes, in the Adriatic. If a low-pressure system coincides with a rising tide, the water dome that the meteorological low pulls up rides on top of the tide itself. This compounds the amount of water being pushed by winds across the sea and toward land. When the two conditions merge like that, it is called a storm tide or a storm surge.

Two types of major winds nearly always drive the storms in the Adriatic. First, the *bora* is a strong, cold wind that blows from the northeast onto the Adriatic region of Italy and the Balkans. Most common in winter, when the Venetian lagoon is most vulnerable to high water, it can reach speeds of more than sixty miles (one hundred kilometers) per hour. Second, the sirocco, a warm, humid wind that blows northward out of Africa, begins as a dry wind. But it picks up moisture as it moves ahead of the low-pressure centers that travel eastward over the southern Mediterranean.

If a storm-driven high tide is being buffeted by the *bora* from the north, the dome of water can be pushed down the Adriatic from its northern edge near Trieste and crash into the southern edge of the Venetian lagoon at Chioggia, the area's main fishing port.

If a sirocco is pushing the storm tide up the Adriatic from the south, this surge of millions of gallons of additional water can push into all three inlets to the lagoon, or, as in November 1966, across the barrier islands of the Lido and Pellestrina. And if the winds hold the extra water there for several hours, as they did during that massive 1966 flood, and the water cannot reverse its flow back into the Adriatic, the following tide can come in on top of the first, wreaking havoc on the city, its outlying islands, and its people.

Of course this is all like a lottery, in which Venice is the only player. The odds of the city being the focal point of such a combination of weather and tides are high, and that is why floods occurring at levels like the one that hit the city in 1966 are rare. Historians estimate that this kind of high water— about six feet (nearly two meters) above relative sea level—has occurred only about five times in the human history of Venice. This is so infrequent that generations go by without any direct sense of what such high water can do. Who, for example, is left to remember the horror of the famous 1906 San Francisco earthquake, which devastated an area that new generations continue to flock to and build on? This denial, even in the face of lesser subsequent events, reflects human nature.

The bigger problem for Venice, and one unique to the twentieth century, will not likely be a repeat of the 1966 flood. Flooding of that magnitude is a long way from becoming a regular event. Rather, it is that sea levels are rising all over the world because of a phenomenon known as global warming, and regular minor and medium flooding is expected to increase in frequency. Eventually Venetians and tourists alike could be walking through water several times a month rather than just once in a while.

In 1997 the Intergovernmental Panel on Climate Change (IPCC) estimated that by 2100—just a century from now—the mean annual global surface temperature will increase by between one and three and one-half degrees Celsius, and that global mean sea level could rise at the extreme end as much as three feet (ninety-five centimeters) over the same period! The IPCC report was in the process of being updated in early 2001 by the World Meteorological Organization (WMO) and the UN Environment Program. The IPCC had suggested that the average rate of warming would be greater than any seen in the past ten thousand years. And its estimate of global sea-level rise represented a rate two to five times higher than what has been experienced over the past one hundred years.

Of course, as Venetians and millions of others living in coastal environments around the world are realizing, these climatic factors will have a dramatic impact on the social and economic well-being of coastal inhabitants. The IPCC estimates that 46 million people a year are potential victims of flooding from storm surges. The sixty thousand permanent residents of Venice's historic center certainly have lots of company.

This increase in mean sea level at Venice's very doorstep means the minor storms that ordinarily in ancient times would not have put St. Mark's Square under water now do so regularly. To illustrate the impact of a significant sea-level rise over the next several decades, picture this: Imagine that nothing is done to raise the pavements along the edges of the lagoon at the Piazzetta San Marco or to improve an ancient drainage system that acts as a reverse conduit to carry high water *into* the piazzetta and square. Then imagine that sea level has risen by twenty-three to twenty-seven inches (sixty to seventy centimeters) above what it is today. This would permanently put water into the piazzetta and square—day in, day out. It may be a minor inconvenience now for Venetians to pull on rubber boots a few times a month in order to walk to work, but what would the inconvenience be when it becomes a daily event? Slipping on rubber boots would be as common as clipping on a cell phone is today. Then there is the problem of the damage done to the city's very fabric by the repeated action of water— its stones and the buildings formed by those stones.

Most responsible scientists, after years of debate over whether global warming really exists, now generally accept the concept. What many disagree on is how long the trend will last. Is it a short-term cycle that will reverse after a few more decades, or is it longer term—something that can be measured in geological times of thousands, or hundreds of thousands, of years? IPCC scientists estimate that even if global greenhouse-gas emissions are stabilized by 2100, global warming will continue to raise sea levels. In a proposed summary statement for the IPCC's 2001 updated global warming assessment, the scientists said: "Global mean surface temperature will continue to increase and sea level will continue to rise due to thermal expansion for hundreds of years after concentrations of CO_2 have been stabilized, owing to the long timescales on which the deep ocean adjusts to climate change."

Scientists believe that the earth's temperature increased by at least 1.1 degree Fahrenheit (0.6 degree Celsius) over the last century. Within the last twenty-five years, temperatures seem to be rising at a quicker rate. Some scientists estimate that temperatures have jumped in the past two decades alone by one-half a degree—a rapid increase when compared with trends of the previous eighty years. Go back even farther in time. Some estimates put the world only five to nine degrees warmer than it was in the last ice age—about the time when the northern Adriatic was dry land, tying what is now Italy and the Balkans into one landmass. The IPCC's proposed summary for its 2001 report stated flatly: "The rate of sea-level rise during the 20th century was about ten times greater than the average rate over the last 3,000 years."

On a more seasonal basis, scientists during the late summer of 2000 were saying that average springtime temperatures in northern Europe have risen by more than two degrees Fahrenheit during the past two decades. This is because wind patterns have blown warm, moist air off the North Atlantic to northern Europe.

Scientists are also quoted as saying that the earth's ice cover is melting in more places and at higher rates than at any time since record keeping began. According to the Worldwatch Institute, global ice melting accelerated in the 1990s, the warmest decade on record.

On March 24, 2000, *The New York Times* reported that a group of scientists from the National Oceanographic Data Center in Silver Spring, Maryland, believes that the world's oceans have "soaked up much of the global warming of the last four decades, delaying its full effect on the atmosphere and thus on climate." This is disturbing because it is the warmer atmosphere that has affected climate through the last half of the twentieth century, and the seas are feeding the atmosphere as they begin to release even more heat. "Some experts believe that about half the greenhouse warming is still in the oceanic pipeline and will inevitably percolate to the air in the decades just ahead," the *Times* article stated.

Another study—this one an analysis of freeze-and-thaw records for twenty-six bodies of water in North America, Asia, and Europe—suggests that these waters are freezing about 8.7 days later over the past century and a half and are thawing in the spring about 9.8 days earlier. The Associated Press quotes John Magnuson, a researcher at the University of Wisconsin (Madison): "It is clearly getting warmer in the Northern Hemisphere. This is very strong evidence of a general warming from 1845 to 1995 in areas where there is ice cover."

Many scientists linked this kind of evidence to what is known as the "greenhouse effect," caused by human-made pollution and concentrations of carbon dioxide in the atmosphere. According to one report quoted in the *International Herald Tribune*, "Loss of the ice would not only affect the global climate, it would raise sea levels and lead to regional flooding, damaging property, and endangering lives."

Even this observation is controversial. The melting of Arctic ice in the Northern Hemisphere might not affect sea levels as much as the melting of Greenland ice or of Antarctic ice in the Southern Hemisphere. Arctic ice floats on the sea, like ice cubes in a drink. Due to the effects of displacement, the blended water from melted ice cubes in a drink do not overflow the top of the glass. The Greenland and Antarctic ice sheets lie frozen on the ground, and if melted would add to the world's seawater. But there was good news in late 2000—at least for the next one hundred years. In the case of the West Antarctica Ice Sheet, according to IPCC projections for its 2001 report, "Major loss of grounded ice and accelerated sea-level rise is now believed to be very unlikely during the 21st century."

According to these reports, the real problem is the warming of sea water because of atmospheric warming. A UN–sponsored panel has predicted that average global temperatures will rise from two to six degrees over the next one hundred years if current greenhouse gas emissions are not curtailed.

In addition to rising seas in areas such as the Adriatic coastline, such warming would allow crops to be grown in areas that are too cool for them now. An Associated Press report has pointed out that Georgia in the United States could become as well known for oranges as it is for its peaches, and higher levels of carbon dioxide would increase crop yields because plants need the gas for photosynthesis.

But that is an optimistic viewpoint. Such climatic changes from one part of the planet to another would have devastating effects as well. For example, Africa-like desert conditions are hopscotching into southern Italy and are moving north up the peninsula. Much of the Italian south—in antiquity a region so agriculturally rich and diverse that it lured successive waves of colonists and conquerors—is becoming desert. Summers are drier and hotter, and winters are warmer than they were just a decade ago.

Obviously, in geological time, such cyclical shifts occur over millions of millennia. The dry, desertlike interior in the U.S.

West, where I live, was once rain forest with vegetation-chomping dinosaurs everywhere. In more recent times, ancient cities built along the Mediterranean shoreline of Egypt are being discovered deep within the sea just off the modern coastline. A warming trend over the millennia, boosted by shifts in landmasses due to plate tectonics and earthquakes, has progressively brought the sea over what was once dry land.

I needed answers to global warming questions and what the phenomenon does to sea levels around the globe, so I called Henry Pollack, professor of geophysics at the University of Michigan. I was drawn to him because news reports in early 2000 detailed results of his studies dealing with temperature changes worldwide. His research, as reported in the February 24 edition of *The Washington Post*, indicates that at a majority of his test sites worldwide, data show the earth has warmed by an average of 1.8 degrees Fahrenheit since 1500, with 80 percent of that occurring since 1800 and more than 50 percent since 1900. Pollack and his colleagues did not use tree-ring analysis—a traditional method—to come to these conclusions, but instead lowered thermometers down 616 boreholes left around the globe by oil and geological drillers and others.

Pollack chose this method because he knows that heat moves two ways: down into the earth from the planet's sun- and air-warmed crust, and up from the earth's molten core. Researchers lowered the thermometers, subtracted the bottom-up signal from the readings, and then read from the deep rock itself—some boreholes were a quarter-mile deep—a history of temperature shifts over time as they propagate down through the rock. Pollack found that over one thousand years, heat pulses penetrate only about sixteen hundred feet.

In the same *Washington Post* article, reporter Curt Suplee wrote that any warming detected during the sixteenth, seventeenth, and eighteenth centuries was probably not caused by human activity but came about through the gradual recovery from a prolonged cold period that gripped Europe from 1400 to 1850. It was not until the middle of the Industrial Revolution, in the early nineteenth century, that atmospheric carbon dioxide levels began to rise.

I asked Pollack to provide a quick education in global warming.

"Sea-level rise does not respond to local circumstance," he says. Melting ice caps are not as significant a factor in increasing mean sea level as the heating of seawater by an increasingly warmer atmosphere.

"As the atmosphere warms, so does ocean water," Pollack says. "If oceans represent a big bathtub, you heat up the water and the water rises higher in the tub because water molecules expand when heated. If the water is near the top edge of the tub to begin with, during heating it spills over onto the land."

This fits the Adriatic Sea scenario, where the northern ends of the Gulf of Venice and the Gulf of Trieste actually resemble the curved end of such a tub. The water here and elsewhere around the globe is warmer, pushing the Adriatic higher up onto land, and, over the centuries, the sea level is rising. Over the past century alone, Pollack says, relative sea level has risen about four inches (ten centimeters).

Combine this sea-level rise with storm tides, and you have a recipe for Venice's problems as well as for similar flooding problems elsewhere around the globe.

"These may seem like small numbers, but this small amount has big impacts in the natural world," Pollack continues. "When Darwin sailed through the Beagle Channel in 1834, he saw many glaciers tumbling into the sea from the south Patagonian ice fields. Now those ice fields are a ways inland."

A Knight-Ridder News Service story dated August 24, 2000, reports that progressively warmer springs in northern Europe "have whacked a population of birds out of sync with the caterpillars they eat." Birds there are laying eggs earlier than they used to. For example, Knight-Ridder reports: "In the Netherlands, late spring has been warming up, while early spring has remained cold. Caterpillars appear in response to the mid-spring temperature swing, before the bird eggs—delayed by the cold—can hatch."

Pollack puts all this in perspective: "Remember also that ten centimeters is a tenth of a meter, and the rise of sea level by only 3.28 feet (one meter) is enough to inundate southern Florida."

Like some scientists who think in geological terms as opposed to human terms, Pollack has a global view of rising seas, rather than looking at just their effect in a local context. There are plenty of places in danger, not just Venice, he says.

Consider the Maldives, a drop-dead-gorgeous chain of 1,192 coral atolls in the Indian Ocean, off the southern tip of India. Ever-rising seas regularly flood many of these atolls, including the island-nation's capital of Male, only inches above sea level. Male is partly ringed by a six-foot concrete sea barrier known as the Great Wall of Male, but officials there are not in denial about the inevitable. They know that the wall will keep the sea out for only a few more decades. They are building up an artificial island six feet above sea level, where the population, now numbering about 280,000, would move when the "great flood" comes.

Also endangered by a combination of subsidence and the global rise in seas is Bangkok, Thailand. This Asian city was once known as the "Venice of the East" for its numerous wide canals. Now mostly paved over to accommodate roads, these canals, called klongs, were Bangkok's traditional means of waste disposal. In addition, factories and housing estates have consumed thousands of acres of land once used as drainage systems, and the groundwater underlying the city is being consumed at a rate double the amount that can safely be removed without affecting the soil. According to a correspondent's August 25, 2000, report in the *Pittsburgh Post-Gazette*: "The Thai capital may be completely below sea level within 50 years. . . . Bangkok is sinking by as much as five centimeters [nearly two inches] per year. Already, six square miles have fallen below sea level. . . . Despite the potential for disaster, the government has taken no action"—ostensibly because government officials "are unwilling to alienate industry and land owners before the general election."

Closer to home, Pollack points out, more than half the U.S. population lives within fifty miles of a shoreline. Rising seas eventually will create havoc there as well.

"Why are we fighting to save Venice?" Pollack asks rhetorically. "Maybe that is the story you should be following. There is a certain attitude along the eastern U.S. seaboard: You don't fight with nature, you move. The early settlers along the East Coast built houses so they could move them. The attitude is that the ocean is slowly gaining ground along the modern shore, and you can't win the fight along shifting beaches, and you can't fortify a beach so it won't move. In the past, of course, people were more mobile and would simply move when water increasingly invaded their homes. Now we don't have those choices. We own property and we can't just wander.

"I am not suggesting [moving] for Venice, of course," he adds. "But rising sea levels should cause people to rethink what they do at sea level."

For the short term, Pollack believes, there will not be a significant change in what global warming will do to the planet in terms of rising sea levels. People in their thirties today can expect to see warmer temperatures in their lifetimes. And they will also see continued sea-level rise; biological, agricultural, and precipitation patterns will shift. And perhaps they will be growing oranges in Georgia.

"I don't think all these changes will be thought of as good," the geophysicist says. "Some places will get better agriculture and other places will get worse agriculture. Wars have been fought over instabilities much smaller than this."

CHAPTER FIVE ~

Acqua Alta

The rate at which Venice is going is about
that of a lump of sugar in hot tea.
—JOHN RUSKIN,
    LETTER TO GEORGE RICHMOND

Before the twentieth century, high-water disasters of the kind that slammed Venice in November 1966 were rare. A high-water incident that would cause Ruskin to think that the end of Venice was nigh is now commonplace. If left entirely up to nature, a flood of the magnitude of the 1966 event would be a rarity. But humans, whose lifestyles and industry contribute significantly to global warming through greenhouse-gas emissions, have increased the probability that this type of flooding will occur more frequently. Humans also allowed the city's infrastructure and defenses to deteriorate, created new channels within the lagoon and deepened existing ones, and permitted thirty years of industrial pumping of groundwater from deep beneath Venice—a practice that hastened the city's sinking and was finally halted by government fiat in the early 1970s. The seas are rising much more quickly than nature would ordinarily allow, and Venice—as well as countless other coastal regions around the world—is in greater jeopardy than ever before.

A high-water record, kept over the past century, shows dramatically how flooding, no matter how minor, has gone from the unusual to the commonplace. Water enters St. Mark's Square at about twenty-seven inches (seventy centimeters) above mean sea level. This is routine, and tourists and residents alike have grown accustomed to seeing water at this level rising through the city's drains into the open area directly in front of St. Mark's Basilica. At many high tides, water can often be found there quietly lapping against the magnificent colored marbles and granite columns that front the foundation of this impressive church, and tourists must enter by means of elevated walkways.

In one year alone—1996—there were ninety-nine tides over thirty-one inches (eighty centimeters), including seven storms in which the tidal level was greater than forty-three inches (110 centimeters) and two storms greater than fifty-one inches (150 centimeters). That was an exceptional year. Generally St. Mark's Square is flooded fifty times a year, compared with seven times a year in 1900 and twenty times annually during the 1950s. Or, in another context, the minimum high-water mark to flood St. Mark's Square—twenty-seven inches (seventy centimeters)—was reached 1,013 times between 1970 and 1979.

But for exceptionally high waters, measuring more than 3.5 feet (1.10 meters), the progression over the last century and a half has been dramatic. In the forty years between 1867 and

1907, the water went above that elevated height a mere seven times; in the forty-seven years between 1907 and 1954, that height was exceeded twenty-two times; and it topped 3.5 feet twenty-four times in the ten years between 1954 and 1964. Keep in mind that at 4.6 feet (1.4 meters), 90 percent of the city is flooded. It was inevitable that the events of November 3–5, 1966, would take place.

Floods at 4.9 feet (1.5 meters) or more above mean sea level—the 1966 level, remember, was at 6.37 feet (1.94 meters)—are predicted to occur every fifteen years, and they have happened, in modern times, predictably, in 1951, 1966, 1979, and 1986. A flood that peaked at 4.7 feet (1.44 meters) occurred in November 2000. It is inevitable that such levels, and higher ones, will occur on an ever-increasing scale.

Archaeological research tells us that from the early fifth century to the eleventh century—the period when the mosaic floors of the churches at Torcello and San Marco were laid—Venetians had raised ground level by six feet.

New research conducted by Albert Ammerman and a group of colleagues takes the known development of the lagoon back much farther than the first recorded chronicles of the early fifth century. Their studies show that today the current sea level is sixteen feet (4.9 meters) higher than it was six thousand years ago when the lagoon was formed. And, they warn, the trend of sinking land and rising waters continues in league with global warming and geological shifting.

According to a news release from one of Ammerman's sponsors—the National Geographic Society—the scientists conducted specially tailored acoustical studies, using new dating techniques. They determined that relative sea level rose rather slowly in Venice—about three inches (7.6 centimeters) per century—between 4000 B.C.E. and C.E. 400, immediately prior to the first invasion by the barbarians and the early use of the lagoon islands as places of refuge.

After that, as construction of the city began in earnest over the next few centuries, the sea level increased at an average rate of five inches (12.7 centimeters) per century, and that level has accelerated during the twentieth century to as much as ten inches (25.4 centimeters).

Systematic monitoring of the height of tides has been possible for barely more than one hundred years. The first gauge, placed in 1897, now sits near the church of Santa Maria della Salute just across the water from the Doges' Palace and the Piazzetta San Marco. The zero mark on the gauge represents relative sea level at the time the instrument was placed. Now, of course, with the natural sinking, or subsidence, of the lagoon caused by ongoing compression of the Po River sediments and the unnatural sinking caused by twentieth-century extraction of groundwater for industrial purposes, relative sea level in reality is nine inches (twenty-three centimeters) above the zero mark.

The impact of this twentieth-century phenomenon is certainly increasing the frequency of high-water incidents in Venice. As UNESCO stated in a 1983 report:

It is important to note that when the height of the tide reaches 1.3 m, 62 per cent of the city is covered by water. For a height of 1.2 m, the percentage drops to 33 per cent, for 1.1 m to 15 per cent and for 1 m to 5 per cent. Between 0.7 m (when

Acqua Alta ~ 95

water appears in St. Mark's Square) and 1 m, the flooding
only affects only a few central areas, the *acqua alta* familiar to
many tourists.

It is also important to note that these heights are relative
to the zero mark on the tide gauge. What many people do not
often consider is the fact that the real zero level, because of
natural and unnatural sinking of the city's sediments over
the past century, has moved twenty-three centimeters higher
than the fixed zero mark on the gauge. This casts new meaning on the numbers denoting the high tides in the statement.
The twenty-three-centimeter rise above 1897's zero mark and
what should be real zero today was computed in 1983 by scientists at the Venice-based National Research Council, or
Consiglio Nazionale delle Ricerche (CNR). In the nearly two
decades since then, that rise has remained unchanged.

Looking at the 1966 crisis, for example, the adding of
twenty-three centimeters to the 6.37 feet (1.94-meter) storm-
tide level relative to zero on the tidal gauge puts in a different
perspective the "real" height of 7.1 feet (2.17 meters) above
relative sea level.

Almost everyone agrees that more frequent winter flooding of
Venice, even at the lower, more routine levels, is an increasingly prevalent phenomenon in this century. Of course, it is
possible that human interference has little to do with the
impact of the rare, gigantic storm systems—such as the one
that fueled the November 1966 catastrophe—that, strictly by
chance, ride on top of exceptionally high tides. It could be
that there is no way to absolutely guarantee the safety of Venice
from such storms, no matter how high the city's perimeters

are raised or how well its lagoon is defended at the three entrances.

It would be like trying to protect every square mile of San Francisco from massive killer earthquakes. New buildings can be constructed to higher standards, but severe damage is inevitable if the earthquake is strong enough. Elsewhere, people routinely build subdivisions within floodplains that will flood on average every 100 or 500 years, ignoring the possibility that everything might be lost in one giant flood that would be prohibitively expensive to defend against for such a rare occurrence.

Consider the folks around Los Angeles who build homes hard against the San Gabriel Mountains. They know, as naturalist John McPhee describes in his 1989 book *In Control of Nature*, that every few years massive debris flows blast out of canyon mouths, sending boulders "as big as a Chevrolet" down on their houses and towns. Many of these Los Angeles residents rebuild on the same spots as soon as the debris is cleared away, even though they know that in a few years or a few decades, the same disaster can strike again. As McPhee writes, "they would rather defy nature than live without it." He quotes one Los Angeles resident who lives in the mouth of a San Gabriel canyon: "People often ask why we continue to live here. We have a fire nearly every year and the floods follow. . . . Each time we have a disaster, only one or two families move out, but there are hundreds standing in line waiting to move in. People live here, come hell or high water."

Humans, thinking in terms of average life spans and not geological, or even historic, time frames, typically make the choice "in the here and now" when deciding where to live and to build. The Venetians were no different over the centuries than McPhee's twentieth-century Angelinos, and they are no different today.

The tides that flow into and out of the Venetian lagoon do so with routine precision. The early Venetians knew their importance and worked diligently to preserve their integrity. Twice-a-day high tides move into the lagoon, and when they recede a few hours later, the accumulated sewage that pours forth from buildings—soapsuds from kitchen sinks and the day's laundry, and effluents from toilets, all raw and untreated—is carried from the canals to the Adriatic beyond the barrier islands of the Lido and Pellestrina. These dregs are replaced by fresher seawater, and the cleansing cycle begins again a few hours later.

This is why, through history, Venice has had no need for a conventional sewer system of pipes hauling sewage away from the city and, in more modern times, to treatment plants. The lagoon and its tides are the sewer system, and that is why Italian law is quite rigid in decreeing that nothing must be done to the lagoon to alter this vital process. The Venetians, in their own time of the republic, were even more rigid, decreeing death to anyone who did not follow strict laws regarding water.

For centuries the process worked so well that Venetians gave it little thought. Entire generations would live between infrequent high-water disasters—much as some people who live near or on top of fault lines or within floodplains never experience an earthquake or flood. Their ancestors may have and their progeny might, but they themselves never felt the earth tremble and saw buildings tumble. So it was with different generations of early Venetians.

The Italian news service ANSA produced a report in 1996 charting the thirty years of travails Venice has faced since the 1966 flood as it searched for a solution to the city's flooding woes. The report detailed the many centuries that Venetians struggled with high water, listing, for example, the flood in C.E. 527 that reportedly destroyed Malamocco. In 589, nearly 250 years before what we know as the historic center of Venice was inhabited on a grand scale, ANSA reports that the entire lagoon delta was hit by a "cataclysm" of some sort that swept away roads and changed the courses of rivers. The people reportedly said at the time, "We are living neither on land nor on the water." Other inundations were reported over the subsequent centuries, principally in 782, 840, and 875. In 1102 a great flood erupted during a major earthquake. In 1240 the chronicles tell of water sweeping through Venetian streets at the height of a man, and in 1268 comes the first discussion of victims. Then "the water rose from eight o'clock until midday. Many were drowned inside their houses or simply died of the cold," according to the ANSA report.

Floods took place over the intervening centuries as well. Some resulted in "more than a million in gold" in damages to goods and houses. Rainwater cisterns, jealously protected against invasion by seawater, were often breached.

But closest to the November 1966 catastrophe was a flood on Christmas Day, 1794, three years before Napoleon shut down the republic for good. A newspaper article of the time describes the event:

> After the blowing of icy tramontana winds which suffered us all extreme cold, we are dominated by the sirocco in this beneficial season. But its visit produced great disorders. A full tide of swollen and enraged sea made the waters in the lagoon

and inside the canals grow so much, that it came into the great *Piazza* from one end to the other, and all the streets subjected to its extraordinary flooding.

No depth was given. Perhaps this great catastrophe of 1794 was no more significant than many of the floods that now routinely affect Venice.

Given that it takes a long time for Venetians, both historically and in modern times, to conceive of a need, design plans, and implement public works, government leaders finally decided in the fourteenth century to build up the sea defenses along the barrier islands. These were initially basic, impermanent structures that needed constant reinforcing and replacing. Especially heavy seas in the late 1600s washed away three hundred years of such rudimentary efforts, and it was only then that the Venetian Republic, in its last century of life before Napoleon forever changed things, launched a massive plan, executed in the mid-to-late 1700s, to build up the sea defenses of the Lido and Pellestrina.

Instead of clay-and-reed structures, the republic used huge blocks of Istrian marble carried across the northern Adriatic to where its craftsmen cut, fitted, and mortared the stone into place. To understand the size of the undertaking—if Venetians could divert mighty rivers, this task must not have been considered too insurmountable—consider these figures: The biggest seawall on the island of Pellestrina and, farther south at Sottomarina near Chioggia, would be 5,297 meters long. It would become 4.5 meters high. Its base would be 14 meters thick. The first stones were laid in 1744, the last in 1783—and the republic died fourteen years later.

Napoleon handed Venice and much of northern Italy off to the Austrians, who continued to maintain and rebuild the seawalls despite a series of destructive storms in the early 1800s. The Venetian newspaper *Il Gazzettino*, in a historic retrospective of these defensive efforts published only a few weeks after the 1966 flood, reported that until the late 1930s the seawalls had been annually reinforced with about fifteen thousand tons of Istrian marble. ANSA quotes this retrospective as saying: "The quantities of rock brought from Istria greatly decreased after 1934, and by 1938, the operation had stopped altogether."

Venice had gone into the fold of a unified Italy in the 1860s, and less and less attention was paid to its infrastructure and lagoon defenses all the way up to 1966. It seems that over recent history, the international community has worried more about Venice's future than have the Italians. Venice's sea defenses fell under a handful of government bureaus that squabbled and ignored her problems for decades. Authors Fay and Knightley, in their 1976 book, *The Death of Venice*, report: "Work on the sea walls was first reduced to an absolute minimum and then virtually abandoned. By the 1960s the ludicrous situation was reached in which the Italian government was spending an average of only one dollar a yard per year to maintain Venice's sea wall defenses."

On top of all this, the lagoon was being transformed in ways unimaginable to its original inhabitants. Giant channels were cut through the lagoon, and the three entrances were widened and buttressed by giant stone jetties—all done to accommodate larger twentieth-century ships.

The 1983 UNESCO report says:

Since the nineteenth century there has been a steady reduction in the surface area of the lagoon. In 1791 it covered a

total of 56,300 hectares. By the end of the nineteenth century, some 5,000 hectares had been wholly or partially enclosed for fish farming, some areas had been filled in and a
railway bridge built across the lagoon. During the present
century, some 2,500 hectares of the lagoon have been re-
claimed for agriculture, a road and an airport have been built
on 800 hectares, and new fisheries—resulting in the extension
of the enclosed area to about 8,400 hectares—have been developed. In the 1950s, a second industrial zone occupied
1,250 hectares and in the 1960s a third industrial zone [now
abandoned] was set aside. . . . As a result of these various
encroachments, the free area of the lagoon today is only about
70 per cent of what it was at the beginning of the nineteenth
century, while its waters have become increasingly marine in
nature as a result of the widening and deepening of the
mouths of the lagoon and of the reduced inflow of fresh
water.

Throughout, the name "Venice" was given to the entire
lagoon—including the mainland communities of Mestre and
what later became the center of the industrial zone, Porto
Marghera, near the village of Marghera—which put into motion political battles that saw the mayor of historic Venice also
become mayor of these zones. Loyalties were divided between
preserving the historic center and pushing moneymaking, job-
creating development.

This modern-era economy began fairly early in the twentieth
century. The area was impoverished through the teens and
early 1920s, when a series of Italian leaders transformed the
lagoon—especially along its mainland crescent—into an industrial zone, keeping the historic center for tourists and the

fringes for real moneymaking activities. Initially the impacts of these changes were small, and it was easy for Venetians to retain local control.

The industrial zone's greatest growth came during the reign of Mussolini. And, Venice being Venice, the city, including Porto Marghera, was spared the destruction of intensive Allied bombing during the later years of World War II. Following the war Porto Marghera blossomed for the same reasons that the Venetian Republic flourished from the thirteenth to the seventeenth centuries: Venice is the closest Western European port to the Middle East. As Fay and Knightley say: "It was natural that, as Europe's demand for oil grew greedily after the war, Porto Marghera should grow with it."

Beginning about 1925, the government allowed the business owners to pump groundwater, located in a broad, deep aquifer that underlies the Venetian lagoon. Reportedly thousands of wells were drilled, and the subterranean water bubble that had undergirded the lagoon for millennia began to deflate.

As part of the Po River basin and sitting on that river's sediment, Venice sinks naturally at a faster rate than other coastal areas along the Adriatic. Ravenna, to the south of Venice and at the southern extreme of the Po River delta, sits on even deeper Po River sediment and is sinking naturally at an even more accelerated rate.

But the water extraction from beneath Venice accelerated its natural settlement process. Albert Ammerman believes that if this pumping had never been allowed, it would have taken until about 2050 before Venice would have sunk naturally to the point where it is today in relation to the rising sea level.

The groundwater withdrawal was halted in the early 1970s. Many nontechnical people believe that, due to the end of industrial water extraction in 1973, the bubble beneath the city should reinflate and push the city upward. But a series of hydrologists I talked to debunked this notion.

"In 1975 we measured a little rebound in the historical center. But this is not a real gain against subsidence," says Dr. Laura Carbognin, a hydrologist with Italy's CNR. Rather, she describes it as the reaction of a sponge when it is pressed down. "If you push on a sponge and lift your hand, it will recover," like the slight rebound of the below-Venice aquifer she and her colleagues measured in 1975. "You remove the pressure and the soil says 'Ahhhh.' That is positive behavior, but then the soil settles and becomes stable."

So while water in the aquifer has been recharging over the years since industrial pumping was stopped, the soils beneath the city have already compacted, and natural compaction continues as well, "at a very low rate, I agree, but it is still in progress," Carbognin says.

Carbognin's CNR colleague Dr. Maurizio Bonardi interjects: "Don't forget that the load on the sediments of Venice stays even though extraction of groundwater has stopped." Essentially the water was extracted for nearly five decades, with the most critical phase of depressurization beginning in the 1950s. As water was drawn out, the sediments compacted under the weight of the city's massive buildings, and even though underground water is trying to come back into the aquifer, the compaction continues because of the natural processes and the unrelenting weight of the city. By the time water extraction was stopped in the early 1970s, the land and lagoon area around Marghera had subsided more than 4.7 inches (twelve centimeters) and, around Venice, 3.1 inches (eight centimeters).

While the human-caused sinking of Venice has slowed, global warming and its impact on rising sea levels are the new concern. This is tied to the phenomenon of eustacy, and de-

scribes the variation in sea level that relates to global climate
changes. During cold eras, such as the last ice age, which ended
ten thousand years ago, the continents retain rainfall and
snowfall in the form of glaciers and ice fields. Sea level, as a
result, is lower. Throughout this period, as we have seen, the
northern Adriatic reached only partway up the Italian and
Dalmatian coasts, and the entire area around what is now the
Venetian lagoon was dry land all the way across the Adriatic
to what is today Croatia. As the ice age ended and glaciers and
ice fields began to melt, the northern Adriatic crept upward,
eventually creating the Venetian and Grado lagoons, and isolating former high-elevation Dalmatian landmasses as islands.

This natural atmospheric-heating cycle is expected to continue well through modern times and well into the long view
of the far-distant geological future. It explains the conditions
of rising seas that the early Venetians as well as their twentieth-
century counterparts had to live with. But human-caused
global warming, driven by the introduction of greenhouse
gases into the earth's atmosphere, is compounding this natural
warming.

All these factors together have led to an average annual sea-
level rise in the Venetian lagoon area of 1.27 millimeters over
the past one hundred years. This rise, combined with the increased frequency and heightened power of winter storms
throughout the eastern Mediterranean, create the storm-surge
tides that lie at the crux of Venetian *acque alte*.

Such calamity was certainly not in the mind of Francesco Salvini when, at the age of thirty-six in November 1966, he had
a plum of a job. A Venetian by birth and trained as an electrical engineer, he worked for the national electric company,

On November 4, 1966, with water coming down from a record 6.3 feet (1.94 meters) above sea level, this view greeted Venetians looking southwest from the corner of the Doges' Palace across the Basin of St. Mark's, toward the church of Santa Maria della Salute. CAMERAPHOTO-EPOCHE. VENEZIA

A *carolina* (traditional Venetian boat), left high and dry after the 1966 *acqua grande*, sits in Calle Larga, near the church of San Giacomo dell'Orio in Venice's San Polo quarter.

Crews working to restore and rebuild the city's interior canal system, and to raise pavements to hold back high tides, prepare to dredge a small canal.

SARAH QUILL

RIGHT: A worker prepares a portion of the San Polo canal wall to receive a waterproof covering. The plastic tubes are used to push additional sealants behind the stone. JOHN KEAHEY

BELOW:Colgate University archaeologist Albert Ammerman points to the approximate height of the 1966 flood. The base of the pillar in the background shows the floor of the building's original entryway. Venetians raised the entryway over the centuries to keep it above rising water.

JOHN KEAHEY

The Thames Barrier, near Greenwich and east of London. JOHN KEAHEY

Claudio Boniciolli, president of the Venice Port Authority.

JOHN KEAHEY

Consorzio Venezia Nuova engineer Maria Teresa Brotto.

JOHN KEAHEY

Lady (Frances) Clarke, president of Venice in Peril, in the garden of her Venice home. JOHN KEAHEY

Venice Mayor Paolo Costa at a campaign stop in Campo Santa Margherita during the April 2000 campaign. JOHN KEAHEY

National Research Council scientist Roberto Frassetto. JOHN KEAHEY

Insula President Paolo Gardin at Ponte San Polo, a sixteenth-century bridge overlooking the San Polo canal, where workers are rebuilding and waterproofing its sides. JOHN KEAHEY

Professor Gherardo Ortalli, Italia Nostra board member, at Campo del Traghetto on the Grand Canal, near the Gritti Palace Hotel. JOHN KEAHEY

In the distance, the industrial area of Porto Marghera sits in contrast to Venice's historic center. SARAH QUILL

A typical *acqua alta*. A man wades along the *fondamenta* on the Grand Canal near the Rialto Bridge. SARAH QUILL

Water, at nearly four feet (1.20 meters) above sea level, threatens to float the *passarelle* (duckboards) set up at left for pedestrians. SARAH QUILL

ENEL, in Verona from 1954 to 1964, when he was called back to his home city to head ENEL's operations there.

As a native Venetian, of course, he was no stranger to high water. No Venetian could avoid familiarity with the phenomenon during the middle part of the twentieth century, when portions of the city were periodically flooded during winter months. Salvini, now in his seventies and retired, is sitting back in a comfortable chair in his tastefully appointed living room. He struggles for my benefit with his English, a language he likes to practice as often as he can. He talks about a major flood in 1953, which he calls "the first high water of modern times." This *acqua alta* came into the city at 1.60 meters above zero on the gauge at the Salute. It caused a few, but not insurmountable, problems and led the electric company to elevate its system of transformers and ground-floor household and commercial plugs throughout Venice to positions on the walls at 1.90 meters above the Salute's zero mark.

This worked for a long time—precisely thirteen years. Then disaster struck the city early in November 1966 on the heels of a spring tide—the tide that follows a full moon. The high tide was pushed up the Adriatic the night of November 3 on a storm surge, supplemented by water gathered beneath a low-pressure system. Before the water went down nearly twenty-four hours later, it would crest the following day, November 4, at 6.37 feet (1.94 meters), 1.57 inches (4 centimeters) above the post-1953 level of transformers and plugs.

As soon as the rising salt water hit 1.90 and assaulted that equipment, the city went black. All power was down, and all telephone service—its equipment maintained at the same level on the ground floors of buildings—went dead as well. Fuel tanks holding diesel, then a common fuel for heating (now replaced by natural gas), were breached, and the water became thick and oily, turning black and smelling of petroleum.

"It was terrible," recalls Salvini, who lives comfortably in his two-story home in the Venetian district north of the train station. He lived in this same house in 1966, but the family has always resided on the second-floor level. During the flood the canal outside his door overflowed into the family garden and into the ground-level entrance, creeping slowly up the lower stairs.

"I went to a major transformer station—there were three in Venice then—plus four hundred smaller transformers spread throughout the city. A communications line was raised and we were able to speak to one another, but there was nothing—absolutely nothing—we could do. We had to put out the service in all the town; the blackout was complete."

Complete except for the local hospital. "We made sure the special backup line was working for the hospital. It was an underwater cable, and its transformer was higher."

It took Salvini and his crews, many imported from throughout northern Italy, a full week to restore power to the city. Each one of the three major transformers and all four hundred of the smaller ones were damaged beyond repair. New ones had to be put into place. Normally Salvini had a crew of 150 workers. Those numbers swelled to 400 as the utility workers toiled in wind and rain. He seldom slept during those long seven days, and he saw little of the city during the height of the crisis because his job was to position himself on the Tronchetto, that portion of Venice near the train station where repair parts and new transformers, shipped in by truck and boat, were unloaded. And he often had a rough time of it.

"There was a war on the Tronchetto," he says, describing how he had to clear enough space on the giant docks to receive and hold all of his rapidly arriving gear, space that was coveted by others involved in the recovery and rehabilitation of the city. There was not enough room for everyone and everything, and turf wars were inevitable.

"I spent from five in the morning until late at night organizing the materials: transformers, cables, all the material to completely change Venice's electrical system. I assigned my regular Venetian workers to operate the repair boats full of the outside workers, because my own men knew the city, and the outside workers did not.

"One morning it was impossible to defend the space we needed to get everything. Everyone was fighting, taking space from everyone else. I put the transformers in a circle; I made a fort with enough space inside for just me. People were arriving in trucks and they did not have the patience for your problem." This went on for a week, until all the transformers were installed and power was turned back on.

A variety of images stand out in the minds of Venetians who were in the city when the storm-driven high water hit: the frantic scrabbling of canal rats up the walls of the houses; later, the memory of those sounds was replaced by the fixed images of carcasses—rats, cats, dogs—and of mattresses and other bedding and furniture floating in the canals. Mixed into this mess, compounded by thousands of gallons of diesel fuel, were crates of vegetables and fruit, swept from the market near the Rialto. Maurizia De Min, an archaeologist and now with Venice's Superintendence of Architecture, based in the Doges' Palace, was in Rome when the storm hit. She returned to her family home ten days later, and even after that length of time mattresses, furniture, and other debris were still floating everywhere.

Thirty-four years later De Min still recalls seeing the abundance of rat carcasses, floating "by the thousands," after ten days of routine high and low tides. Luckily, like the Salvinis, her family also lived in a second-floor apartment and was not as hard hit by the flood as were ground-floor dwellers. It was the ruined furniture of these "lower-down" families that floated freely in the lagoon's historic waters—either carried there by the retreating floodwaters or tossed into the canals by distraught homeowners clearing out their soggy interiors. "Now few live on the ground floor in Venice," De Min says.

For Venetians today who were children during November 1966, the memories are less grim. Giovanni Caniato recalls that at age eleven he and his nine-year-old brother broke out the family's rubber dinghy at the height of the flooding and paddled through the city's formerly dry streets from a point near San Samuele, which is three *vaporetto* stops beyond the Ponte dell'Accademia toward the Rialto Bridge, all the way to St. Mark's Square, a distance of slightly more than a half mile.

"It was charming," Caniato remembers fondly. "We do remember the black water, caused by the diesel fuel. Italians call it *gasoil*." Others I spoke with who were children then recall doing the same thing, only instead of a rubber dinghy many used the duckboards the city stacks up to make *passarelle* when the water gets high. Only this time the water was too high, and the duckboards floated off their bases, a delightful toy for Venetian children while their parents were more concerned with saving possessions and even wondering where their next meal would come from.

In 1996 ANSA, a cooperative of Italian newspapers, produced a special report on the flood and the fallout from its aftermath over a thirty-year period. The publication, sponsored in part by the Consorzio Venezia Nuova, sets the stage for a section it calls "That day":

> It was the night of November 3–4, 1966. By 10 o'clock that evening the water was already lapping over the city gunwales, and it was still rising. In the early hours of Friday, November 4, it reached the impressive height of one metre and 27 centimetres. Not that this was anything out of the ordinary in itself, all other things being equal. On February 22 of the same year it had reached one metre 26 centimetres, and on the famous night of October 15, 1960, there had been a tide that reared up 1.45 metres.
>
> But there were so many, too many meteorological factors conspiring against Venice that night: the phase of the moon, the wind, a particularly sharp fall in barometric pressure, and even, it appears, an unusual swell in the Adriatic—a phenomenon known as *seiche*—all contributed to the freakish event that was later likened to the whole city having a heart attack.

The rising spring tide, a reasonably unspectacular event for Venetians in the twentieth century, was caught in a once-in-a-million situation. A multitude of variables had come together that created a disaster of unprecedented proportions in modern Venetian history, one that may never be repeated. It was a dice roll with unexpected consequences.

It had been raining for several days all across northern Italy. Rivers were swollen, and the rain was being driven across Italy by an African sirocco that had formed over Sardinia and moved eastward over mainland Italy toward the Adriatic. According to one contemporary newspaper account, seawater pushed "up against the lagoon outlets and the river mouths that had been swollen by days of rain." The high tide that began building at ten o'clock during the night of November 3 should have dissipated by five the next morning—at least that was how the natural ebb and flow were supposed to work. But the rising, pushing storm did not abate, and its winds held the previous evening's high tide in the lagoon. Held against its natural will, water did not go down as nature intended. "The sea had not drawn off the water that had built up in the lagoon, and the level started rising again, right up to a water mark never before reached in living memory: one metre ninety-four centimetres," ANSA reported.

Meanwhile, elsewhere in the lagoon, because of the telephone blackout, residents in the historic center did not know that a few miles to the southeast seawater was sowing destruction along the *barreni*, or lagoon island barriers that protect Venice from the sea: the Cavallino Peninsula to the north, with its produce farms, fishing villages, and cattle herds; the upscale Lido with its five-star hotels and well-apportioned homes of locals; and the blue-collar fishing villages of Pellestrina to the south of the Lido, separated from its sister island by the narrow Malamocco Channel.

Along these barrier islands, also known in the Venetian vernacular as *lidi*, or sand spits, gales of more than sixty miles an hour whipped up waves that swept over them. ANSA reports that, on Cavallino,

a tidal wave swept away cattle, farm machinery, crops and fishing fixtures, erupted into houses, and ripped boats off their moorings. . . . Farther on, along the Lido, the freak waves were tearing through bathing establishments, smashing hundreds of cabins and wrenching the sand off the beaches.

The violence of the force-eight sea also punched disastrous holes in the lagoon's artificial defenses, the sea ramparts called "Murazzi" which the old Serenissima republic put up in the 18th century; strong, tall walls augmenting the natural defenses.

These were the walls that had fallen into disrepair in the decades following the Austrians' turnover of Venice to the Italian state in the 1860s, and which the Italian government, by 1960, was spending just a dollar a yard per year to maintain.

The tides, climbing one on top of another, were not the only culprits. The rivers, whose mouths the Venetians centuries ago had diverted from the lagoon directly into the Adriatic, were rolling over their banks and over the banks of the diversionary canals, flooding the coastline adjacent to the lagoon's boundaries. The Sile and Brenta Rivers particularly contributed to the problem, pouring fresh water from the land into the lagoon while from the other direction seawater was being pushed in by the winds and riding on the tides from the Adriatic.

Water managers made a crucial decision on November 4 in order to save vast areas of farmland and coastal buildings. The dikes of the Sile River, which for hundreds of years had protected the lagoon from high spring runoff, were breached at the tiny village of Trezze, today only a cluster of three or four buildings. This poured even more fresh water into the lagoon. Water authorities focused on the dikes at Trezze because the Piave River was flooding at five places above the Sile, forcing the Piave's waters down into the already swollen waters of the Sile.

Meanwhile, the Brenta River, south of Venice and near Chioggia, went over its banks without human intervention and poured millions of gallons of out-of-control fresh water into the lagoon as well.

Of course, an event of this kind created episodes of high drama throughout the lagoon. In retelling the stories today, many Venetians who object to the massive projects being proposed for the mouths of the lagoon to safeguard it from another devastating flood point out that there were no deaths from the high water. "What is the problem?" I heard Venetians say, over and over. "The water goes up; it goes down. No one is hurt. This has been happening for centuries and we are still here!" These survivors point out that Venice's 1966 flood was unlike what happened over much of central and northern Italy, where, according to the ANSA report:

> rivers were breaking their banks and sowing death and destruction. On November 6, the toll [in that part of Italy far away from Venice] was 61 dead, a score wounded and 15 missing, but by November 10 the Interior Ministry was talking about 96 dead and 14 missing, and by November 19 the official final toll was 110 dead (nine of them rescue workers) and six missing.

Florence, for example, a city equal to Venice in art treasures, was split in half by the raging Arno River, its low-lying churches and buildings filled with water, mud, and debris to heights topping six feet. Several Florentines died in the river's rushing onslaught, compared to no direct deaths in Venice as the water simply rose up to a point breast-high on the average-size person, and then slowly retreated. A friend arrived in Florence the night of November 5, unaware during a long train ride from the south that the Arno had flooded. "The entire city was dark," he recalls. "We were led across the street by candlelight to a small *pensione* that agreed to take stranded visitors in dire straits."

Despite the Venetians' memory of no deaths in their city, however, the Italian media reported two deaths, albeit far from the historic center but within the lagoon, both near Chioggia at the lagoon's southern end: ". . . a fisherman named Vittorio Vianello, 50. He died of an apparent heart attack while trying to bail water out of his craft, which was about to sink during the storm. . . . At [Sant'Anna] a young farmer, 30-year-old Mario Tonello, died of a heart attack after seeing how badly damaged his farm was."

Since those fateful few days in 1966, water has run high in Venice, but certainly not close to the 1.94-meter mark. Between 1966 and 1995 Venice was invaded more than two hundred times by water more than one meter above average sea level. Remember: This measurement is compounded by the fact that the real "zero" on the tidal gauge at the Salute should be nine inches (twenty-three centimeters) above where the zero was locked into place more than one hundred years ago. So when the measurement reads one meter above zero, in reality it is 1.23 meters above today's mean sea level.

The ANSA report states:

In the 50s, the Marciana area was submerged only six or seven times a year, while now the average is 40. According to information from the city's tidal warning center, 1995 shows 42 cases where tides were at or greater than 80 cm, 18 of which occurred in the second half of December. The most

persistent tide was on December 31st, when the water rose to
112 cm [there are 100 centimeters in a meter]. In all of 1995,
there were only three cases of tides around a meter high:
December 23rd, which saw tides of 104 cm, and May 13th
and August 28th, with tides 100 cm high.

This growing trend, ANSA reports, caused some scientists
to predict that within sixty years, "Venice might be submerged
in high water every day if no remedy was found for carbon
dioxide emissions which cause a rise in temperature, thus
melting the polar icecaps and raising the level of the world's
seas." But as we have seen from the IPCC projections, the
polar-ice-cap contribution to rising seas today is generally not
considered part of the problem.

There appears to be irrefutable evidence that Venice's
problems will not go away. Water, which for centuries safe-
guarded its citizens against a multitude of enemies, is now
itself becoming the enemy. And while a storm tide like the
one that happened in November 1966 may be rare, its impact
awakened the world to Venice's possible fate: As the Adriatic
rises in concert with the world's seas, Venice has the potential
of being constantly bathed in water reaching high into its
buildings and eating away its art.

Newspaper columnists, in articles written just days after the
flood, condemned the bureaucratic lethargy that had led to a
breaking down of lagoon defenses. Dino Buzzati, writing for
the *Corriere della Sera*, decried overbuilding in the lagoon. "No
longer having any sandbanks to settle on, the tide goes back
out more quickly, and not having found that natural outlet,
it flows into the streets and St. Mark's Square more easily."

Count Alessandro Marcello del Maino, an authority on Venice's history with water, was interviewed by Buzzati and said: "A natural device [the ebb and flow of unimpeded tides] that has lasted [more than] ten centuries has been destroyed by people wholly ignorant about the environment." Count del Maino also condemned a project to deepen the Canale Malamocco from the Malamocco entrance to the lagoon, south of Venice, for oil-tanker access to the industrial zone at Porto Marghera. The canal project had not been carried out by the time of the 1966 flood, but it was completed more than a year later, and today's critics of how the lagoon has been managed believe that the project contributes mightily to the increasing frequency of damaging high tides flooding the city. This so-called *canale dei petroli* proposal was another "piece of mischief," the count said.

The Times of London, whose writers and readers had their own concerns about repeated flooding in England, sounded the most sonorous warning about the meaning of the 1966 floods. On November 12—a week after the disastrous flood and just as Signor Salvini and his colleagues were restoring electricity and telephone service within the lagoon—*The Times* described the flood as "an alarm sign, a warning of the danger the city must face if it does not find a solution in time." The British newspaper called the event "a useful shock therapy."

And another British publication, *The Economist*, opined: "The negligence in controlling the waters has brought sorry retribution."

Writer Sandro Meccoli, in *La battaglia per Venezia* (The Battle for Venice), sums up best what November 1966 accomplished for Venice when it sounded a wake-up call for the world:

The terrifying drenching of November 4 exposed . . . all the recklessness, incompetence, and negligence [that] were affecting Venice. Seawalls out of repair; churches, palazzi, and houses left to rot; an immense artistic heritage falling into decay; the hydraulic balance of the lagoon, which the Venetians had protected with extremely severe laws for centuries as their most precious asset, broken by digging and landfills dictated, in indiscriminate fashion, by industrial growth.

CHAPTER SIX ~

Saving Venice

The historic city of Venice is in danger of
extinction. The largest lagoon in the Mediterranean, in which the city was established
for safety, now is dangerously challenged by
the ocean.
—REPORT TO THE NINTH WORLD WATER
CONGRESS, MONTREAL, 1997

International reaction to the plight of Ven
ice—and all of northern Italy—in the aftermath of the events of November 3–5, 1966,
was swift. Since words always fly faster than
substance, however, the expressions of concern came from all quarters; the actual
money—quickly promised and arriving in
dribbles over several years—was another
matter.

President Lyndon B. Johnson of the
United States expressed "profound condo-
lences" at the damage wrought by floodwater
to Florence, Venice, and the rest of northeastern Italy. ANSA reports that within days

of the event, the then head of Italy's Industry Ministry who later became prime minister, Giulio Andreotti, took part in the first meeting of a committee that was supposed to organize assistance for damaged areas. Venice's mayor, Giovanni Favaretto Fisca, "stressed the urgent need to strengthen the coastal defense system as a preventive measure against future flooding, which otherwise would be sufficiently damaging to the city." This latter proposal mirrored the typically American phrase: "Closing the barn door after the horses had run away." It would be years before any such defenses were bolstered. The Italian parliament, ANSA says, approved an emergency bill earmarking thirty billion lire in aid, but Fisca declared that the amount was not enough. *Il Gazzettino* reported that the mayor said, "Another 300 billion lire are urgently needed to guarantee the city's survival." Interestingly the money being asked for was not entirely intended for restoring the city's monuments, buildings, and artworks, but for building a project that had been approved four years earlier and never funded: the sea dike at Cavallino, just north of the northernmost lagoon mouth at the Lido's tip. It is difficult to know what the impact of such a dike would have been had it been built as proposed before the events of autumn 1966.

The first call for massive public works had been made less than a week after the floodwaters had subsided, but it took years before the first major works were undertaken.

This slow pace was complicated by political realities. After World War II the Allies did not act to completely restructure the Italian government the way they did in Japan and Germany. After all, Italy had become an ally in 1943, when the government surrendered. For the peninsula at war's end, the

Allies generally maintained the Italian governmental status quo, but they did add another element to the 1948 constitution: a third tier of government between national and local control. This tier was to play a role in the political machinations that occur later in this story.

Italy then was divided into twenty regions. This was done primarily to distribute power in such a way as to make it difficult for someone like Benito Mussolini again to create a dictatorship. It has worked well in that regard, perhaps too well. Governments must now be created through coalitions between the Left and Right, represented by more than a score of parties at any one time, and those governments never survive for long. New premiers are elected, top government officials come and go, and continuity in major works, such as the safeguarding of Venice's lagoon, is nearly impossible to achieve. In the fifty-five years between the end of World War II and the end of the twentieth century, nearly sixty governments have risen and fallen.

Authors Fay and Knightley, who wrote the searing 1976 indictment *The Death of Venice*, which graphically detailed the long history of Italian government negligence toward maintaining its crown jewel, describe the core problem that has been present ever since Italian unification during the 1860s and that still exists today:

> [T]he very nature of government in Italy, its inherent instability, its system of political favours, and its crushing bureaucracy, made it unsuitable to handle a problem like Venice, and is the basic reason for its spectacular lack of success.

The water was down, the city surfaces were drying out, and life was returning to normal, but only a few observers had any real sense of the tragedy the flood represented. The publication *Paese Sera*, as reported by ANSA, pointed out the real danger to the city did not lie only outside the lagoon in the form of nature's climatic whims, which occur rarely and cannot be adequately predicted and completely controlled, but within the city's very foundations.

Paese Sera declared: "The danger is actually 'inside' the city at this point, inside its very foundations. In this flood, the sea has broken its age-old alliance with Venice, which had anyway been showing cracks for a long time." This warning was one of the early oblique references to the fact that not all of the salty seawater went out with the retreating tide. Some remained, lodged deep within the city's bricks, which sit above the impermeable layer of Istrian marble foundations, laid in place at then-appropriate elevations when the tides and sea level were much lower. Because sea level was rising and tides had grown higher and more frequent, seawater regularly ebbed and flowed above the impermeable Istrian stone, lapping regularly against the exposed bricks, which did not have enough time to properly dry out between high-water cycles. This regularly replenished water would move up through the bricks through capillary action, eventually working its way inside structures to gnaw away at the magnificent paintings, marble carvings, and frescoes created centuries ago by the artists of the late republic.

Over the later centuries, many opinions had been expressed about what was eating away the city's structures. The French believed that a strange breed of rock-eating bacteria was devouring the Venetian stone; others thought pigeon droppings were doing the damage. These exotic theories aside, the real destruction of Venice is due to the silent water seeping almost daily into the bricks.

In reality the 1966 flood did not begin the deterioration process; it just drew attention to what had been going on for years: Mean sea level was climbing higher, millimeter by millimeter, until the permeable brick layers were consistently reached by successive high tides. But, during those decades, the Venetian and national governments had turned a nearly blind eye to the molecule-by-molecule destruction. The city's monuments and artworks were in a deplorable condition by the time of the 1966 flood. One of the benefits of this latter-day tragedy is that the flood created a growing international awareness of the deeper, inner problems of Venice—the repository of some of the Western world's greatest treasures.

Fay and Knightley put it this way:

> Venice is a city beset by misfortune, suffering from severe neglect, caught in a cycle that is destroying her. Because she has been neglected, few of her citizens want to live there. Because fewer Venetians want to live in Venice there is less urgency to remedy the neglect—nearly two out of three buildings need attention. The results of this cycle can be seen everywhere.

The authors exhaustively detail individual examples of how the city is crumbling beneath the very feet and almost before the very eyes of the masses that flock to this "living museum." One of their more poignant phrases—"It was built in the fifteenth century and ruined in the twentieth"—could be used to describe many of the buildings within the city's historic core. They used those words to describe Santa Maria dei Miracoli, a lovely little church with a beautifully restored statue of the Virgin and Child above the front entrance. In recent years, thanks to donations from the international community, led by the privately funded American committee called Save Venice, the church has been saved by the best of the restorer's art. But in 1976 the Miracoli, along with dozens of other artistically and architecturally important churches and buildings, was close to being lost. In the Miracoli, despite a still-earlier ill-conceived renovation that did further damage to the interior marbles, the beautiful stones were heavily encrusted with salt, because walls repaired earlier had not been allowed to dry thoroughly. Salt, brought by sea tides rising repeatedly against the now-exposed exterior brick and, true to the laws of physics, carried through to the church's interior, was still doing its damage a full decade after the "great flood."

Prior to 1966 the Italian parliament had passed a series of well-intentioned special laws for Venice. This was and still is unique for Italy. It is rare that a special law is created for a specific place. There were no special laws for Florence, which suffered mightily and experienced significant loss of life during that same flood. Ravenna, the former Roman capital of the Western Empire and a major Adriatic seaport south of Venice, has no special laws, and it is sinking at a much faster rate than Venice. There were no special laws in the aftermath of the earthquakes that occurred in and around Assisi in the late 1990s. There were no special laws for the recovery of areas affected by massive mudslides around Naples in the late twentieth century. But Venice has always been special for Italians—and for the international community as well—in ways that are difficult to describe.

The first special law for Venice was passed in 1937 and involved planning controls on Venetian buildings; the second, in 1948, was intended for the development of Mestre on the mainland and was part of the drive to continue industrialization in the lagoon as Italy strove to become a major marketplace for Middle Eastern oil.

The third special law (1956) actually promised money to help Venetians deal with increasing pollution within the lagoon and to restore deteriorating buildings. Not much got accomplished, however. Just five months before the November 1966 flood, a fourth special law was passed to provide billions of lire for more restoration and improvements. Immediately after the flood, the government offered billions more to repair seawalls.

Despite bureaucratic lethargy, some positive steps were taken. A special committee had been established in 1966 to conduct scientific research and collect technical data on how to protect the lagoon from rising storm-surge tides. This group became known as the *Comitatone* (big committee). It would figure in subsequent special laws.

As far as significant financial resources being expended on Venice in the immediate aftermath of the flood, Fay and Knightley report: "But then, as the extent of Venice's problems emerged, a paralysis seemed to grip the politicians." Nothing was spent and no projects were launched. All that really took place was meetings of the *Comitatone*.

In 1969 Indiro Montanelli, a journalist for *Corriere della Sera*, took the mayor of Venice to court, "claiming that he and his colleagues should be stripped of their powers because they had spent not a [lira] of the government grants. But Montanelli's ingenious flourish was overtaken by events: By 1971 the various political parties in Rome had agreed that Venice needed a fifth special law, both comprehensive and very expensive."

Special Law 171, passed in April 1973, was the first to declare that Venice and its lagoon were a problem of "essential national interest."

Law 171 simply asked Italy for a "united effort" to safeguard the city. This phrase was part of the universal text applied to all special laws directed toward Venice, ANSA reports, and it sparked "one of the most heated debates on federalism and centralism between the right-wing coalition government and left-wing opposition." The Left accused the government of following a centrist plan "aimed at regaining a stranglehold over local and regional matters and killing off local government."

Passage of this most important law kicked off the chain of events that eventually led to the creation a decade later, in 1983, of the Consorzio Venezia Nuova. That is the organization that was ultimately given a monopoly to define Venice's problems, come up with solutions, and then build—and profit from—those solutions. The law took into account the *Comitatone*'s work over the preceding seven years, which supporters believed would come up with the technical solution for Venice's high-water woes. It was in this special law that the recommendation to build mobile gates across the lagoon mouths was first mentioned, touching off rancorous debate that continues today. Both government and opposition members of parliament agreed that mobile gates were the only solution, but the opposition felt that the small amount allotted—three hundred billion lire, or roughly five hundred million dollars, based on the mid-1970s exchange rate—doomed such a solution to failure.

ANSA quotes one member of parliament: "Narrowing the mouths of the ports or building mobile flood barriers are unattainable objectives," given the limited funds. It would take trillions, not billions of lire, to build mobile gates, which has been borne out as the plan to build the gates remains in limbo. Politicians today, just like those involved thirty years ago, continue to wrangle and agonize over making the final decision. One member of parliament summed it up: "[I]n the true style of the worst kind of politics, the measure contains mere statements of principle rather than concrete operative tools." Other members, growing more aware in the 1970s of environmental concerns involving the lagoon, wanted the law to take things even farther. They were hoping that it would force closure of Venice's ports, something unlikely to happen even today, as Venice's twenty-first-century leadership recognizes the need for economic development within the entire lagoon: The region needs more than the tourism drawn to the city's historic center.

Despite the rancorous debate in 1973, Special Law 171 passed. While it did not call for the ports to be closed, it did mandate a halt in the development of a new third industrial zone, in which lagoon waters were being filled in by earth to expand the chemical, petroleum, and container-port operations at Marghera. That area remains undeveloped today and will probably never be developed—in fact there are calls for the lagoon to be restored there. Special Law 171 also spelled out precisely the responsibilities of the state, regional, and local governments. For example, the state would fund interventions (the mobile gates) concerning water from canals and the sea; restoration of buildings; and reinforcement of bridges, canals, and foundations. The Veneto Region would be responsible for water-pollution control, and the Venetian government for some restoration of the city's historic infrastructure. Even today, with still another special law in effect along with four ordinary laws directed toward Venice, this division of responsibilities generally survives.

Special Law 171 allocated three hundred billion lire, for use between 1973 and 1977, to pay for urgent projects and to provide incentives to private industry to control pollution and restore property.

Foreigners were elated over the passage of this special law and what it would mean in the preservation of such an international treasure. These foreigners were involved through special private committees—Venice in Peril in Britain, Save Venice in the United States, for example—which were set up to pay for the restoration of individual works of art and specific buildings in Venice. Fay and Knightley, who interviewed politicians of the era, determined that the Italian leaders themselves did not share the enthusiasm of foreigners. Deep down, these leaders knew the deadlines and the money involved "were more optimistic than realistic."

Despite such concerns, Special Law 171 was a start. A Commission to Safeguard Venice was formed, whose membership included a representative of UNESCO (the United Nations Educational, Scientific, and Cultural Organization). Having a foreigner on such a commission was controversial in that it allowed a non-Italian to have a voice in internal matters of state. A promised technical and scientific committee was formed much later. Other delays held back progress toward working out the specific methods for safeguarding Venice, promised by the new law.

And when vital sections of the law were published, after a long delay through the summer and winter of 1973, key elements of the parliament's intent were omitted. And in 1974 the people concerned about Venice's ultimate survival started asking: Where was the money that the law had promised?

The problem was, the cash was locked up by a continuing debate between those who wanted Venice physically saved by massive public works and those who felt lire would be better spent developing the third industrial zone across the lagoon in Marghera. This kind of debate sounds familiar to many people living in developing nations. Special interests were driving it, and conservationists believed that the sure way to destroy Venice was to listen to the economically driven industrial interests.

While this fight was going on among groups of Italians, frustration was growing among foreigners who wanted, at all costs, to save Venice, its art, and its culture. The details outlining how the money would be spent still had not been released by mid-1974, and what is now known is that the government had a draft document but had not released it because, Fay and Knightley say, the document "leaned toward the conservationist view, and rejected substantially [the] development of a third [industrial] zone." Fueling this nondisclosure were local politicians who supported additional industrial development.

Then the government fell and the new administration, headed by Aldo Moro, shifted its allegiance away from the industrial developers and toward the conservationists. But another mystery sprang out of all this confusion. When guidelines on execution of the special law were finally released in April 1975, two years after the law was passed, they contained what amounted to a compromise, designed—in typical Italian fashion—to appease everyone and, ultimately, making it difficult to get anything done. In that document the Left was appeased by the promise that there would be no loss of jobs in Mestre's industrial zone. The industrial developers were quieted by a vague promise that the third industrial zone could—perhaps, maybe—be expanded. This ended up being the creation only of a container port, as opposed to expanding chemical and petroleum operations. And the conservationists, who knew that development of a container port would be least invasive to the lagoon's fragile ecosystem, were appeased as well.

The document announced that the intent of Special Law 171 would be followed. It ordered that an international competition be held to come up with the best way to protect the lagoon from *acqua alta*, said the seawalls must be strengthened, and demanded stricter pollution controls.

No sooner had this document been released than new debates began to surface over its interpretation. The area set aside for development of the third industrial zone started to grow when one official said the zone needed double the space that had been agreed to. Fay and Knightley sum up this phase: "It began to look suspiciously as though the [liberal politicians most enthusiastic about saving Venice] had won a round, but not the fight. Like other victories claimed at other times in Venice, it was possible that, like the city itself . . . on a hot, hazy day, the Law to Save Venice was just an illusion, a marvelous dream."

Despite everything, the government finally had a plan. Now it needed the three hundred billion lire, or five hundred million dollars, to put it into action. In 1973, an organization known as Consorzio di Credito per le Opere Pubbliche (Credit Consortium for Public Works), or CREDIOP, was organized. Major international banks agreed to lend the money. Chase Manhattan of New York, Security Pacific of San Francisco, the Bank of Tokyo, and the European Banking Company were named, and merchant banks, such as Lehman Brothers, were enlisted to lead the credit consortium. By making the saving of Venice the focal point for this fund-raising, the loans were guaranteed to go through. If the money was being raised for Italian public works in general, bankers might not be so willing, since many outstanding loans to the Italian government were already in the marketplace. The name *Venice* assured that the money would be raised effortlessly, and it was.

But what then happened is shrouded in mystery. The money was supposedly in the treasury, but it was not being spent. When the people interested in saving Venice started asking the government when it was going to be spent, Fay and Knightley report, the government responded by replying, "Spending what?"

It appears the money was being used elsewhere. Government officials and bankers were not necessarily speaking with forked tongues, Fay and Knightley say, but "they were speaking a different language and had different priorities from the laymen whose sole concern in all this was to see that Venice was saved." Questions asked through 1973 and 1974 elicited this response: "[T]he bankers knew all along that all the money would not go to Venice." It appears that "None of the money raised . . . by the 'Venice loan' was to be spent in Venice. And to add insult to injury, none of the money raised in Italy had been spent there either."

It appears the money went instead for "general needs," with only a small percentage—8 percent—earmarked for Venice. Here are Fay and Knightley's conclusions, drawn after a series of conflicting interviews in the mid-1970s with the then-key players, who could not seem to agree on which version of the story to tell:

> During 1973, Italy was running a heavy balance of payments deficit, and government expenditure was rising fast. A 300 billion lire loan reduced the deficit and government spending

at a stroke. . . . That, in terms of government finance, was a perfectly satisfactory explanation: the economic managers in the Treasury were, no doubt, quite pleased. It was only in terms of saving Venice that the explanation left so much to be desired, because it showed what a low priority the city would have during a severe and prolonged economic crisis. . . . The 300 billion exists only on paper, in an annual list of funds appropriated but not spent which is issued each year by the Italian Parliament, and called the *residuo passivi*.

Venetians and Italians in general, never ones to accept that government always acts in the best interests of its citizens, "would go on believing that the loan had been fiddled, filched, or diverted." Some of the money arrived, but there are disputes over what happened to it. "Not until substantial sums of money did arrive would the cynicism which informed so much opinion about the Italian government be dispelled." And, of course, inflation was rampant. The 300 billion lire ostensibly provided in the 1973 special law was the same amount that Venetian officials said they needed in the "great flood's" aftermath in 1966. That meant inflation had whittled down the amount and how far it would spread, if it were ever spread at all. In reality, the prevailing notion in the mid-1970s was that Venice would need 450 billion lire to accomplish the works that the 300 billion were intended to accomplish seven years earlier. Today the amount is significantly higher.

Fay and Knightley, in their usual pithy prose, summed it up: "The fact is that politics in Italy *are* different, and politics in Venice . . . are unusual even by Italian standards."

The Venetian bureaucracy in the mid-1970s was, by comparison, unchallenged by Italian bureaucracy in general. The city—remember that Venice by this time included the mainland towns of Marghera and Mestre as well as the historic center—managed the lagoon through the Venice Water Authority, or Magistrato alle Acque (magistrate of the waters), an ancient department of government with roots well back into the Middle Ages. At one time, when doges ruled the city, the department was a model of speed and efficiency. It had to be: Preservation of the lagoon was paramount to the city's defense. And an early doge had provided incentive for the magistrates by declaring that a magistrate would be well rewarded as long as he did his job properly—and quickly put to death if he made a mistake.

By the time the bureaucratic twentieth century rolled around—a more compassionate era that removed the threat of death that for centuries had hung over the bureaucrats' heads—the Magistrato had evolved into a frustrating maze of rules, regulations, and delays.

This was the sorry state of affairs for much of the 1970s, as people wondered back and forth where the money was that had been appropriated, and then lent to Italy by some of the world's largest banks, to safeguard the lagoon. Little could happen in a political environment that was constantly shifting as governments came and went, top bureaucrats were shuffled, and paper trails became ever harder to follow.

Through all this, Venetian leaders were locked in a debate over how the city should be planned for the future. Venice then as now was rapidly losing population as ordinary citizens found living conditions intolerable. Officials were desperate to find ways to stem that outflow.

Numerous town plans were put forth and scrapped, redrawn, and scrapped again. University architecture students were relied on to redraw how portions of the historic city should look, and they did so in haste to meet a January 1, 1975, Italian government deadline. The government said it needed such a plan if money was to be disbursed.

This hastily drawn plan called for massive reshaping of the Venetian skyline. Many of the areas, except for the historic core of the city, would be rebuilt into a more modern landscape. Private gardens were to be made public, an inordinate number of day-care centers were to be established throughout the city despite the fact that Venice's population, particularly of children, was declining. Privately owned parking lots at the city's perimeter were planned, new streets were to be cut through historic areas—a process some described as "using a sledgehammer to crack a nut."

All this, of course, terrified those who cherished the city's historic past. And, if the plan was not forthcoming, the Italian government threatened to turn over the power to control the city's destiny to the now-ponderous, top-heavy, and bureaucratic Magistrato alle Acque, an agency that Venice's citizens knew would be unable to get anything done.

The threats finally worked, but the town plan had to pass the city council chamber. The threat to turn everything over to the Magistrato and the promise to start flowing money that had been earmarked for safeguarding the lagoon into the city did the trick. But many observers of Venetian wiles and ways know that those approving this dramatically unpopular redevelopment plan for the city must have believed that even if it was passed to meet the national government's conditions, the work to change the city forever would not take place. That is what happened. Little if any of this work has become reality as the city goes into the twenty-first century some twenty-five years after the vote in the city council chamber. The plan was passed over some 750 individual objections lodged by council members, but then it met another delay—this one fortuitous—in the next layer of government heaped upon Italy by the Allies in the late 1940s—the regional government. The Veneto regional bureaucracy sat on the plan throughout the winter and spring of 1975.

And UNESCO, its leaders frustrated that Venice had not done much about preserving its city after the 1966 flood, intervened. A conference was called. Leaders argued that the first goal should not be to rebuild major portions of the city simply to replace the old with new, but to stop the migration of Venetians to the mainland. Fay and Knightley reported that UNESCO officials felt this could be done only by providing restored housing at low rents, decent schools, and hospitals.

Most important, UNESCO said, the plan lacked "any analysis of what Venice contained, *and what it was good for* [emphasis added]." One leader worried: "Venice is on the water, and yet it hardly uses the water. . . . Venice has become a city without a role, colonised by tourists and by Milanese and Turin industrialists. They use Venetian labour in their Mestre factories but they ignore the place the workers come from."

The regional experts determined that the destructive self-serving plan passed in the city council chamber was "useless" and a "grave error." It was urged that the city council rethink the matter, under the guidance of special consultants and using programs at the University of Venice.

The reality of all this was that little happened with the town plan. Like many proposals, it drifted away into filing cabinets. Years would pass before much would be done to deal with the city and its problems.

While the financial and political machinations were playing out through this period, work dealing with Venice's plight was actually being carried out, however. International committees were beginning to restore works of art and long-ignored buildings, and scientific groups were studying ways to protect the city. Out of this early scientific work emerged the concept of building gates across the lagoon mouths—the concept still being pushed nearly three decades later. And UNESCO—one of the city's greatest champions, under the leadership of René Maheu—worked diligently to "internationalize" Venice's problems. This international organization created a presence in the city in 1973, occupying a suite of rooms in the old state apartments of Vittorio Emanuele III in one of the long, rectangular buildings lining St. Mark's Square. But Maheu knew the task was formidable. Fay and Knightley report his words, spoken near the time of his retirement in 1974, after eight years of his personal crusade to save the city: "[Venice's problem is that it is] one of the most refined cities in the world. I am afraid that its very refinement makes it less susceptible to change."

UNESCO's actual scientific offices are today in another palazzo located along the Grand Canal. Its equally grand rooms are occupied by Pierre Lasserre, UNESCO's director of the Venice office, and his staff. In 1988 UNESCO's Regional Office for Science and Technology for Europe (ROSTE) was brought to the city and housed in this headquarters as well.

Lasserre has the look of an orchestra conductor—he is solidly built with arms that appear perfect for waving a baton, and he carries a head full of jet-black, naturally curly hair that moves with his every motion and falls back into place perfectly.

We meet in his palazzo office. It is huge, large enough to hold twenty clerks in cubicles, and it is old. An artist's fifteenth-century rendering of a palace along the Grand Canal hangs on one wall; the chandelier over the long discussion table we are sitting at is eighteenth century; three seventeenth-century portraits of once-famous, but now-forgotten Venetians line one wall. "They have always been here and they will always stay here," Lasserre says, giving insight into his belief that the demise of Venice is greatly exaggerated.

He says that Maheu more than anyone in 1971 "launched the campaign to alert the world community of the renovation needs of the city following the 1966 flood." Maheu approached the Venice task much in the way that he handled saving ancient Egyptian structures that were threatened by the rising waters of the Aswan Dam across the Nile River.

"Before 1971, Italians were concerned about the future of their city," Lasserre continues. "Buildings were in poor condition. It appeared as if the idea of Venice disappearing into the mud, presented by eighteenth-century engineers and nineteenth-century writer John Ruskin, could be coming true."

From 1971 to 1978 the overriding concern was saving the city's heritage by restoring individual pieces of art and individual buildings. Beginning about 1975, Lasserre says, the emphasis started to shift toward finding better ways of water management and control. Much of this emphasis was driven by Italian scientists such as Roberto Frassetto, whose work in the early 1970s began suggesting mobile gates as a solution to higher and higher tides.

A turning point, Lasserre says, was a meeting in 1981 sponsored by the Italian foundation CINI, on its grounds on San Giorgio Island, located to the east of the Doges' Palace within the lagoon.

"I attended this meeting as a young marine biologist," Lasserre says, adding that he was captivated by the discussions.

"They talked about various options for saving the city. Shall we enclose the city and some of the major islands to protect them against the weather and rising waters? This was a serious question being asked even then. Or should we work to save the integrity of the lagoon?

"Today, the thinking has moved away from building walls around the key islands—they are completely pro-lagoon," he says of the scientists who have been working on solutions for several decades.

My interview with Lasserre was one of the earliest in my education about the problems facing the city and the controversy swirling around the multibillion-dollar project of the mobile gates, which still hangs over the politicians' heads in Rome. He said something very revealing at a time when I thought nearly everyone backed the gates concept: "It is obvious that something has to happen in forty or fifty years. The [mobile gates] could be called for, or perhaps we will find ways to close the lagoon. This will take one or two generations to solve." Lasserre pauses. Then, he says, "It is very Venetian to work this way." For him the issue is far from being decided. It appears that the same is true for the politicians as well.

The distinct possibility that it could take one or two more generations for Italians, Venetians, and concerned members of the world community to resolve the issue of how to safe-guard the lagoon mightily frustrates one scientist in particular.

He is oceanographer Roberto Frassetto, an Italian World War II hero. A navy frogman who was captured during an attack on Alexandria in Egypt, he received the Italian equiv-alent of the U.S. Medal of Honor. Educated in engineering in Italy following the war, he finished his doctoral work at Columbia and Yale Universities in the United States.

Frassetto has been involved in the Venice safeguard debate almost since the 1966 flood. In 1968 he founded an institute within Italy's National Resource Council that studies geophys-ical and environmental problems affecting the city and the lagoon. It was this courtly gentleman who, with other scien-tists, conjured up the concept of placing mobile gates at the three mouths of the lagoon. He pushed this concept through the 1970s and was largely ignored by Italy's politicians—a group of people for whom he has little regard. The concept would not be accepted until 1982, thereby validating his early work in the eyes of the political and scientific establishment. But by this time Frassetto had fallen out of favor and was essentially kicked upstairs. The institute he had founded was turned over to someone else.

He was kicked up but not out. A consummate scientist, Frassetto had done significant work trying to determine how Venice could develop an early-warning system to alert au-thorities at least six hours in advance when a major storm surge could be expected. This work spawned worldwide climatologic and oceanographic studies, and he turned his attention from Venice to global studies on climate and its causes.

I sit down with a man in his seventies whose face shows the age and stress of the years spent fighting for the gates he believes are essential to saving his adopted city. We are in another palazzo situated in fading splendor along the Grand Canal, a short distance toward the Rialto Bridge from UNESCO's offices. Outside this palazzo a handful of powerful-looking motorboats, with the research council's insignia on their hulls, are tied up to their poles sunk deep in the mud of the Grand Canal.

Frassetto is in a somber mood as we meet in a long, empty conference room whose heavily leaded windows look over the canal. He shares a small office with a colleague far back in the bowels of the building; the conference room gives us more privacy.

His opening remarks underscore his frustration.

"The only thing that has been done [since 1966 to safeguard the lagoon] has been to increase the understanding of all the mechanisms connected with the safeguarding of Venice, both scientifically and technically. But the idea is the same, the problems are the same, and as far as action is concerned, very little has been done."

The work within the city to dredge canals, rebuild building foundations, and raise pavements higher to forestall rising water from flooding neighborhoods is, in Frassetto's view, "a very small part of the problems of Venice."

The decision to do the greater works, the multibillion-dollar undertaking of building the gates, he says, continues to flounder.

"The politicians are uncertain. They prefer to take the attitude of wait and see, which is a bad and expensive policy, as everybody knows." He points in frustration to Britain, Germany, Holland, and Russia—nations that "have already provided defenses of the critical areas of their coasts to protect them from floods." It galls him to know that while he and his team have proved repeatedly, to his mind, that the gates are essential to Venice's survival and can be built to work long into the future, these other governments have studied the problem, come up with solutions, and implemented them, while Italian politicians continue to avoid the decision about the gates.

"The fact is that 'prevention' is not a term that is interesting for transient politicians. They care about their chair [elected office] and their immediate problems, and do not want to spend time dealing with long-term problems that involve prevention."

It is obvious that Frassetto's thoughts about the politicians responsible for deciding Venice's fate have not changed much over the years. In Fay and Knightley's *The Death of Venice*, he is quoted: " 'There is an illness in government today, and Italy has it worse than most. When a politician takes power then he also must take responsibility. The pleasures of power are among the rewards for taking that responsibility. But in Italy the people who take power decline responsibility.' "

Our discussion took place in early spring 2000 in the midst of regional elections over nearly all of Italy. Politicians whom I managed to reach were noncommittal about whether the gates would be approved, preferring to wait out the regional results. Then when those elections were over in April, the same politicians said that the Center-Left coalition was fighting for its political life and they would withhold comment until the coalition's battle with the Center-Right threat was resolved. That would not be done until spring of 2001, following national elections.

I began to see Frassetto's point. Trusting such a decision

to Italian politicians in the midst of a struggle for their political lives *is* a study in frustration for the non–political scientist.

"All the politicians will say, 'Tomorrow, Venice will be saved,' or 'I will do,' or 'We will do,' or 'The party will do,' et cetera and et cetera. This is election nonsense. When the election is gone, nothing [will happen]. Everything will return to the drawers of the politicians and the bureaucratic organizations.

"It will only be a miracle if they decide. Even a crisis [like the 1966 flood] has an effect that is very temporary," Frassetto continues. "Everybody complains during and immediately after, but then ten days later we go back to the same thing. There are flashes. Elections and crises are flashes that don't have an effect."

All this said, Frassetto concedes that dramatic decisions to take steps against the threat of flooding in other nations stem from the fact that in those places there is the potential for massive loss of life. Venetians are not likely to die in the midst of rising waters—over the centuries the lives of very few have ended that way. Frassetto mentions the giant multimillion-dollar barrier built across the river Thames in London during the late 1970s and early 1980s. It is a barrier with gates, much like those he wants to see built across the three entrances to the Venetian lagoon.

"The first gate [for Venice] was presented in 1970," Frassetto says, "so my institute was the one that proposed and made a meeting and got the [construction] firms to tell us what kind of technical information—geological, meteorological, and so forth—they needed to build this kind of defense. So among the several solutions that emerged there was the gate that lies at the bottom and is hinged at the bottom and is lifted up by compressed air.

"In thirty years, despite jealous engineers making all attempts possible to ridicule the gates—there is no better solution. This is the only solid and intelligent solution for Venice," Frassetto says, bringing his hand down for emphasis on the table's highly polished surface. "Decision makers are not deciding, so they are not to be called decision makers. They are 'undecision' makers!"

The kindly professor appears to me to be tired, frustrated, worn out by of the years of battles. I ask him, "Do you believe you will live to see the gates built?"

He laughs, a short subdued snort. "I think I will die without seeing any solution." I then ask, "Will I see it—I am fifty-four?" His one-word answer, accompanied by a slight shrug of the shoulder: "Perhaps."

Then I ask: "Do you ever feel like giving up the fight?"

At this question Frassetto begins a remarkable transformation. He pulls himself upright in his chair and his eyes take on a new, fresh look. His transformation from an attitude of defeat to one of being prepared to accept the challenge is remarkable.

"I am not tired," he says with finality. "If I were, this would be giving up. Actually every day I find something that is worth investigating. I find and research," he says. "Why is it called 're-search'? It is called that because it never ends. Improving knowledge and *affidabilità*—reliability. We have to demonstrate without a doubt that something is happening and approach the truth. The truth is very difficult to approach one hundred percent. But we are going toward a greater and greater confirmation of what we say and what we find."

———

During the 1970s scientists like Frassetto formed commissions and committees, studying and restudying the concept of the gates. The ever-rising, unpredictable Adriatic was busy as well. While water has never lapped as high against the city's stones as it did in 1966, it has come close. On December 23, 1979, it hit 5.4 feet (1.66 meters), or just 11 inches (twenty-eight centimeters) short of the 1966 height.

UNESCO continued to apply pressure to get Rome to start directing money toward the lagoon. Meetings were held at which Rome's representatives smoothly made glib promises. UNESCO's Maheu diplomatically acknowledged that Italy's economic crisis of the times could forestall the arrival of funds to help Venice, but following a particularly combative meeting in July 1974, he did say that UNESCO's continued presence in Italy depended on whether the national government could reverse "a state of affairs in which we cannot produce results or even make encouraging noises."

Another issue erupted and caught non-Italian participants by surprise. The Italian government was (and still is) dependent on private committees to raise funds worldwide from wealthy benefactors and corporations, and then to use those funds to restore art and buildings suffering grave damage from years of neglect in general and the 1966 flood in particular. But the government, while withholding its own funds for building extraordinary measures to safeguard the lagoon, was taxing this foreign money at an astonishing 12 percent.

Sir Ashley Clarke, a British resident who made Venice his home shortly after the 1966 flood and whose widow, Lady (Frances) Clarke, still lives in the city and carries on much of his work, headed the British private restoration committee known as Venice in Peril. He protested the tax at that 1974 meeting, and an Italian official abruptly dismissed his concerns, saying this was no time to be complaining about taxation.

Fay and Knightley report that Maheu intervened by asking the official from Rome: "Do you mean that if we help to save the fabric of St. Mark's, that money is taxed?" Yes, the official replied, "implying that if the voluntary funds were to be in Venice, *it was to be on Rome's terms* [emphasis added]." Later in the 1970s, perhaps driven by the realization that the taxing policy would do little to spur the arrival of foreign capital to restore Venice, the government backed down and granted tax exemptions.

Fay and Knightley report that following the meeting at which Sir Ashley raised the tax question, the Socialist politician Giuseppe Mazzariol commented, out of earshot of the Frenchman, Maheu:

"The problem is 174 years old, but Maheu wants it solved by September," said Mazzariol. "We're not in such a hurry. We've made tremendous efforts to understand the problem, and we are getting fed up with all this Anglo-Saxon pragmatism. Give us time; the score is 0–0 at the moment."

UNESCO had been promised during the July 1974 meeting that a meeting would be scheduled with the responsible politicians in September, just before Maheu was scheduled to retire. But when the appointed month arrived, "there was no longer a government in Rome to provide the politicians." Again decisions about money for the safeguarding of Venice were put off. The Commission to Safeguard Venice continued to meet regularly. Few decisions were made, and local Venetian politicians often criticized UNESCO for meddling in local affairs. The Save Venice law had been passed, but few of its provisions had been implemented.

After eight years in Venice, UNESCO seemed unable to move the government off dead center, and Maheu, who died in December 1975, only fifteen months after leaving UNESCO, realized, perhaps rightly, that it was not the place of his organization "to take the initiative, organize a great international fund, and gather a collection of international experts" to take over the job of saving Venice. In a final interview with Fay and Knightley, the tired UN diplomat, who had spent years fighting for the city and making its cause an international one, had concluded: " 'The Italians must save Venice.' And would they? 'They must. They have a duty to save Venice for the world.' "

CHAPTER SEVEN ～

Saving the Sublime

You save the art; and you *must* save the art, because one hopes this may be a phase, a cycle, and therefore the water will go down again. The reason why Venice is one of the unique cities is that so much has remained from previous centuries. It has been a backward city, if you like, but no other city has retained its heritage in quite the same way.
—LADY (FRANCES) CLARKE

The effort to save Venice is managed on two levels. There is the job of protecting the lagoon and the city itself; and there is the job of protecting what makes the city: its art and its heritage. The Consorzio and its legions of scientists and engineers want to take care of the first; the international art world is concerned about the second.

The November 1966 flood was a seminal event because it alerted the Italians and the international community to both problems. The overwhelmed Italian government, in the flood's early aftermath, appealed to

UNESCO, which responded on both levels. Regarding the salvaging of art masterpieces and ancient documents, the government's first thought was for the treasures of Florence, where the raging Arno River, in addition to drowning numerous Florentines, smashed into churches and museums at heights of six feet or more, trashing paintings, frescoes, books, and irreplaceable documents. And the world's art community did respond.

The efforts in Florence led to a resurgence in the restorer's art as well as to many breakthroughs in restoration science. These breakthroughs not only repaired the ravages of the flood but also corrected centuries of misuse, bad treatment of masterpieces, and decades-earlier botched efforts at restoration that only hastened the deterioration of many works. Such techniques continue to be used today all over Italy and elsewhere in the world.

A Briton with a lifelong love affair with Venice describes what life was like following 1966 for people concerned about the deterioration of art and the buildings that house the masterpieces as well as residents:

"The Italian government's appeal for worldwide help in the days following the flood was especially for Florence, which was the priority at the time," recalls Lady (Frances) Clarke, now in her early seventies and a longtime Venice resident.

"But once the Florentines got their house more or less in order they said, 'Thank you very much, but we can manage by ourselves.' The Venetians jumped in and said, 'We still need help!' "

Lady Clarke's husband, Sir Ashley Clarke, had been involved in creating what was then known as the British-run Italian Art and Archives Rescue Fund, and as efforts began to focus on Venice, the name was changed to British Fund for

Venice. The American organization was called the Committee to Rescue Italian Art. Today, the British group is called Venice in Peril, and one American group is known as Save Venice. They are among twenty-nine private committees representing nations throughout the world.

"We transferred our attention to Venice and started to work on the Church of the Madonna dell'Orto, which is up on the north side, in Cannaregio, and we've gone on here ever since," says Lady Clarke. The work on that church was pivotal. It had been the parish church of famed Venetian artist Jacopo Tintoretto and contained eleven of his masterpieces. Sir Ashley died in 1994, and Lady Clarke has assumed his role with Venice in Peril. She spends much of her time in the former royal apartments, where John Millerchip, a fellow Briton, coordinates the activities of the more than two dozen private committees funded by private benefactors and corporations from around the world.

It is a costly venture. These groups have saved and restored hundreds of paintings, tombs, stone monuments, building facades, and the very internal portions of buildings themselves. For example, from 1987 to 1997, Save Venice spent nearly four million dollars to restore the fifteenth-century Church of Santa Maria dei Miracoli. The organization and its donors provided the money while Italian restorers did much of the work. It was a monumental task that was originally supposed to take only two years to complete and cost barely a million dollars. But as restorers dug deeper into the church, its nearly fatal problems exposed themselves.

Old parts of the building had disintegrated and would fall apart at the slightest touch. They were rebuilt using original materials and methods. Salt, from the repeated action of the floodwaters from the canal adjacent to the church, had to be removed from the stones.

This kind of work goes on and on throughout the city. And while this priceless repository of some of Western civilization's greatest art is threatened, there are places in the world where basic human needs are under constant threat.

I pose this question to John Millerchip, a quintessential Englishman and longtime Venice resident. White hair and a full white beard frame his face. He appears to be in his mid-fifties and is incredibly thin, appearing almost weightless. We meet in his offices in the apartments once used by the House of Savoy, Italy's former royal family—"their Venetian pad, as it were," he quips.

The issue of saving art in Venice from floodwaters that never kill anyone does seem to be in conflict with problems elsewhere. After all, thousands die in raging floods in Mozambique and in Bangladesh, and even elsewhere in Italy, hundreds have died in recent years from mudslides and earthquakes.

Millerchip does not attempt to justify spending millions to save art in contrast to those greater tragedies. These works represent our Western civilization in the minds of many, and that status alone puts them on the level of the sublime.

"I continue to invite [the private] committees to ask themselves that question every chance I get," he says dryly. He adds, "Many view Venice as the most restored city in the world. So what are we doing here when thousands are dying, starving [elsewhere]? The reason has to be more than that we just enjoy coming here year after year."

So priorities have to be set. UNESCO and other international organizations are involved in easing conditions in Africa

and elsewhere as well. Meanwhile, Venice's art, after decades—
and even centuries—of neglect, needs saving.

"High water was regularly seeping into walls and was being
carried up into frescoes and so forth," Millerchip says. "It was
not a matter of, like in Florence, cleaning a few paintings,
restoring a few facades, and moving on.

"We do this work and we hand it back to the Italians, the
Venetians, without conditions attached."

Now the situation of increasing floods and seemingly un-
stoppable high water may change this approach, Millerchip
says. "It is increasingly important that we attach conditions of
maintenance with our work. We came to realize that we must
'consolidate the container [Venice]' before we deal with the
contents."

If, after the private committees spend millions to restore a
major structure and its contents, and visitors begin to see, say,
a crack developing across a fresco or dust collecting beneath a
bench, Millerchip says, "We want to ask them [the Italian
maintenance people], 'Why?' It's a matter of keeping things
tidy; keeping it clean." There must be monitoring at all levels,
he maintains, from the cleaning people on up.

"If not, Venice will find itself where it was in 1966. They
may not have another flood like that one, but they will find
themselves with the need to restore more and more, over and
over again. And restoration is a threatening activity: We always
risk degrading the article.

"You need a culture of maintenance. You must be aware
that if you neglect your property it will degenerate."

After three decades of saving individual works of art and
historically important public buildings, the private committees
want to go further, says Millerchip.

"We want to look at the fabric of residential buildings, euphemistically called 'minor architecture.' Take, for example, a building here that dates back to 1500 or before, and it was last touched in the last half of the nineteenth century. We have produced plans that are conservation based. We want to try to keep respect for materials and layout—not to create a museum but a house to live in."

And, he adds pointedly, it has to be used to benefit the public—the Venetian family that is contemplating a move to the mainland because of deterioration, costs, increasing periods of flooding, or few jobs. It must not be done for a wealthy Swiss, or Briton, or American. "It has to be used for people who are less well off, or less able, such as elderly or handicapped people.

"This works on the premise that if the building is used, it will be maintained." Millerchip acknowledges that by respecting original buildings—by not bringing in bulldozers or using modern bricks or reinforced concrete—you do incur greater costs than if you tear it down and rebuild it to modern standards. This makes the concept a tough sell, but the private committees are trying.

If the entire lagoon is in danger from the rising sea, why save individual buildings or integrated art when the whole environment is threatened?

Millerchip seems bothered by the question. "I don't know why you asked that, really. It is clear that continual floods endanger frescoes. But the two are not immediately connected. The question of floodgates is tied to the economic future of Venice, indeed of Italy. Those kinds of solutions are not amenable to the kind of money we can wield. It can come only from the government."

In other words, the private committees do what they can, piece by piece, and count on the government to do what it must eventually do: come up with a solution for *acque alte*. Millerchip's American colleague, Melissa Conn, director of Save Venice, puts this perspective on the question of why preserve art when the container is in danger: "It is sort of like thinking if you live in California, don't fix your roof because there might be an earthquake. You have to mow the grass; you have to keep things going. Saving the lagoon is very important. The ecology of the lagoon is something we are all concerned about, but these monuments have to continue. If we were to ignore them, then there would be nothing left."

Conn does not want to take a position for or against the proposed gates. But Millerchip does not hesitate a bit. In his view the mobile gates are not the solution. He is like many of the residents of Venice with whom I talked over a period of several months. Many of the organizations they work for support the gates because something, after all, must be done to save the city in the long term, but when asked for their personal opinions, that support does not carry through.

"Do the work on the lagoon first [all the restoration proposals other than the gates themselves], and monitor that work to see how it affects the problem of rising water," Millerchip suggests. "Monitor the trends of global rise of sea levels." Once this trend has been established, "then that is the moment to make decisions about whether to protect Venice from the sea.

"If we delay the gates, is there a real, immediate threat to the existence of Venice? Is Venice going to be exposed to unreasonable danger?" The pro-gates folks say yes; most Venetians, believes Millerchip, say no.

"Remember that the water in 1966 was deepest for only ten

minutes. The deepest area was the Piazza San Marco. Much of the rest of the city was just above shoe level. The [pro-gates people] have to tell the truth! It was never two meters. Quit bandying two meters as a threat! The lagoon has come within twenty centimeters of the 1966 level [1.94 meters, six centimeters short of two meters] three times. The inner lagoon rehabilitation has to have priority."

Meanwhile Millerchip's associate, Lady Clarke, worries that the lack of action by the Italian government regarding a decision on the mobile gates will continue to bother the deep-pocketed benefactors who support art restoration in the city.

"People in England, or America—anybody who is collecting money for Venice—ask, 'What are the Italians doing about the flooding?' "

She is eager to see that something gets done and done soon.

"The water may go up and then go down, but meanwhile the damp courses of the houses, which are made out of this impermeable marble, have by now long gone under water level. You've got the saltwater rising through the bricks, as you see everywhere, and the bricks are starting to crumble."

Lady Clarke faced this problem with her own home, built in the early 1600s along a small canal parallel to the huge Giudecca Canal just a few hundred feet away. Several years ago she had workers pull out the crumbling bricks that made up the walls of her home, bricks that were repeatedly sloshed with saltwater as the canal in front washed over the *fondamenta* where she regularly walks her dog, Hannibal.

"It is very normal to do this system of replacing damp wall through a system called *scuci cuci*, which means to unsew and to sew. You take the old brick out and replace it, section by section, with a special kind of brick made of a special water-resistant consistency. This is the traditional way of doing it. A few feet up, workers place a damp course of impermeable material that stops saltwater from moving up into the rebuilt wall."

Lady Clarke realizes that all this is temporary—for naught, if nothing is done about the flooding. "It's a time scale. Is the work raising the *fondamente* going to be sufficient before we get another big flood? They are becoming more frequent, and they have come close [to the 1966 level]. Maybe they've already waited too long. And now they are running out of time."

CHAPTER EIGHT ~

New Laws and the Consorzio

We now understand the forces at work in Venice and we know how to act to save it for ten, twenty-five or fifty years. We can't pretend, however, that the solutions we offer are final; every generation will have to do its bit. But we have to begin now, because if we don't then there is no doubt that the next generation will be too late. . . . [The technical people] can get on with saving Venice for the next ten to fifty years while science moves on to the long-term investigation needed to save it for the next thousand years.

—DR. ROBERTO FRASSETTO,

QUOTED IN *THE DEATH OF VENICE*

Roberto Frassetto, the beleaguered grandfather of the mobile gates, who fears he will not live long enough to see the construction of his solution for Venice's flooding, did see acceptance of the gates concept in the early 1980s. As 2000 wound down, he could take comfort in the fact that the gates remained the only technical solution still supported by all decision makers. In the early 1980s the politicians, it appeared, finally seemed to be listening.

The flood of December 23, 1979, while not as damaging or dramatic as the 1966 event, spurred a new flurry of activities, and parliament was gearing up to pass still another series of laws to deal with the problem. This ultimately led to passage on November 29, 1984, of a new special law for Venice, Special Law 798. This law differed from the toothless Special Law 171 in that it favored a more experimental, or flexible, approach to the safeguarding of Venice. It did not tie target dates to completion of specific projects, and it allowed for step-at-a-time implementation of projects only when they were proven and ready. It was abundantly clear that the rigid timetable of interventions favored by Special Law 171—interventions that never materialized anyway—would not work for such a complex problem. It especially would not work in such a complex political environment—where the only constant is change, with which Italians have lived for decades.

The more cynical Italians would say that it was easy for the politicians to pass these laws, knowing it would be years before projects would be realized, and that in the meantime the money for those projects could be used to further political goals elsewhere.

Despite its different approach, Special Law 798 did capitalize on some of the best ideas that came out of earlier attempts to safeguard the lagoon. For example, Special Law 798 reestablished a committee (the *Comitatone*, or "big committee"), to be chaired by the prime minister. This had been the name given to the group created out of the chaos surrounding the "great flood" of 1966. Sitting on the body are various govern-

ment ministers, including the prime minister and his appoin-
tees to the Ministries of the Environment and Public Works,
the mayors of Venice and Chioggia, and other mayors from
neighboring local councils. This group is responsible for overall strategy, coordination, and control.

And, once again, the new special law spelled out specific responsibilities for the various levels of government: The state is
responsible for overall safeguarding of the lagoon and the restoration of environmental balance there; the Veneto Region
deals with pollution in the rivers and streams throughout the
drainage basins, or catchments; the Province of Venezia has the
ambiguous task of "the conservative restoration of the heritage
under its authority"; and the city councils of Venice and Chioggia are responsible for maintaining urban structures.

This special law also called for interventions to protect the
lagoon and to develop a plan to restore buildings, preserve
Venice's historic town plan, its environment, and its economy.
The 1982 acceptance of a plan calling for mobile gates, to be
built below sea level across the lagoon mouths, one entrance
at a time, was not specifically mentioned in Special Law 798
when it passed two years later. This was in keeping with the
law's appeal for flexibility and experimentation. But the 1982
concept, which essentially remains intact today, still has the
support of bureaucrats, politicians, and many scientists. Ironically, the 1982 price tag for the gates project was set at 550
billion lire or, in the exchange rate of the time, 367 million
dollars. Today, with the gates still not built and a decision
delayed through late 2001, the price tag has jumped considerably to somewhere between 2 and 4 billion dollars.

While Frassetto's worst fears that the gates will be delayed
until a major catastrophe inundates the city once again might
still be realized, the 1982 action did set the stage for smaller-

scale, long-overdue infrastructure improvements to the city fostered by Special Law 798 in 1984.

In effect, this special law has generated improvements. While work continues on the design and testing of mobile gates, money is being spent to repair crumbling bridges, dredge canals, raise the *fondamente*, and improve sewage systems.

What the special law hasn't been able to do any better than its predecessors is to move politicians—principally the ever-changing occupant of the prime minister's chair—off dead center to authorize their actual construction. After all, a flood of the magnitude of the November 1966 catastrophe was at that time considered a once-every-eight-hundred-years event. The lowering of that prediction to a once-every-two-hundred-years event has not done much to spur on politicians who generally look ahead only as far as the next election.

Following passage of Special Law 798, a series of "ordinary" laws directed toward Venice were passed as well, beginning in 1991. Law 360 was directed toward finding a solution to the exodus of Venetians from Venice's historic center to the mainland. In 1992 Law 139 further allocated the responsibilities for safeguarding the lagoon among the various layers of government, particularly the region and the central government. In 1995 parliament passed a decree calling for urgent interventions for historic Venice and for Chioggia, including the development of waste-disposal facilities that could eventually lead to a traditional sewage system for the two cities—complete with pipes and treatment plants—as opposed to letting the tides do the work.

And a year later parliament issued a decree that would continue funding in the amount of 185 billion lire (nearly 116 million dollars) to keep this variety of existing projects on track.

So progress is being made. The far-reaching 1982 plan

called for restoring seawalls, work that was begun in the mid-1990s and is still under way. It also said that work would be done to the banks of the lagoon, and that Venice's canals, which had not been maintained for more than a generation, could be dredged of their toxic mud, and their crumbling stone sides waterproofed and repaired. All this is taking place. Work to raise the height of Piazza San Marco and install a waterproof membrane to keep water from gushing up from below was scheduled to begin in 2001. The first phase could take four or five years and cost 50 billion lire (23.8 million dollars). The only major project that is not happening is the gates themselves. As the end of 2001 approached, no one was willing to bet that they would be begun any time soon.

Optimism reigned in 1982, following two years of frenetic meetings and strategy sessions. Officials of the City of Venice Safeguard Commission also, according to reports from the Italian news service ANSA, were "on the same wavelength in calling for preliminary works to reverse pollution and safeguard the coast." The news report added: "It appeared that at the end of two hectic years the works that had eluded everyone for decades could be performed." The works, as outlined, were called the *Progettone* (big project). More precisely the title was the "Feasibility Study and General Project for the Defense of the Venice Lagoon from High Water."

There had to be a way to pull all this activity together. Out of that need was born the Consorzio Venezia Nuova, or Consortium for a New Venice. Created by government fiat, the Consorzio is made up of about fifty of the largest public and private civil-engineering and construction firms in Italy. This gave a virtual monopoly for the rescue of Venice to a group of Italy's largest for-profit firms. Such a monopoly could never be created in the United States. There it would require several independent groups, all bidding for a variety of contracts. They would compete for the right to determine what solutions needed to be developed for problems within the lagoon, how those solutions should be designed, and then who should build them.

The Consorzio was created in the years when Italian contracts and money were routinely funneled to "friends of friends," as one official wryly described it. And it was created before the 1990s crackdown by judicial magistrates on major business executives throughout Italy who were believed to have profited from a variety of favors and scams.

To its credit the Consorzio has weathered the wave of investigations that swept the country in the last decade of the twentieth century, a fact that has not stopped cynical Italians from continuing to believe that money is being poured into a bottomless hole, and that the Consorzio was making billions of lire from a project—the mobile gates—that would never see the light of day. Even today, in the dawn of the twenty-first century, there are those who believe that the Consorzio is content to have the gates continually delayed because it gives the organization a reason to exist—and continue to draw billions of lire annually in government funds.

The first agreement between the government and the Consorzio was signed on December 18, 1982. Its terms followed Italian law at the time and were limited. It allowed the group to conduct a handful of studies and tests, and the document gave the Consorzio the right to construct barriers at only one location—the Lido mouth—among the three entrances to the lagoon. The local Venetian government had since 1980 liked the idea of giving an all-encompassing franchise to a consortium of public and private companies, but prevailing Italian law had blocked such an arrangement. Those laws were modified and the monopoly allowed.

Then came Special Law 798. By reestablishing the *Comitatone*—or all-powerful committee of government ministers, regional, and local officials—the law gave the committee the power to supervise Venice's water board, known today as the Venice water authority, or by its ancient name (dating back to 1501), Magistrato alle Acque. The historic agency had been abolished in 1806, following Napoleon's conquest of the republic, and was reestablished one hundred and one years later, in 1907, to supervise the water system and catchments of northeastern Italy. Some of these functions have since been further dispersed among other twentieth-century agencies. Today, the Venice Water Authority, which has grown into a large, slow-moving bureaucracy responsible for activities in and around the lagoon, supervises the work of the Consorzio Venezia Nuova.

But Rome—not Venetian authorities—maintains strict supervision of the Consorzio. This is because the Venice water authority has been placed under the national Public Works Ministry—not under regional, provincial, or local Venetian control as it was for centuries before modern times.

The Consorzio's first major project was called, aptly, the Progetto Venezia (Venice project). According to ANSA, "The project mapped out studies and experiments on the lagoon's hydrodynamics and pollution, and general subprojects for preliminary works within the lagoon and at the mouths." The prime minister at the time, Bettino Craxi, described the project as "the first of a new generation of public works" that would place technology at the service of the environment.

ANSA reports that Craxi also named the date for the completion of the works: 1995.

Out of this Progetto Venezia came the first proposal for testing gates at the lagoon's three mouths. The mid-1980s concept is little changed from Frassetto's original mobile-gates proposal dating from the early 1970s. And, at the beginning of the twenty-first century, the theory remains intact: seventy-nine mobile gates, lying in wait on the Adriatic's floor, would be dispersed across the three lagoon mouths, ready to rise up at the approach of a storm surge riding on top of a high tide. The gates would be able to hold back nearly three feet (one meter) of high water. As the tide began to recede, the gates would be lowered back into place to allow the lagoon to flush out itself.

The test of a prototype gate, launched in 1988 and designed to sit in place until 1992, was named Modulo Sperimentale Elettromeccanico. Pundits began calling the project MOSE (Moses), an allusion to the biblical leader's ability to part the seas.

MOSE was a full-scale model consisting of a single gate. To great fanfare, the gate and its giant yellow superstructure were towed by two tugboats down Venice's Giudecca Canal, the major waterway that skirts the historic city's edge and the pathway for large tourist ships that sail into Venice through the Lido entrance. Venetians and tourists alike lined the *fondamente* to watch as MOSE was placed, hours after it began its journey across the lagoon, near the mouth of the Lido harbor, in the Treporti Channel between Sabbioni and Sant'Erasmo. ANSA describes it thus:

> This was an enormous steel caisson measuring 20 × 17.5 meters mounted on a hull 32 × 25 meters on which four piers rose to a height of 20 meters to support a crane. The

crane was used for the replacement of defective parts. The hull also housed the control center and personnel . . . when it came time for Moses to get his feet wet, there was considerable anxiety for a time because a huge air bubble trapped in the gate caused the caisson to swerve. Then everything worked according to plan. Approaching noon the yellow gate had been raised and allowed to float for a quarter hour before sinking it beneath the surface, where it disappeared like a sounding whale. This event, historic in some ways, rekindled debates and polemics—and not only among the environmentalists.

The price tag for this single-gate structure was enormous: 20 billion lire, or 13.3 million dollars. The date chosen for the placing of MOSE—November 3, 1988—was significant. It was one day short of the twenty-second anniversary of the 1966 flood. The structure sat in place for four years, and its obnoxious yellow-orange exterior, turning more brightly orange in the light of nearly 1,460 sunsets, hard against the skyline, forever implanted in Venetian minds how the final gates project, if it was ever built, would look. Whether that vision was reality did not matter then, and for many does not matter now.

Ironically the special laws that fund the project and all the works throughout the lagoon forbid any support system for the gates to rise above the level of the lagoon mouths. Unlike the Thames Barrier, which sweeps across the Thames Estuary near London while supported by a massive visual intrusion of steel and concrete, Venice's mobile gates would be completely submerged, superstructure and all. They would rise up only when a storm surge threatens the city during high tide, their defenders say, and then slip back beneath the waves until the next high-water warning shrieks from the *acqua alta* sirens placed throughout the lagoon. The experimental model, the MOSE, with its visually repugnant superstructure, was designed that way to house the scientists and technicians who conducted four years' worth of experiments.

How this image of gates became the symbol for Venetians to disparage is frustrating for engineer Maria Teresa Brotto, assistant to the Consorzio's director general.

"This is a *laboratory*!" Brotto says sharply, tapping a fingernail against a photograph of the MOSE superstructure, which now sits rusting away in a lagoon backwater. I ask: "So because it is above the water, Venetians believe the final gates will be above the water as well?" "Yes," Brotto responds.

Her colleague, Monica Ambrosini of the Consorzio's press office, says that the Venetian press, when it publishes stories about the debate surrounding the gates, repeatedly illustrates the articles with pictures of MOSE.

"Many oppose the project because it is too expensive or because they believe it will harm the environment of the lagoon," Ambrosini says. "But the bigger problem is this," she says, pointing to the old MOSE picture. "I think you know this very well: Not everyone reads the newspaper with attention. So they look at the images, and they can imagine other things."

Furthermore, engineer Brotto adds, "The MOSE was the laboratory. You wouldn't call this MOSE." She is now pointing to a drawing of how the gates would be housed underwater and out of sight. They are "mobile gates," she says. MOSE was a "physical model"—nothing more.

Everywhere I went in Venice asking ordinary Venetians— shop owners, restaurateurs, tourist-trinket sellers—about the gates, they would respond, "Oh, you mean MOSE," and they would raise one hand above the other as if to indicate height.

It seems that the Consorzio engineers and its media spokespersons do have a public-relations problem. Their once-clever acronym and the image it conjures have come to haunt them.

Despite its image, however, MOSE did what the Consorzio needed it to do. Repeated tests over the four-year period that the massive hunk of curved metal sat in the Lido entrance, dodging tourist ships and other craft making their way along the lagoon's eastern edge, helped designers come up with more functional gates proposals. Scientists, according to ANSA, were able to improve a hinge-connector system on the test gate, and they came up with a way to remove sand deposited in the gate housing. They also figured out how to operate touchy compressed-air systems that were easily fouled by the same kind of sea-life encrustations that fix themselves onto the hulls of steel ships. And after tests of the gates' paint systems Consorzio engineers and other scientists are satisfied that the underwater structures could last half a century or more—as are the Thames Barrier operators about their steel-and-concrete monster.

But as time went by, the organized opposition to the gates had time to build its case against them, either for financial or for environmental reasons. The more time that was required to gain answers to the gates' technical mysteries, the more time there was to raise questions.

Around the beginning of the 1990s, officials began to realize that they needed to "think outside the box" and put the Venetian lagoon within the wide context of the Upper Adriatic.

In other words, they began to take a macro view of the problem of shipping and commerce overall. After all, Ravenna has its own flooding problems, as does Trieste—and in their own way their ports are just as commercially viable as Venice's.

At the same time, the Supreme Council of the Public Works Ministry was able to step back and view the micro needs of historic Venice. It was at this point that serious thought, made financially possible by the sweeping Special Law 798, started to be given to protecting the interior of the city from the medium-height floods that more regularly coursed through the canals and walkways than did super-high floods. Serious consideration also was given to the long-held environmentalist view that oil tankers should eventually be eliminated from the lagoon itself. And the Supreme Council went a step farther by raising the possibility that the fish farms be reopened to the nat-ural ebb and flow as they had been in preceding centuries. In later centuries the farms had been cordoned off from the main lagoon and the free flow of the lagoon tides, thereby promoting flooding in the historic center by reducing the area that once accommodated unhindered tidal motion.

So, during this period the Public Works Ministry asked that the gates project be halted until the lagoon itself could be cleaned up. Driving this decision were conditions that appalled residents and tourists alike. Summertime water quality was so bad that massive fish kills were reported in the lagoon, and tons of algae were blooming in the midst of pollutants that were overly enriching the water on top of the sewage present in a city without a sewage system. Mainland runoff was full of agricultural fertilizer, and this fueled the algae and insect problem. Today, during the summer, special boats ply the waters, harvesting tons of algae daily. Officials believe the water quality improved over the decade of the 1990s. Nutrient levels were reduced, they say, through construction of municipal and industrial treatment plants around the lagoon's edges.

ANSA reports: "The city of Venice, however, was strongly critical of Public Works Ministry's request to halt the gates project and, acting on March 15, 1995 on the basis of the findings of a technical working group, proposed subjecting the project to an assessment of environmental impact."

The environmental assessment of the mobile-gates project and the other major projects for the greater lagoon was so ordered, leading to even more delays in the long-awaited decision to go ahead with the gates' construction. But all these political and scientific machinations worked to the delight of local Venetian politicians and residents, who for decades had worried about the deteriorating condition of the city itself. With the bigger gates project undergoing a rigorous environmental review during the mid-1990s, work began on the long-neglected canals and structures that make up the historic city's interior infrastructure, or *insulae*.

CHAPTER NINE ~

London and the
Thames Barrier

In Venice, as the high tide hard against the
fragile brick goes down, the water pulls away,
bit by bit, the molecules of the fabric of the
city. It happens over and over, day by day.
How long before Venice crumbles?"
—DAVID WILKES

It is the rare kind of morning in London
when the sun shines and the sky is so shock-
ing a blue that a visitor can be persuaded to
leave his umbrella in a hotel room and venture out into the city, unafraid of the damp
and primed for high adventure.

I am standing umbrella-less on Westminster Pier, just a few short feet downstream from the bridge of the same name.
David Wilkes should arrive soon. He man-
ages the operations of the Thames Barrier—
a collection of massive steel gates that rise
up, on command, from deep within the
riverbed and close when super-high tides,

driven up river on the cusp of massive storms, arrive from the North Sea. His title is acting area manager for Britain's Environment Agency and, when we met in late March 2000, he was just a few days away from leaving London and taking a new job closer to his family home in Yorkshire. He would relocate from London to Leeds, in the north of England, to manage flood defense and water resources for most of western, eastern, and southern Yorkshire. Before being asked in 1999 to serve as acting area manager, Wilkes had been the agency's "tidal defence manager" for five years. He knows firsthand what high tides, combined with storm surges, can do. He has strong opinions about the need to defend cities from what he views as the irreversible trend of rising seas.

Wilkes is certainly aware of the problems in Venice. At conferences, he has spoken about how Londoners dealt with their flooding problems over the centuries, and what finally motivated them to build massive gates to safeguard their historic city from storm-driven tidal surges. Like the Italians, he knows that any reasonable act to safeguard a major international city is excruciatingly expensive, and that in a hundred years, or perhaps less, something else equally expensive will have to be done once again. The seas are rising, and scientists, thinking in terms of human, rather than geological, cycles, cannot predict whether that cycle will eventually hold fast or reverse.

I was drawn to meet Wilkes after I read a speech he delivered before a Venice in Peril symposium held in April 1998 at the Courtauld Institute in London. In it he asserted: "Cities on water are very special. They have unique problems—not least the fact that the sea, which is their lifeblood, can also threaten their existence. But as well as problems, such cities have their own distinctive brand of beauty and energy. Many are centers of civilization, or economic giants, sometimes both. They deserve our protection."

I knew Wilkes could help me understand the depths of the problems of Venice, one of the "centers of civilization" he referred to, by talking about the problems of London, one of his "economic giants."

After we communicated via e-mail, telephone, and the postal service, he agreed to show me the Thames Barrier, a massive engineering feat that is similar in theory and magnitude to what engineers have proposed for Venice. As an added bonus, he promised to give me a tour, by boat, along the Thames through London to help put into perspective what the river means to the city and how the English have tried to strike a balance between nature and human needs—something Italians struggle with in the Venetian lagoon.

I am an hour early for our ten A.M. meeting and—as I watch tourist boats of all sorts of shapes and sizes pull up to Westminster Pier one after another, take on passengers, and depart—I ruminate about London's long history of living with and battling water. It is a history that goes back well beyond Roman times, when the unfettered, uncontained Thames naturally ebbed and flowed up and down its length, from the North Sea to more than forty miles inland, periodically affecting the native peoples and the invading Romans alike.

Precisely how it affected those early peoples is not known. But written records, beginning with King Canute in the eleventh century, tell us that London has a thousand-year history with flooding. Canute is famous in English lore because tradition has him sitting on his throne and ordering the sea to go away. Historians believe that this seeming act of arrogance was not arrogance at all, but a calculated demonstration by the king to his courtiers and other followers that there were limits to what he could achieve.

Some people who believe the myth say that King Canute was sitting somewhere along the east coast of England when he issued his order to the "sea." But like much of myth that springs forth over dusty centuries as stories are told and re-told, that is probably not where the king demonstrated his powerlessness over natural forces. Modern historians know that King Canute was likely sitting on his throne very close to where Westminster Abbey now is, and close to Parliament as well, when he made his "command" to the waters carried by the Thames, which were invading inland London in the form of the rising sea tide.

There are records of major debilitating floods in 1099, 1236, and 1663, when Samuel Pepys wrote of "all of Whitehall having been drowned." Pepys painted a vivid picture, describing men rowing up and down London's streets in wherries—long, light rowboats pointed at both ends, used to transport passengers on the river.

During the 1800s there were six fairly big floods. In fact, the historic City of London would probably have been flooded many more times if it had not been for the low-slung bridges that crossed the river at various points. These early bridges were enclosed, and they effectively acted as barriers, forcing the storm-driven tides to pile against the bridges' downstream walls. An early version of London Bridge was such an enclosed structure. It likely prevented the highest volumes of water from coming upriver—a sort of ancient wooden version of the modern, technical, steel-and-concrete wonder known as the Thames Barrier.

To understand what these floods could mean to a city of seven million souls, one needs to consider this reality, laid out by Wilkes in his 1998 "Venice in Peril" speech:

> Sixty square miles of London lie below high tide level. That area contains many famous streets, built on mud and marsh—and vulnerable. The basements of each and every building in that area could be flooded out with water reaching ground-floor level and, in some places, up to ten feet deep. The homes of three quarters of a million Londoners are liable to be affected by a major flood, with far-reaching disruption of gas, electricity, water supply, sewerage, and telecommunications systems. Floodwater could pour into the Underground system at the entrance to any one of the twenty-six tube stations and down countless airshafts. The potential for widespread loss of life is huge.

Wilkes then presented his audience with the price tag for such a disaster: "A major flood in London could easily cause direct damages of twenty billion pounds [$34 billion]. It would take twelve months to get the city working again. Meantime, trade and commerce would move elsewhere—and probably never return."

Later in his talk, he compared this cost of a single flooding disaster to what it took, in pounds sterling, to build the barriers: 530 million pounds (approximately 901 million dollars). Ignoring inflation, that means that by early 1998 it cost roughly 17 million pounds (nearly 29 million dollars) for each closure of the gates since the barrier opened in late 1983. By 2030, Wilkes said, the Environment Agency expects the gates to have been closed 250 times, at an average cost of 2 million pounds per closing (3.4 million dollars). Wilkes believes that given proper care and maintenance, the barrier should last another hundred years.

Without the barrier, Wilkes asserted in his speech, each time London was threatened by a major storm surge, authorities would have to consider temporary closure of the city's historic center and the Underground in the interests of safety.

The first major flood of the twentieth century hit London in 1928. That event was unusual because it was a freshwater flood, largely fueled by a relentless rainfall over the lands that drain into the Thames. And it just happened to coincide with a big tide moving up the river. The volumes of water pouring off the land joined with the seawater heading upstream, filling the river from bank to bank and pushing hard against London's thick stone river walls. Those walls, which had been substantially rebuilt during Victorian times, were breached at Hammersmith and Millbank. Fourteen people died in their beds. Millbank, where the original Tate Gallery—now called Tate Britain—is located on the Thames's north bank, is just upstream from the Houses of Parliament. Hammersmith is another five miles upriver, also on the north bank.

The 1928 flooding spurred renewed interest in finding a way to safeguard the city from future catastrophes, first debated around 1906. Parliament ordered the river walls raised another twelve inches. That was done in 1930, and the walls that visitors to London see today remain at that standard. Other floods of varying degrees periodically occurred following the raising of the walls.

In 1953, for example, London was still a war-scarred city, with heavy World War II bomb damage remaining, particularly in the East End. During a stormy January night a massive weather depression arrived after crossing the North Atlantic from the east coast of North America, dragging millions and millions of tons of additional water into the North Sea.

As this surge tide moved around the northern end of Scotland and down the east coast of England, it breached sea defenses between Newcastle and Hull, and all the way around East Anglia. One-third of East Anglia was submerged that night. Two hundred people died, and ten times that number of cattle were drowned. As the tide moved farther south and into the Thames Estuary, it seemed that London was going to be completely swamped and overwhelmed by one of the largest storm-surge tides that had ever been known. Perhaps fortuitously, at least for Londoners, the earth embankments in Essex and Kent failed under the weight of the water, which spilled out into farmland. The flooding caused many tragic deaths and a lot of damage to agriculture, but the earthen banks were breached just sufficiently, and the brunt of the surge was spread out, so that the tide reached central London barely at the level of the river-wall tops.

The devastation of the east coast and the realization of what might have happened to London were so great that it refocused public attention on seeking a flood-protection solution for the city.

But even with this near miss for London fresh in everyone's minds, another fourteen or fifteen years of "How can we do barriers? What about shipping?" followed.

Then, in September 1969, another big storm-surge tide swept down the east coast of England. On this occasion it was once again very severe in the East Yorkshire city of Hull, on the Humber Estuary: One-third of Hull was flooded.

By chance the London Flood Committee was meeting that afternoon—September 21, 1969—when news of the Hull disaster reached the city. The tide was due to reach London three hours later; the committee members left their comfortable quarters, opened their traditional black umbrellas to the pouring rain, and went to the banks of the Thames, where they watched in silent horror the waves lapping over the tops of the walls throughout central London.

On the riverside of those walls, between the Vauxhall and Blackfriars Bridges, the Victorians who built the walls had carved distinctive lions' heads, one after another, along the top edges. Londoners like to say that the city should beware when "the lion takes a drink." On this day in 1969, the lion was getting a very good drink—drowning, in fact. The line of heads, complete with full-flowing manes, was fully submerged.

That afternoon was so vivid in the decision makers' memory that they decided they must have a barrier for London. Finally things moved quickly. The antibarrier shipping lobby was quieted, and in 1972 the Thames Barrier Act was passed and designs approved. Work started the following year. The barrier was completed by 1983, opening in October of that year.

The first ideas for a barrier for London had been proffered in 1906 and 1907, but it took another sixty years before there was sufficient public will to finance and build one. In those intervening sixty years, as we have seen, there was serious flooding in 1928, with a loss of fourteen lives. There was a near miss in 1953 and another near miss in 1969.

The length of time taken by this process should give the Venetians and the Italian government heart. They have been seriously debating the need for barriers to the lagoon for a mere thirty years.

———

My thoughts shift back to the present as David Wilkes, aboard the *Thames Champion*, pulls up, right on time. Wilkes and the boat's master, Fred Saunders, are true to their roles in the government bureaucracy: They are wearing ties, covered by sweaters, covered by waterproof jackets showing Environment Agency crests over their left breasts. They have been caught on this river too many times to trust a sunny, cloudless sky in the heart of southeastern England, just a few miles from the temperamental and tempestuous North Sea.

Wilkes, in his early forties, is clean shaven and the consummate Englishman. He is polite, and he knows this Thames-story business forwards and backwards, having given this tour many, many times to dozens of visitors over the years. He speaks efficiently and precisely. His storytelling is captivating. He never uses his tone of voice to convey disappointment or to make judgments about what people in the past did or did not do to protect the city or the river environment along the Thames, which he obviously holds sacred to Britain's honor and economy. And he is very much the historian. Nothing he describes happens out of context in the here and now; he is always able to understand today's events in the context of what occurred decades, or centuries, before.

His department's boat, the *Thames Champion*, is a clean and sleek, nearly forty-foot-long (thirteen meters) riverboat with enclosed cabin and a particularly comfortable passenger chair to starboard of the efficient master and coxswain. Saunders adroitly maneuvers the wheel and she slips from the pier, her bow pointed hard against the current, for a short journey upstream. I am told we will go as far upriver as Battersea and then reverse course, passing Westminster Pier once again en route to Greenwich in the heart of the Thames Estuary and the point near where the Thames Barrier stretches across the river like a gleaming silver necklace clasped around the city's throat.

With luck the clear skies will hold, and I will be able to watch the setting sun bounce golden off the barrier super-structure, which resembles the upturned hulls of Viking ships—once a scourge along these coasts during the first millennium.

Here, just beyond Westminster Bridge, the river through modern London has been channeled and made much nar-rower than it ever was in earlier times. People lived here along this river for centuries before the Romans established this in-land port, using superb engineering skills to construct what was likely the first bridge across the tempestuous river that then was more or less left to its own devices.

Wilkes, whose sphere of responsibility within the Environ-ment Agency is called the "South East Area of the Thames," is a veritable font of facts.

"Here at Westminster," he says as we head upstream beneath the famous bridge, "we know that the river was 750 yards [686 meters] wide. Today it is down to 250 yards [229 meters]." By progressively building into the river over the centuries and narrowing the channel in the name of development and com-merce, Londoners inadvertently increased the speed of the tide's ebb and flow. From Wilkes's 1998 "Venice in Peril" speech, I knew the basic science of all this. It taught me that the moon's gravitational pull causes two high and two low tides every day.

But ever-shifting weather is what tosses uncertainty into the astronomical mix, and where problems of tidal unpredictability arise. In an attempt to grapple with this unpredictability, Thames Barrier engineers construct two weather forecasts daily, year round, and constantly look at North Atlantic and North Sea conditions thirty-six hours ahead of each passing moment. This phenomenon of weather on top of the gravitational influences of the moon and sun is, of course, true for locations worldwide, and most particularly true for Venice at the head of the Adriatic.

The physics behind it is straightforward. High atmospheric pressure forces the sea level down; low pressure, which typically accompanies storms, raises it, and wind can pile the water up into a "hump." Technically speaking, a surge is the difference between the actual tide and what had been the predicted height of the tide due to the movements of the moon and sun.

In the North Sea—the northern Adriatic has its own similar set of phenomena—this could be the scenario: There could be a deep depression, a low, off North America, forming in the Gulf of Mexico. Moving clockwise toward Europe, toward Britain, it could be two thousand miles in diameter, creating a one-foot-high dome, or hump, of water beneath it, also two thousand miles in diameter. These are the first seeds of potential disaster. This massive dome, moving across the North Atlantic and carrying millions and millions of tons of seawater, could arrive at the top of the North Sea at the same time as the tide is entering the sea around the north of Scotland. Because the North Sea's shape is rather like a funnel, this additional volume of water on top of the regular tide would flow down from the funnel's widest end along the east coast of Scotland and England to the Straits of Dover, at the narrow end. At the top of the funnel Scotland and Scandinavia are five hundred to six hundred miles apart, narrowing to twenty miles between Dover in England and Calais in France. The water would be squeezed at the narrow end, making it even higher along those southern coasts, and forcing it onto low-lying land or up river estuaries.

These are classic Thames Estuary surge conditions, which can make the water level six to twelve feet (two, three, maybe even four meters) above the level of the tide expected because of the pulls of the moon and sun. Such conditions, which lead to a risk of flooding, can occur four or five times a winter and are critical only when the astronomical levels of the tides are at their highest, usually over the two or three days that follow a full moon.

It is like a game of chance—a matter of timing that brings on storms at the same moment as superhigh tides. Venice and the northern Adriatic play such a game, as do hundreds of coastal and island locations worldwide.

"Where the palace of Westminster stands, there is a patch of high ground, known as Thorny Island," Wilkes says above the hum of the *Thames Champion*'s engines. He is pointing out the fully developed spot on the north bank beyond the high walls lining the river that act as a barrier to the river at high tide. There sits one of the most famous pieces of real estate in the Western world, the Houses of Parliament. The idea of an "is-land" being there is hard to fathom in modern times, but centuries ago it was a marsh where the unfettered river channel split in two and separated a bit of land from the river's north bank. Now only the narrower main channel of the river re-mains, the northerly meander of the split channel, and Thorny Island itself, lost beneath a giant, modern city.

"But over here to the south of the river, where the London Eye [a giant Ferris wheel—type structure that opened in late

1999] is now, is very low-lying marshland." Without the stone walls that were built long, long ago lining both sides of the river, the tides each day would flood vast portions of what is now city.

At nearly thirty feet (nine meters) the difference between high and low tides today is dramatic, and it can be much more during storm surges. Unlike what happens when Venice is flooded—there the rising waters can be like a new tourist attraction, with hundreds of gleeful tourists splashing through knee-deep water in St. Mark's Square—tens of thousands of lives have been lost as the North Sea raged out of human control over recent centuries.

The last remaining swamps around London became Battersea Park, built in 1850 on the south bank between the Albert Bridge and the Chelsea Bridge. Again, to keep the river out and the park dry, a new section of high wall was constructed at precisely the same height as earlier walls along the river.

"If you look behind you [to the north side of the river], you can see that the top of the walls is roughly at the level of a saloon car [sedan] driving along the road on the protected side of the river," says Wilkes. "And then, as you look farther inland toward Chelsea, you can see the ground level is falling away. Typically, on the north side of the river, street level is six feet below today's high tide. Those walls essentially keep two high tides out of the city each and every day."

The tides that roll through the city high on the waters of the Thames are massive and powerful. There are a number of reasons for this, including the human impact on the river, such as narrowing the channel that forces the tides to run faster and higher than they did in ancient times. The tides following the full moon each month are especially high and powerful. These can run at five or six knots, although the tides go in and out over time at the same rate as normal ones. A person walking typically moves at two knots, so these full-moon tides—known as spring tides—move at three times walking speed. (The word *spring* has nothing to do with that season of the year, but with the tidal situation following the full moon, when the friction effect of the ocean on the surface of the earth is at its greatest.)

Conversely, the smaller range within high and low tides occurs when there is a new moon, or a small moon, when the sun and the moon act against each other in terms of gravitational pull. These smaller tides, in which the distance between high and low is barely discernible—the Venetians call this condition *acqua morta* (dead water)—are called neap tides. The water with neap tides does not come up as high, or drop as low, as water during spring tides, when the differences between high and low tides are the most dramatic.

The Thames is tidal as far as Teddington, twenty miles upstream from London Bridge. In fact, Teddington literally means "tide and town." But while the tides go far upstream, the saltwater ends at about Greenwich, only a few miles from the North Sea.

Now we are heading downstream toward Greenwich, its costly Millennium Dome, and the location of the Thames Barrier. We pass Tate Britain on the north shore and the headquarters of the British Secret Service, MI6, on the south shore. Along this stretch, just as the *Thames Champion* nears Parliament, Wilkes points out the stone lions' heads that line the embankment walls along both sides of the river, between Blackfriars Bridge and Vauxhall Bridge. These are the very lions that got that famous "drink" in 1969, when Parliament was finally pushed into action.

"You can see that the top of the lion heads is level with the top of the walls," he says. "The height of those walls was fixed, during the 1870s, when those embankments were built as a housing for London's main interceptor sewers (a piece of engineering masterminded by an eminent Victorian, Sir Joseph Bazalgette) and the last major reclamation of land along the Thames took place.

"Without a Thames Barrier—and in the face of increasing high-tide frequency at ever-increasing levels—those walls would need to be more than two and one-half meters above the level of the existing walls to give the present level of flood protection."

Here Wilkes pauses. He scans the riverbank on each side and says quietly: "You know, from Westminster, the City of London, and the Tower Hamlets, which run in sequence from upstream to downstream, it is not a very wide band for a floodplain. This plain takes you only a block or so into the city on the north side of the river; the floodplain on the south side extends up to two miles inland. If there was flooding, probably the first thing people would notice would be flooding of the Underground railway system—there are twenty-six stations within that defended area that have their entrances below high-tide level."

He pauses again, then resumes: "Just imagine the scene eighty to ninety feet below the streets of London, with the river Thames pouring past the ticket barriers, down the stairs, down the escalators of those Tube stations." It sounds like a disaster movie in the making, but Wilkes is not thinking of the movies. "The potential for loss of life is just horrendous," he says finally. "It is so important that the barrier operates effectively."

Ironically, Londoners were aware of this risk during World War II, and were concerned about Nazi bombers that conducted nightly raids into the East End, trying to bomb away the entire Docklands area. If one or two of them had been slightly off course, and a bomb had blown away the river walls near one of those Underground tunnels, Londoners would have faced serious flooding with a potential loss of life as great or greater than that accomplished by single night's bombing.

"Maybe they were unlucky. Maybe they didn't know about this potential," Wilkes muses about the Nazi bomber pilots.

Today, from the middle of the river, it is easy to see that the current ratio of river to embankment height affords travelers a pleasant cruise through London. If the Thames Barrier had not been built, and those embankment tops had been pushed another seven or eight feet (2.1–2.4 meters) higher instead, engineers would have created the illusion of sailing through a tunnel without the roof. The tops of trees would disappear, and only the tallest buildings lining the river would poke into view.

"From the city side, you would not be able to see the river or its boats at all," says Wilkes, his face showing the sadness such a situation would hold for a city so dearly tied to its river.

The *Thames Champion* is nearing Greenwich on the ever-widening river's south bank, just upstream from the Thames Barrier. As we pass Greenwich, I can see the famed nineteenth-century tea clipper, the *Cutty Sark*, lodged in her place on shore, now a tourist attraction. Nearby is Sir Francis Chichester's *Gypsy Moth IV*, the small boat the sailor sailed alone around the world in 1966. En route to this point, we have come downriver past historic London with Wilkes, who is as much historian as engineer, pointing out sites steeped in legend. We glided past Deptford, which had been the heart of the Royal Navy for centuries. It was there that Sir Walter Raleigh, probably met by Queen Elizabeth I, returned from his North American adventure with potatoes and tobacco. The massive piers, running parallel to the south embankment, are slightly concave—the better to nestle the curved hulls of the giant wooden sailing ships against the shore.

On the north bank, across from Deptford, also a haven for pirates—the "hard men," as Wilkes calls them—is the Isle of Dogs, for centuries a marshy area that is actually a peninsula and not an island. We have already passed the beach just downriver from the Tower Bridge, where the British government, in the seventeenth and eighteenth centuries, often tied convicted pirates to stakes and let them drown as the tides washed over them three times—that means they were left there approximately a day and a half before they were cut down and their remains disposed of. Near the Isle of Dogs, at a place called Rotherhithe, is also the point from which convicts were exported to Australia. A yellow-brick building on the north shore behind this beach has been converted into a theme restaurant, where, Wilkes says wryly, Australian tourists can reconnect with their roots.

The Thames Barrier is now coming into view. In the midday light its steel tops, designed to look like upturned boat hulls, show dull against an increasingly gray sky, the blue of the early morning now gone. I count ten gates stretching in a line across the river. It is wide here, probably close to six hundred yards across (548.7 meters), nearly three times the river's width at Westminster Pier far upstream, where our journey began. The width of the river at the barrier is close to the prehistoric width of the river at Westminster.

Six of the ten barrier gates can be sailed through. Four— three on the north side, one on the south—are too shallow for most river craft. River traffic—from big ships to small do- ries—moves through them and over the gates that are held at the ready deep in the riverbed below. The four main gates, each two hundred feet wide (61 meters), are the same width as the central span on Tower Bridge, farther upstream, where shipping traffic still passes through when its drawbridge is raised. This width is also about three feet wider than the Pan- ama Canal, and at high tide the water at the barrier is four feet deeper than that of the Panama Canal.

These are not the only gates. Nearby, a bit farther down- stream on the north bank, is the entrance to Barking Creek. It has a guillotine-type gate that drops like an executioner's blade onto a subsurface concrete sill, closing the creek's mouth against the same storm-driven high tides that force the closure of the barrier gates across the Thames itself. If that Barking Creek opening were left unsealed, the tidal surge, rebuffed by the Thames Barrier, would go up the creek, flow around the north side of the barrier itself and defeat the main Thames tidal defenses.

Everything along the river that is designed to keep water out of 75 square miles (194 square kilometers) of London is under the purview of Wilkes's Environment Agency. His area of responsibility runs from just downstream from the barrier, near Dartford, to the upstream tidal limit at Teddington. That includes nearly 120 miles (192 kilometers) of raised defenses such as the river walls and earthen dikes. Beyond Dartford, it is about 30 miles (48 kilometers) to Southend and the open North Sea coastline. Other Environment Agency regions manage defenses along that stretch.

Through March 2000 the barrier was activated against storm-driven high tides thirty-eight times, for an average, since 1983, of a little more than twice a year. (When I visited Wilkes in March 2000, the last time the barrier had been raised was the preceding Christmas.)

"We had a very, very stormy period in a run up to, and over, the Christmas period," Wilkes recalls. "The Christmas of 1999 was unprecedented in that we closed the Thames Barrier and used all the Thames defenses five times in succession, or over five following tides, or twice daily. First was the second tide on Christmas Day, two on the December 26, and two on the twenty-seventh and into the twenty-eighth."

I was not likely to see such a closure during my brief visit to London. It was nearly April, the typical last month of the storm-tide season. "We are probably okay until the end of August, early September," says Wilkes. "We cannot say 'never' because the weather always has a habit of catching you unawares. The tides are always still as high, but through the summer we usually don't see the combination of high tide with weather depressions over the North Atlantic."

Wilkes takes me into the barrier compound—a high-security place where a uniformed guard meticulously checks Wilkes's credentials and mine before admitting us. I cannot tell if the guard knows Wilkes by sight, but he gives his boss the same close scrutiny he gives me. The headquarters is on the river's south bank, the same side as Greenwich, and the airportlike control tower on top offers a magnificent view of the artistically inspired series of gates that stretch nearly a third of a mile across the massive mud-colored river. Below us, ships of all sizes are almost always moving through the barriers, both up- and downstream. It is a parade that has been going on in this river, in and out of this great European city, for centuries.

I meet Colin Carron, tidal control engineer, who is in charge of making each day's decision whether to keep the gates open or to close them. I ask about false alarms, or whether a closure, which always disrupts the steady flow of shipping, was ever made when it wasn't necessary.

Carron begins answering the question cautiously.

"The way we try to minimize false alarms is to forecast as accurately as possible, using mathematical modeling, what the tides will be," he says.

Wilkes breaks in at this point, knowing that I want a more direct answer.

"We have a factor, a safety line, of ten inches—two hundred millimeters—below the closure criteria, and I know that something over 90 percent of our closures have been within that range. If a decision were taken here that we close the barrier, and the actual tide was more than two hundred millimeters away from our published closure level, then we would critically review why that happened. If it is within two hundred millimeters of closure threshold, we'll defend that."

At this point Wilkes's tone turns very, very serious.

"Because with variability of tides, the weather, and winds, we are not dealing with an absolute, precise science, and I will always encourage people to err on the side of safety rather than say, 'Oops! We're sorry that we flooded London. We underestimated things.' "

Then, after that context, I get a direct answer to my original question. "We've had one or two 'wide-of-the-mark' events out of thirty-eight closures," says Wilkes, still uncomfortable using the words *false alarms.*

When the decision is made to close the gates, all the necessary warnings are made and upriver traffic is halted. Ships and boats queue up and wait it out. A typical closure lasts six hours.

"We've continued to learn over the years," says Wilkes. "In the early days, we were raising the gates quickly, over a period of half an hour. It was causing a negative wave upstream from the barrier and a reflecting wave downstream, which was becoming a nuisance for boats." This, he says, caused them to rock heavily, especially those tied up at London piers. "Now a typical closure takes an hour to complete, but it can go much faster if conditions warrant. During my six years here, I never had to do a crash closure. But if it comes to it, there is a basic decision: Do we get the barrier closed quickly and risk inconveniencing ships on moorings, or do we protect London and protect the people?"

Like the promoters of gates for the lagoon of Venice, who say those structures would last for one hundred years, Wilkes offers the same life estimate for the Thames Barrier. While its useful life for depreciation purposes is 2030, Wilkes and others believe that the barrier will easily work until 2100.

"The gates we have here in 2003 will be twenty years old then, and they now are still on their original paint system, which recent tests tell us is good for another five or six years. With a new paint job every thirty years, I see no reason why they won't last one hundred years."

Then Wilkes talks about Venice, which like London grew up near and on the water. "Both are seaports. Both are very special cities because of their culture, their heritage, and their architecture. But there is a major difference: In Venice there is no major threat to life when the water rises, while there is a very real threat to life in London because of the height of the tides.

"London also is different because it is spread out along the banks of the river; it offers a linear flooding problem, whereas Venice is contained within a cell, a lagoon."

Of course Venice needs to build defenses, Wilkes believes—both major defenses like the proposed gates as well as the raising of Venice's pavements that is now being done routinely. He believes global warming is a reality that will force, in a single life span, the sea upward to the point where Venice, London, and probably one hundred or more coastal cities worldwide will be in continual danger.

By 2030 Wilkes expects that the Thames Barrier will be modified to adapt to new, progressively higher sea levels. The same thing will happen to Venice. Whatever is built there will, in another generation, probably be modified or replaced with an even more dramatic plan.

After sixty years of debate it finally took a near catastrophe in 1969 in full view of government decision makers to spur England to approve construction. It will probably take a similar near catastrophe to force Venetians and the Italian government to accept the inevitable.

"It nearly always does" take such a disaster, says Wilkes of such crisis-driven decision making over tough, money-gobbling issues.

It is the end of a long day and Wilkes drives me to the Trafalgar Tavern—the traditional site of Lord Nelson's final meal on land before he sailed to meet the combined French and Spanish fleets in 1805. The tavern reeks of history: Apparently there has been a hostelry on the site since the mid-1700s. It was originally called the George Inn, and by the time of Horatio Nelson's meal, it was known as the Old George.

We take our places at a window table overlooking the river. Earlier, when we passed the tavern while aboard the *Thames Champion*, the river had been near low tide and was a short distance away from the building. Now, late in the evening, high tide is approaching, and the Thames is lapping against the building, inches away from our feet and just below the level of the tall window that gives us a spectacular, moon-brightened view of the river and its traffic.

Wilkes sets aside his engineer's mantle and picks up that of a historian.

He says that in 1805, 195 years before, when Lord Nelson ate here, "perhaps in this very spot," he muses, the top of the tide came up to the bottom of this window, much as it does now. Over the years, the normal high tide got slightly higher, but not much. There is now a plate of reinforced glass that covers a foot or so of the six-foot-high (1.8-meter) window's bottom portion to keep the high tide away from the original glass and its casing.

Wilkes continues: "Because of global warming, 195 years from now, in 2195, the high tide riding on the Thames could be six feet higher than it is today. The water could reach to the top of this window."

What this means for London, Venice, and the rest of the world's coastal cities, Wilkes will not venture to guess. But it appears likely that any solution reached in this decade for Venice, like the Thames Barrier, will be short term in the grand scheme of things.

"Nothing really lasts forever, does it?" the engineer and historian suggests as he takes a sip from his amber-colored pint.

CHAPTER TEN ~

Insula—Saving the City from Within

The problem of saving Venice is not only about defending the city from the *acqua alta*. There's another part of the story that we need to confront and that has nothing to do with the Moses dikes and which the media seem to ignore.

—MASSIMO CACCIARI, FORMER MAYOR OF VENICE, *ITALY DAILY*, 6 DECEMBER 1999

There are those involved in the debate over how to save Venice who believe that since Venetians have lived with fluctuating water levels for centuries, the only steps that should be taken to preserve the city are "ordinary maintenance." They want the kind of routine maintenance that Venetians conducted century after century. There is clear evidence that as structures were built over the centuries, foundations were placed higher than foundations of earlier buildings to account for the gradual rising of the sea.

And, particularly in St. Mark's Square, archaeologists know that pavements were raised as well, to stay ahead of the imperceptible rise in mean sea level. But there is little new construction in the city today; most work is restoration work. So property owners and contractors do not tear down and rebuild new. They renovate, increase the height of foundation stones, and add impermeable brick and moisture seals well above old foundations.

In general, this kind of work—preservation and protection of old structures—was not done for most of the twentieth century. The city has suffered mightily in the hands of its modern protectors. Many Venetians believe that this internal problem—not the mobile gates—is the place to begin. When these measures no longer keep out high water, then it will be time to come up with a farther-reaching solution.

One of these advocates against the concept of the gates is prominent Venetian civil engineer Paolo Pirazzoli, who divides his time between Venice and France, where he is a member of the National Center for Scientific Research. His work for the French center and for UNESCO for several years has dealt with studying global sea-level rise.

"From time to time I come to Venice"—he maintains a home in the city's historic center, near the Peggy Guggenheim Collection—"and I follow what is happening here," he says. His belief is that the gates would offer some protection to the city for only a few years, but then the sea-level rise would exceed their protection level. "Then you must construct something else entirely. It is impossible with this kind of project; they [the mobile-gates advocates] cannot adapt [the gates to higher water]."

We are meeting in a small neighborhood bar near the Guggenheim. Pirazzoli is sipping a wonderful-looking red orange juice from the Sicilian blood oranges that blanket this city's fruit-vendor stalls.

"My answer about what to do instead of the gates is given as a Venetian. This attitude is difficult for people who are from the outside to understand," he says, nodding to me as an obvious outsider. But when he refers to outsiders, I know he is also speaking about the Italian scientists and engineers from elsewhere in Italy who believe the gates are vital to saving the city. Anyone who is not born a Venetian is an outsider here, even if they have lived in Venice for decades. Venetians view most of the Italian staff of the Consorzio, for example, as outsiders.

Pirazzoli continues. "Venice has always had high water. It is part of the life here. To know that you will have some flooding is acceptable, especially if you know two or three hours before by a series of alarms. I don't know if it is possible to defend against that. You would have to defend against the sea, from the rivers, from a lot of things."

That is why he does not believe that the 1966 flood would have been prevented by the mobile gates had they been in place then. Consorzio engineers believe that waters as high as 9.84 feet (three meters) above mean sea level would be stopped. The 1966 level was 5.2 feet (1.6 meters) short of that, but Pirazzoli points out that much of the water that flooded the lagoon to such record heights came from the mainland when the rivers overflowed. The gates, he points out with conviction, would not have prevented that from happening.

Environmentalists opposed to the gates use Pirazzoli's celebrity and reputation as a sea-rise expert to bolster their position. A few days after my conversation with the esteemed

Venetian scientist, I meet with Gherardo Ortalli, a professor of medieval history at the University of Venice and university *prorettore*, or vice-rector. Also a member of the national board of Italia Nostra (Our Italy), which has long championed environmental causes and restoration efforts, Ortalli is an outspoken opponent of the mobile gates. He filed a lawsuit (unresolved as 2001 drew to an end) with the European Union protesting the Consorzio's status as a state monopoly.

Ortalli is the opposite of the calm, deliberate Pirazzoli, ever the rational, calculating scientist. The professor cannot sit still. He moves around the large office located in a medieval building just off the Grand Canal, digging through stacks of paper to find a document. His phone rings constantly. He transforms as he picks up the receiver. He is calm and cordial with the caller, who would never detect his hyperactivity. But when he hangs up and resumes his conversation, he again becomes a bundle of movement.

"We have spent an enormous amount of money, and we haven't done anything except sustain the Consorzio," he says. No one knows whether the earlier projects—the building up of the barrier islands following the 1966 flood—will work to hold back a similar event, or whether the current projects to rebuild the city's infrastructure by raising pavements and dredging canals will work. But, he says, it is all a step in the right direction.

"They will not damage anything. Complete them first and see what they accomplish, and then see if we still need the gates. It is only a question of good sense," he says, his hands rising in frustration along with his voice.

Then his frustration boils over.

"We don't have anything," he says of Italia Nostra's financial clout compared to the interests supporting the mobile gates. "We don't have the money to fight this. No one listens."

Like Pirazzoli, Paolo Gardin is the opposite of the passionate, always moving Ortalli. He is tall, gracefully thin, laconic, and has a quiet, relaxed air about him. A delightful man in his sixties, he is proud of his English, which was sharpened in the 1970s when he worked in Kentucky for Armand Hammer's Occidental Petroleum and for the Italian petroleum giant ENI-AGIP. Gardin was treasurer for a mining company in Lexington known as Island Creek, which was part of a joint mining operation there owned by the two petroleum giants. A Venetian by birth, he also was at one time chief executive officer of Italgas, the job he held prior to becoming president in the late 1990s of a purely Venetian creation known as Insula.

Insula has the responsibility for carrying out the long-delayed infrastructure improvements within the historic center of Venice. In contrast, the Consorzio is responsible for the works around the ancient city's outer edges—the portion that looks outward toward the lagoon as opposed to the canal edges that look inward. Insula has nothing to do, for example, with the mobile gates or the massive rebuilding of jetties and beaches along the Lido and Pellestrina barrier islands that protect the lagoon from the Adriatic. However, Insula companies often bid for Consorzio projects because they have workers and the equipment close at hand. Sometimes Consorzio crews and equipment do work for Insula. This symbiotic relationship bothers many Venetians and gate critics, who view it as too cozy.

Despite this bigger-picture work, Insula's main responsibility is to do work that protects individual buildings within the historic center. Its heavy equipment, sitting on flat-bottom barges, is busy dredging canals, and its workers are rebuilding those interior waterways, laying new utility lines, and raising the walkways along the canals to new heights to keep rising tides out of the city's narrow stone streets and alleyways.

Gardin's company is one of those uniquely Italian, or Venetian, creations, originally funded by four thousand million lire (approximately two billion dollars). The city of Venice owns 52 percent of the company, and the four major utilities that serve the city through underground systems own the balance. These four are ASPIV, the Venice waterworks company; ISMES, which is part of Enel, the electric utility; Italgas; and Telecom Italia. Each of the four owns 12 percent of Insula's capital.

The name Insula is derived from the Latin word *insula* (island), and it refers to the forty sectors into which the historic center has been divided. The company's mission is clear: Insula is to deal with "maintenance work on the urban system, safeguard buildings along the minor canals, and conduct sanitary and hygiene operations."

Insula's work is the most obvious work to the eyes of the typical Venetian tourist. The Consorzio's work, except for that along the major canals along the lagoon's edge or over on Torcello, several miles away, is more remote. But throughout the city's interior, visitors crossing medieval bridges can easily see that portions of canals are being drained and dredged, and that workers are moving along duckboards laid out along the empty canal's sides, removing broken chunks of the city's original Istrian stone and replacing it with new pieces that are sealed off against the water's intrusion once the canal is refilled.

Workers are rebuilding the steps, used by Venetian boat-men for centuries, which lead out of the canal and up to building entrances. Hanging out of newly sealed stone blocks making up canal sides are dozens of short pieces of rubber hose that snake back in behind the stone. Using these hose sections as conduits, workers pump a sealer through them that will fill in behind the wall. This is supposed to keep the water out from under the fifteenth- and sixteenth-century buildings that line these interior waterways.

Where the stone has yet to be replaced and sealed, water can be seen leaking out of the cracks. It either comes from around the giant steel sheets that hold the canal's water out of the drained portion, or it is water seeping out from beneath the old buildings where for decades—or even centuries—it was allowed to accumulate due to the porous condition of the old canal walls. Until the canal sides are finished, giant pumps sitting high on the empty canal's banks must run periodically to keep it drained. Following some high tides, I have seen the bottom third of a formerly drained canal full of water, the duckboard pathways for the workers floating in the dark, oily-looking liquid. When the pumps bring down the level once again, the boards are replaced and work resumes.

I meet Paolo Gardin on top of the Ponte San Polo, a bridge across the Rio di San Polo that dates back to 1775. This bridge lies along a major pathway through the city that parallels the Grand Canal. It is within the historic center's Dorsoduro quarter, between the Grand Canal and the Giudecca Canal. Thousands of people walk across the bridge each day and can see the work below. Looking toward the Grand Canal, I can see the giant steel plates that hold back the water from the closed-off section of the San Polo Canal, or *rio*. (The word *rio* is still used because it was one of the original rivers that flowed through the Realtine Islands underlying the buildings here.) A small boat can use the Rio di San Pablo to take a winding shortcut, through interconnecting canals, to the other side of the city, coming out on the Grand Canal near the train station, thereby avoiding the clamorous, sometimes choked-with-traffic, serpentine waterway.

Gardin introduces Giuliano Molon, an Insula employee and obviously the person in charge of this particular canal restoration project. "I must go to a meeting," Gardin says. "Giuliano will show you everything and answer all your questions."

We drop down a short ladder into the now-empty and fully dredged section of the Rio di San Polo. We walk along the duckboard walkway lining the sides of the drained canal and under the bridge. I look up at its date, carved in Roman numerals MDCCLXXV on the side twenty feet or more above us. Molon translates. "Seventeen seventy-five," he announces.

I watch workers rebuilding walls sitting dry just above the gunky, sludge-filled water at the bottom of the canal. One craftsman is mortaring into place special red bricks designed to resist the water's capillary action. Others are filling in newly chiseled-out sections between large impermeable stone blocks with a special cement reinforced with carbon and Kevlar fibers that are strong, long-wearing and temperature-resistant. Where this has already been done, a steel mesh, like fencing along a farmer's field, covers the stone. Here, Molon says, the mesh will reinforce a special coat of impermeable material that workers will apply to the stone's surfaces. This will protect it from the prop wash caused by boat engines and from the wave action of boats as they move through the canal.

Now he demonstrates how the work will protect the surrounding walkways from the regular high tides that typically wash over the tops of the canal's older, lower stone sides. The canal wall is being raised, as it is all throughout the city's interior and along its perimeter, to hold back tides up to nearly four feet (1.20 meters). Molon draws on a page of my notebook a crude profile of the canal, showing where the 1.20 level above mean sea level sits. He draws a wobbly dark line upward, pointing well above the top of the wall, moving toward the 6.3-foot (1.94-meter) point, where the 1966 *acqua alta* reached. It is obvious that when any tide higher than 1.20 occurs—which has happened periodically since 1966—the water will flow over the canals' newly raised tops, down walkways, and into unprotected ground-floor buildings.

As I walk along the duckboards, I see concrete-lined iron drainage spouts, placed at intervals along the canal walls well below the usual low-tide water levels. Occasionally a foul-smelling flush of water spurts out of one of them and tumbles down into the greasy water coating the canal's bottom. I am seeing close up how Venice's sewer system works. Waste flows out of buildings into the canals, where it awaits the next high and low tidal cycles. These cycles occur twice a day, flushing the waste out of the city, into the lagoon, and then through the narrow entrances out to sea. Often, during exceptionally low tides, these spouts are above the water, exposing this process to passersby.

"For thirty years, this city never did anything to maintain the canals," Gardin says a few days later, sitting in his office along a side canal a short distance from the massive parking lot and train station. "So that is why the work just in the canals will take ten years. After that, there will be regular maintenance— much more regular."

Venice, a city that because of its unique setting must always maintain itself, failed to do so for nearly a generation. Its infrastructure began crumbling, and what tourists thought was picturesque decay was really the slow, cancerous death of one of the world's greatest cities. Now, in addition to repairing canals and raising the sides of canals, the company is documenting above- and belowground structures. "All the town will be completely documented. This is our work," Gardin says proudly.

But the work itself is viewed with skepticism by the often-cynical Venetians. This is what seems incredible to the eyes of a casual visitor: The city is crumbling; its government is taking steps to reverse decades of neglect and to rebuild its infrastructure from the lagoon bottom upward; and its citizens, those remaining Venetians who have stayed rather than fled to the mainland, complain. They complain about the disruption in their lives when crews block *fondamente* to replace old stone with new, restore old bridges and fountains, and lay new utility lines.

To understand this cynicism on the part of citizens is to understand the way business has been done for generations in Italy. For example, in Florence many years ago, the stones that were used to pave the large, historic squares of the city were pulled up during a restoration process and, instead of being returned to where they had been trod on for centuries, were secretly sold off by contractors, who installed them in private palazzos and in closed-off gardens. Many Venetians believe that the same thing is happening in Venice as Insula removes bridges that have sat across small neighborhood canals for generations. Some citizens are convinced that workers sell off the originals to the rich and return with poor copies. And the stones of the *fondamente*, some believe, are going the way of the Florentine stone—straight into private estates and being replaced with cheaper stone.

During my stay in the city early in 2000, I attended a meeting in San Leonardo, a former church that had been converted into a public building. It was organized by a Venice resident named Umberto Sartori, who questions whether all the city's neighborhood treasures are being properly restored and whether Insula is returning the originals, once restoration is complete, or copies of the originals.

Sartori and I talked briefly before he was called on to address a gathering of perhaps fifty citizens who came to see a display of photographs of these restored structures and hear what he had to say about Insula's work.

"We are not accusing anyone of anything we see," Sartori carefully begins. "We are just telling what we see. We don't really know who is doing this, because many groups are working in the town; many groups, many different companies."

He says that all he has done is to "take pictures and to observe and to describe what we see: what we have seen before the work and what we are seeing now; what is going away to be restored and what is coming back after restoration." Some of the bridgework and fountain work that return is "a horrible copy," Sartori maintains.

He said he first noticed the difference when he saw what had happened to a fountain that he had passed every day of his life since childhood. "It was perfect, you know. It was black iron. There is no varnish better than the black rust over it." The workers dismantled it, he says: "It disappeared, and after a month it came back, and what came back was not at all the same object."

Sartori also points to the paving stones, which are torn up as the *fondamente* are raised and then replaced. But many of the stones that go back into the walkways are new—not the originals that were removed. The laws that provided the money for the work in Venice specify that the old stuff—the ancient stuff—be reused. Little of the original material is being returned, however, and when Sartori asks about it, he is told that many stones were broken during the removal and had to be replaced with newly quarried ones.

"The new stones cost two hundred thousand lire (one hundred dollars) each. The old, original stones can sell for 1.6 million lire (eight hundred dollars) each." Sartori stops, shrugs his shoulders in that classic Italian expression of defeat, and says, "They get the money for selling the new stones, and also they take away the old ones, which are now rare. There are no more of these to be excavated anywhere." His look says: You do the arithmetic.

I bring these concerns to Insula's Gardin. He knows exactly what meeting I attended and what the citizen charges are. He points out that the authorities have not investigated anything because the citizens are incorrect in their suspicions.

He hands over a document he has prepared, a public-relations flyer, to explain the situation to the Venetian public. "Breakage of the old stones in high," he says, and "we must substitute a new stone for the old one when that happens. The new stones are not quarried like they were in the past because the environmentalists have stopped us from excavating material for such uses as we did in the past. The new stones cannot be shaped by hand as they were in the past. They now are shaped by machines. With a machine, they [look] different. The people are asking: 'Where are the old ones; someone has sold them to someone who wants to put them into his villa!' and it is not true."

About the ironwork on bridges, Gardin has this explanation: Rust, which is causing the metal to deteriorate, is scraped away by workers who strive to protect the ornamentation. Once cleaned, the surface is protected by a varnish and returned to the original site. The varnish makes the iron look different, and citizens, who over decades got used to the look of heavily corroded iron, believe that the original has been switched and a poor copy substituted. Again Gardin repeats: "It is not true."

And Gardin addresses the issue of work in a specific neighborhood taking longer, and bridges and *fondamente* being closed to pedestrians longer than expected.

He points to what happened at the Ponte Donna Esta over the Rio della Frescada, near the Scuola Grande di San Rocco, a museum where some of the Venetian artist Titian's greatest works are displayed.

"There was very big trouble for us because when the mud was taken out, we saw that there were very big holes [in the canal walls] that had been covered by the mud and that we had not foreseen. So we had to rebuild completely instead of rebuild just a little. Instead of two months, we needed six, and the people were very angry."

Crews are discovering this kind of unexpected extensive damage as they move through the city. In the Rio della Frescada, Insula engineers determined that the torn-out canal walls were caused by the tremendous prop wash from the garbage boats that would back into the canal at this point every morning, revving their engines as sanitation workers collect the previous day's accumulated garbage piled high along the walkways.

Gardin says Insula learned a great deal from the experience of uncovering such unexpected damage. "We now try to make much more preliminary monitoring, using sonar to understand the situation underneath. But sometimes this is impossible to determine. When you take away the water and the mud, sometimes you find the situation is much more serious than you thought."

Also, people living in houses along the canals experience settling as the water is removed and other water, which has settled below the buildings, is allowed to escape through the now-damaged canal walls. This leads to cracked walls and numerous complaints from the Venetian residents.

"We have many cases of people we have to pay damages to," Gardin says. "What happens to their houses is not a dangerous thing." Then, with a wry smile, he adds: "They can take profit from this." He is implying that the residents are claiming that old cracks are really new and are taking advantage of Insula's deep pockets to correct, for free, decades of settling and cracking.

All this canal restoration work, expected to take until 2010, is only the first phase of what Insula hopes to accomplish. By the end of this ten-year period, the Consorzio is expected to have completed much of its work along the islands' edges throughout the lagoon, and—if the politicians cooperate and authorize construction of the mobile gates—that project could be completed as well.

By then, Gardin says, Insula will launch its next phase: the construction of thousands of septic tanks throughout the historic center. These tanks will hold and process sewage rather than its being dumped directly into the canals. Around large hotels or hospitals or the city's historic fish market, larger, more dynamic sewage systems will be constructed—the fish-market system near the Rialto Bridge was already under construction in 2000—and waste eventually will be pumped out of the historic center to treatment plants on the mainland.

"This is the work of the next twenty years: the ten years to dredge the canals and restore all the banks, and then twenty to thirty years to develop the sewage system." Eventually, Gardin believes, all of Venice's historic center will be connected to a traditional sewer system that hauls everything from the city through pipes to the mainland for treatment. The idea of the lagoon being Venice's sewer, as it has been for centuries, will disappear over time.

Gardin has other problems as well: What should be done with the millions of cubic meters of mud that are dredged from the hundreds of canals?

"Generally, in the past, getting rid of the mud was not any problem," Gardin says. "They simply used it to construct new islands." He goes to a map of the city and points. "These: Tronchetto, the ferry port; Sacca Fisola [at the southern tip of Giudecca and full of 1950s-style housing units]." All new "islands" made from dredged canal mud.

On Murano, the island where most of the city's glass is made, there is another *sacca* (a Venetian word for "place where the water is very low") "and they opened up land there, where there was once mud and water," by dumping tons and tons of dredged mud.

"You always have to work and to defend" to keep the lagoon from becoming either sea or land, he says. "If you want to improve, you have to make something. The lagoon is always moving; the water is moving mud, silt, sediments; always."

Over the last thirty to forty years, however, Gardin says, concern over what might be in the mud—toxic chemicals, heavy metals—has led to a greater environmental sensitivity.

"We and the Greens [Italian environment activists and a left-wing political party] want to know if the sediment being removed by dredging is dangerous, toxic. Many, many studies were made."

What those studies revealed is fairly sobering. According to a July 2000 report in *Italy Daily,* some 70 percent of the seabed more than a mere 5.9 inches (fifteen centimeters) deep registers mercury tracers well into the danger zone, and 40 percent is above the level scientists say will certainly have adverse effects on fish and other organisms.

The news article, quoting a report by a nonprofit research institution, the Enrico Mattei Foundation, says, "Dioxins, hydrocarbons, pesticides and other toxic stuffs also abound. . . . [T]here are around 50,000 kilograms of mercury floating about heavy waters that also are weighted down by 6.1 million kilograms of zinc, 2.7 kilograms of chromium and 2.3 million kilograms of lead." And, the article says, the problem is exacerbated "by illegal clam fishers who trawl the lagoon and further stir up the sands, spreading the pollutants and further damaging the morphology of the sea floor."

And the clam fishers are not the only ones to blame. As industrialization took hold in modern times, the deepening of the shipping channels increased by 10 percent the amount of water that rides into the lagoon on twice-daily high tides. This additional force picks up the pollutants and spreads them throughout the lagoon and into the city's canals—the heart of Gardin's bailiwick.

It is obvious that this heavily tainted mud can no longer be used to build new islands or reinforce existing ones. In the summer of 2000, those handling the toxic waste proposed a plan to ship some of the polluted sediment to a salt mine near Leipzig, Germany.

For now, the mud is hauled to an island near Marghera, the lagoon's industrial heart and source of many of the pollutants. There it is kept in a repository. To eventually get it out of the lagoon—to the Leipzig salt mine, for example—"it will cost much more money," Gardin says, shaking his head. "Now it costs twenty thousand, thirty thousand lire (ten to fifteen dollars) per metric ton. If you move it far away, you spend ten, twenty times more. When the Marghera site is full, it will hold three hundred and fifty metric tons—and it will be full soon. That is not very big." When asked what happens then, Gardin shrugs. "We will find something else. We have to."

Gardin believes that Insula's work in the city's interior cannot prevent the major, 1966-style floods from sweeping the city, but it can keep the smaller floods from regularly inundating residential areas and flowing into the ground-floor shops and homes of his fellow Venetians. To stop the major floods from happening, he says he truly believes that the Consorzio must be allowed to build the mobile gates, even if they don't safeguard the city for more than half a century. This thinking is in line with conclusions reached by an international group known as the Collegio di Esperti (college of experts). In its evaluation of the Environmental Impact Study that was conducted in 1995–1996 and presented in April 1997, the Collegio concluded that Insula's work in the historic center "is as expensive as the mobile gates, would take 60 years or more to be completed, and would leave the city exposed for a long time to come. Since it would not protect against exceptional floods above 120 centimeters, it should be considered as only a partial solution."

Once the gates are built, Gardin says, another generation

of engineers can come up with other solutions: perhaps turning the lagoon into a walled lake and preserving the historic
intent of Venice for generations to come. A lake protected
from increasingly high Adriatic tides would be possible in the
distant future, he says, because sewers will be designed to elim-
inate the need to use the lagoon as a waste-removal system.
Many scientists believe that in the almost certainty of global
warming lasting for generations longer, the lake concept is not
far-fetched—not if future generations truly want Venice preserved at all costs.

"Sometimes the politicians use our work to make a fight
against the gates, saying, 'Wait and see if the work inside the
city will do the job of stopping the great floods before we build
the mobile gates.' But I am an academician, and I know perfectly that the high tides cannot be defended against in this
way. The danger is in the future. Today is a nice day. There
is no rain, no wind, and the tides are normal. We can say,
'Now there is no danger. Let us wait.' But the problem is
growing toward the time when the seas will rise. The danger
is in the future."

CHAPTER ELEVEN ~

The Works—Saving the
City from Without

I have very strong doubts about the proportion between the big amount of investment for the gates and the results we are certain to have in return from this kind of building. Perhaps we can get more important results studying some different solutions for the city of Venice.

—CLAUDIO BONICIOLLI,
PRESIDENT, VENICE PORT AUTHORITY

Since 1973 the Italian state has given or promised eight thousand billion lire to the dozens of projects proposed for the safeguarding of Venice. The exchange rate over the intervening years has fluctuated greatly, but based on the rate of approximately two thousand lire to the dollar in the year 2000, and accounting for inflation, this astronomical number could translate to an amount equal to some four billion dollars. The money represents what was spent be-

tween 1973 and 2000 and what remains to be spent for projects, including the mobile gates, between 2000 and 2010.

The money has gone via the various special laws to the Province of Venezia, which includes Venice and Mestre; to Chioggia; to the Veneto Region, which encompasses most of the
mainland catchments that supply rivers flowing into the northwestern Adriatic; and to the Consorzio Venezia Nuova.

It has been spent for many of the studies that have examined
problems of the lagoon, for creating the state-sanctioned
Consorzio monopoly, and to pay the salaries of its staff of
engineers, designers, contractors, and public-relations personnel. Early in its history the for-profit Consorzio by law
kept 18 percent of the tax dollars that flowed its way; today
that has been reduced to 12 percent.

The tax money has also paid for a significant number of
public works—short of the actual construction of the controversial mobile gates—that have already been executed or are
well under way. As we have seen, Insula is spending millions
of these dollars for significant works in the historic center—
works that are designed to reverse several decades of infrastructure neglect. And the Consorzio has done, and continues
to do, major works around the edges of the historic city that
border on the lagoon itself; on other islands, such as Torcello;
and along the barrier islands: the Lido, Pellestrina, the tip of
the Chioggia harbor, and the low-lying barrier island north
of the Lido, Cavallino, which runs between Punta Sabbioni
and the Lido di Jesolo. The defense of these islands is crucial
to the plan to protect the lagoon from the whims and vagaries
of the often-rambunctious Adriatic.

The Consorzio, as its public-relations specialists and engineers repeatedly emphasize, is more than just the designer
and chief advocate for the mobile gates, which they believe will

lead to jobs for thousands of workers. This giant conglomeration of fifty or so of Italy's largest companies is in the process of spending 223 million dollars to create new beaches and jetties along the Adriatic side of the barrier islands. The 1966 *acqua granda* breached many of these then-ill-maintained defenses, flooding small villages along the outer rim and allowing Adriatic tides to swamp the inner lagoon more dramatically. This reconstruction work, designed to lessen the impact of storms along the shores of these lagoon defense systems, has been completed along Pellestrina, and similar reinforcing work was getting under way during 2001 along the Lido.

The Consorzio has already spent more than 100 million dollars reinforcing the six jetties found at the three entrances to the lagoon, and it has spent more than fourteen million dollars creating a new system of lights that run along both sides of the so-called *canale dei petroli,* or the canal at the lagoon's Malamocco entrance, which leads oil and chemical tankers to Porto Marghera. The lights, engineers and port officials believe, will lessen the chance of a tanker mishap during heavy fog inside the lagoon. The fear is justified: If an oil tanker ever spilled its cargo within the lagoon, the environmental consequences would be monstrous.

With these projects, and with the promise of major projects to come, this state-created monopoly certainly has, for nearly two decades, carved out a profitable niche for itself and its member-company shareholders. European Union (EU) laws banning monopolies such as the Consorzio came into effect in the years following the monopoly's creation and allowed the organization to be effectively grandfathered in in its original form. But the EU and other powerful lobbies within Italy have nonetheless pressured the organization to put construction of the massive mobile-gates project out to bid. So much so that

Consorzio officials, when speaking to interviewers, now say they eagerly embrace the need for construction bids.

If the Consorzio ever gains approval to begin planning the construction of the gates in detail—a process that will create what is called the Executive Project—that effort alone will pour an additional 113.5 million dollars of Italian taxpayers lire into the Consorzio's coffers. As for surviving the newly mandated bidding process for construction—a process that Insula has been required to face since beginning work in the historic center in the mid-1990s—the Consorzio's participating member construction companies are in a prime position, with workers and massive equipment already in place, to come in at lower bids than any outsider. If this happens, not much will have changed at the Consorzio, and the conglomerate will survive well into the second decade of the twenty-first century. Beyond that, who knows? Will the Consorzio—or one of its offshoots or member companies—manage the operation and maintenance of the gates complex for still more decades to come—if the gates are indeed built? If it does, projections made in 2000 estimate that the cost of maintaining and operating the gates will be 9 million dollars a year.

Even without the gates in the mix, the list of the Consorzio's work plan for the first decade of the twenty-first century is huge. It is scheduled to spend nearly 228 million dollars to raise the height of the outer edges of the lagoon's islands, including the exterior edges of Venice's historic center, to withstand high water up to 1.20 meters. This work matches what Insula is doing within the city's center. Contained within this price tag is the imminent 24-million-dollar project to revamp the subsurface structures and drainage systems of St. Mark's Square and its lagoon-bordering piazzetta—a project that proposes to keep routine high tides, between twenty-seven and thirty-nine inches (70 to 100 centimeters) above sea level, out of the tourist-jammed square. Without the gates at the entrances, however, this basic work will not keep the square free of water coming in at, say, at 3.6 feet (1.10 meters) or higher above mean sea level.

Nearly 126 million dollars are targeted to reestablish salt marshes, those valuable natural cleansing engines so important in the healthy lagoon environments that were lost to early industrial growth, and to dig new canals to improve water flow throughout the lagoon; nearly 150 million dollars have been set aside for a massive environmental cleanup, particularly in the areas around Porto Marghera; and nearly 7 million dollars are earmarked for two new major studies: one into the impact of reopening the cordoned-off fish farms on the natural flow of the lagoon's tides; the other to examine the feasibility of diverting oil tankers out of the lagoon to some offshore on- and off-loading platform in the Adriatic. Such a platform would be connected to Porto Marghera by a massive underwater pipeline.

The mobile gates are included in the budget of some 2 billion dollars out of the 4 billion earmarked since 1973 that still remain to be spent. Some 1.85 billion dollars would go to build just the gates themselves. Many observers believe that that number will easily balloon to somewhere between 2 and 4 billion dollars.

Early in 2001 the mobile gates proposed for the entrances to the Venetian lagoon were nothing more than a handful of models and lots of lines on paper. They were supposed to have been approved years ago, and then approval was scheduled for late 1998, nearly ten years after the MOSE experimental model was lowered into the Lido entrance. The decision was put off again, with late 1999 set as the target. Then the decision was put off because April 2000 regional elections would get in the way, and politicians promised a decision by summer 2000. That never happened. No one associated with the project was able or willing to predict when the prime minister would make the decision. In fact, the prime minister who held the job during the regional elections was replaced by another prime minister after the elections, and this one, Center-Leftist Giuliano Amato, was replaced by a candidate from the Center Right, Silvio Berlusconi, following national parliamentary elections in May 2001.

The scientists and planners long ago had their say. The decision now is a political one, and trying to predict when it will be made, in the midst of government upheaval and with the Center-Left/Center-Right factions locked in battles for their very survival, is impossible.

But since the mobile-gates concept was first proposed in the early 1970s, the basic idea has not changed. Roberto Frassetto, the gates' most ardent supporter outside the Consorzio, believes that the longevity of this idea attests to its strength. One of the project's strongest critics, Albert Ammerman, views this single-mindedness toward one concept as its major flaw. More ideas should have been explored, he says. His opinion, like Frassetto's, has many supporters.

From the very beginning the Italians in general as well as those in government have demanded that whatever is built within the mouths of the lagoon must not be visible above water. Unlike the Thames Barrier across the river's estuary south of London, the skyline of the barrier-island mouths must remain unbroken by structures or buildings. This requirement, spelled out in the special laws, for the moment remains inviolate, just as it is forbidden for engineers to consider isolating portions of the lagoon—beyond the already isolated fish farms—from one another. Instead, part of the Consorzio's plan of action of the next ten years is to find ways to restore free-flowing tides to the parts of the lagoon that were divided off decades ago, principally those fish farms located at the northern and southern ends.

It is possible for the determined visitor without a boat at his or her disposal to travel the length of the lagoon's seaward side from Lido di Jesolo in the north to Chioggia in the south. It must be done by car or bus in combination with ferries. Once the routine is figured out, it could take a long, long day to make the journey.

From the main vaporetto/motor-bus stop at Piazzetta Santa Maria Elisabetta on the Lido—about the center of this chain of barrier islands—I caught a traditional orange Italian motor bus, headed south, with the destination "Chioggia" written high above its front window. The bus travels along the Lido's lagoon-side shoreline toward Malamocco. This ride offers tremendous views across the lagoon and shows the painful juxtaposition of the industrial areas of Marghera and Mestre to historic Venice. The lagoon waters that lap up against the Lido and, farther south, Pellestrina, are fishing waters with numerous marked channels. Beyond, farther to the south, are the channel markers for the *canale dei petroli*, the petroleum channel connected to the Malamocco entrance. The *canale* was opened in 1967, a year after the disastrous flood, and with a depth that is known to increase the speed of high tides that sweep twice a day into the lagoon. Environmentalists want to see this channel filled in or its depth lessened, but the shipping lobby is powerful, and the money shipping provides for this world-class port would be sorely missed from the regional and national treasuries.

Just beyond the tiny village of Malamocco, the bus pauses to wait its turn to board a small auto/pedestrian ferry for a quick ride across the middle channel to the island of Pellestrina. It is hard to imagine that modern-day Malamocco, washed over by the dramatic flood of November 1966 and its residents hauled by boats to barely higher ground elsewhere in the lagoon, sits where the ancient Venetians established one of their earliest governments. That seat of government—which landed here after being moved from Heraclea on the mainland, just a few years later in C.E. 826—was hurriedly moved six miles onto the 117 islands that became today's historic Venice.

These were in the days when the Lido was a series of islands rather than one long, sandy stretch, and Malamocco was on its own island centuries before the channels were filled in and the nine entrances to the lagoon became three.

On this spring day in early 2000, my orange bus glides aboard the Malamocco-Pellestrina car ferry. Pellestrina is unique. It is long and thin, not as wide as the Lido, and less populated. Its residents live in clusters of residential areas with individual harbors opening onto the lagoon. The Adriatic is just yards away from just about anywhere on Pellestrina, and massive dikes along the island's eastern edge—some made up of mounds of grass-covered soil backed up by stone walls, others just stone walls—kept my fellow bus passengers and me from a view of the historic sea.

These dikes along Pellestrina are the ones that were rebuilt and reinforced by the Consorzio during the late 1990s. I wanted to look at them more closely. I climbed down from the bus just in front of a tiny cemetery. But before scrambling to the top of the stone-block wall, I wandered into the *cimitero*, with its array of tiny stone houses, or crypts, lining the sides. Names like *Famiglia Vianello Badan* and *Famiglia Vianello Gallo* were chiseled into the stone over the narrow low doorways. Graves, set in rows through the middle of the enclosure, were well tended, and the space was crowded primarily with older women dressed in black, tending flowers using green-plastic watering cans that hang on hooks near a faucet conveniently placed near the entrance. *Vianello* appears to be one of the more common given names; it is chiseled onto tombstones everywhere.

I walked outside and headed for a rickety wooden ladder lashed tight against the twelve- or fourteen-foot-high (about four meters) wall, made of what appears to be the same kind of impermeable white Istrian stone that makes up the foundations of Venice's buildings. I climbed it and looked east across a sandy beach, perhaps 150 yards (137 meters), to the gray and choppy Adriatic. It is easy to see that at high tide and in the midst of a routine storm, the Adriatic would slam across this wide stretch of beach and pound against this stone wall, but the beaches are intact, protected by line after line of stone jetties—built by Consorzio Venezia Nuova—that run hundreds of feet perpendicular to the wall and out to sea. Before the Consorzio arrived, these beaches were virtually nonexistent, their sand washed away by tides and storms. The stone jetties, line after line of them disappearing into the haze farther north toward the Lido, are what hold in place the new sand, pumped from the sea bottom by special sand-and-gravel ships miles away and hauled to the shoreline, where it was pumped ashore.

I stood clutching my hat in the wind. It was low tide, and

I could see across Pellestrina's narrow southern tip toward the lagoon, where the rotting wooden hulk of a boat perched on an offshore mudflat beyond the channel used by fishermen and the Chioggia ferry. Turning around once again toward the Adriatic, I saw way out along the horizon a long line of tankers and commercial cargo ships, moving like gray specters on their way south from Trieste to the greater Mediterranean beyond.

I climbed down from the wall and walked across the small square to the ferry. Twenty minutes later, after traversing the Chioggia entrance to the lagoon, the entrance farthest south, I stepped onto the pier at the village of Chioggia, one of the lagoon's oldest continually occupied centers. It is a small village that appears to survive solely on fishing and perhaps a few tourists. This is not part of "museum" Venice, but a world apart and unique in its own wonderful way. It shares with Venice only the lagoon and its more famous sister's problems with high water. The mayor of Chioggia sits next to the mayor of Venice as a member of the *Comitone*, which supports the concept of the mobile gates.

The village's canals, lined on both sides by the homes of the fishermen and by a few tiny businesses, were full of fishing boats of all sizes; no gondolas for tourists here. The wide main street was full of people despite the cold, breezy day. This boulevard was likely once a canal, or *rio*, that was filled in when automobiles arrived. It was late afternoon—time for my favorite event in Italy: *passeggiata* (promenade or walkabout), when locals come out, stroll the main streets, and visit with friends and neighbors, recounting the day's events and trading gossip. On a canal to the east of this broad boulevard I saw a man cleaning his short, shallow-bottomed *barca*. He had a plastic scoop and a brush, and with the brush propelled water from

the bright-red-painted deck into the scoop, pouring it overboard, repeatedly and quickly. Across the canal another man
had what appeared to be a brazier, perhaps fueled by charcoal.
Sitting on a seat in his tiny boat, he was broiling long skewers
lined with chunks of what was probably his day's catch, handing
the cooked fish up to the waiting hands of eager customers,
clutching lira notes in their hands.

But this journey represented only half of my plans to go
the entire length of the barrier islands. I still had to make it
to Lido di Jesolo in the far north of the lagoon and travel a
few miles south along the Cavallino shoreline to the northern
tip of the Lido. I went by automobile one sunny afternoon
from Venice's Marco Polo Airport, on the lagoon's mainland
edge, around its northern edge and dropped down toward the
Adriatic to Jesolo. Once there, I followed this finger of land
south and took a road on the side closest to the Adriatic—land
that did not exist hundreds of years ago.

Early drawings of the lagoon show the sea where this particular land now is. Archaeologists believe it was through this
once-open sea that ships trading with the Romans—at the
height of empire and before the lagoon was actively colonized—
entered the Roman port at Isola di San Francesco del Deserto,
just a short distance from the Italian mainland. But centuries
later the shipping channel was completed at the northern tip
of the Lido, and massive stone jetties—designed to protect the
channel and keep it from filling in—were built hundreds of
feet out into the sea. Then, beginning in the Middle Ages,
the silt carried by the Sile River—one of the three major rivers
that had been diverted from the lagoon—began to pile up
against those stone jetties. This created an entirely new landform, on which farms and homes now sit, as well as the road
I am driving on as I try to reach the tip of Cavallino. The

Consorzio is also planning to do much work along this stretch of Adriatic barrier, to protect it from the rising waters of the Adriatic. In 1966 much of the sea washed across this section, inundating farms and killing livestock.

To get to the Lido from here takes another plan. I must get rid of the car, because the ferry that runs between St. Mark's Square and Punta Sabbioni on Cavallino's northwestern edge—with a stop in between at Piazzetta Santa Maria Elisabetta on the Lido—takes only foot passengers.

The most recent plans for the design of the mobile gates are more general in nature than the more detailed schematics that will be laid out in the so-called Executive Project: The Consorzio proposes to build seventy-nine gates in all, each one measuring 65 feet (twenty meters) wide and from 65 feet to nearly 100 feet (twenty to thirty meters) high by 9 feet (3.6 meters) deep, depending upon how deep the channel is beneath a specific section.

The gates would be set side by side across each *bocca*, or mouth, and encased, when submerged during periods of scant tidal threat, in concrete caissons embedded in the floor of the channel. When a tidal threat as high as about three feet (one meter) above relative sea level is imminent, compressed air would be pumped into the barriers to raise them—the air forcing out the water that had held them in place on the channel floor. These gates would rotate on a hinge placed on their seaward edge and float at forty- to fifty-degree angles. Designers say they can be raised in thirty minutes.

Since there will be no fixed barrier on the surface to hold the gates firmly in place, the structures would be able to bob and sway freely as groups of individuals rather than a rigidly held wall of steel. There would be an 80-millimeter gap between each gate to allow for this movement and to combat the inward flows of the tides estimated at twenty-two feet (seven meters) per second. This free range of motion is expected to allow the gates to absorb and dissipate wave energy.

Consorzio engineers believe that the gates would hold back Adriatic tides 6.5 feet (two meters) higher than the water on the gates' lagoon sides, or nearly ten feet (three meters) above mean sea level. The 1966 flood came in at 6.4 feet (1.94 meters), and the gates, say their supporters, would hold back waters five feet (1.6 meters) higher than that. Each gate's bobbing motion, independent of its neighbor, is expected to allow enough gravity-driven water to flow into the lagoon and handle the routine flushing duties the tides have accomplished for millennia. According to the British publication *New Civil Engineer*, water that flows into and out of the lagoon during and after construction "would be reduced by only 2 percent, posing no significant risk of oxygen depletion—most barrier closures will be during the winter, when the danger of stagnation is lowest." And the report continues: The "marginally reduced flow will, in fact, slow the loss of sediments, aiding the regeneration of salt marsh."

If the government ever authorizes the gates-construction project, it is expected to be a gigantic—and as we have seen, an expensive—undertaking. It would be a technical feat equal to the diversion hundreds of years ago of the mouths of the major rivers from the lagoon. For perspective, consider a few comparisons to the 1.85-billion-dollar gates proposal expected to take ten years to complete: The tunnels beneath the English Channel connecting Britain and France with trains between

Consorzio Venezia

Each of the seventy-nine mobile gates are folded away into housing across the bottoms of the lagoon's three entrances. When a storm surge approaches, combined with a high tide to a height exceeding one meter above mean sea level, the gates will fill with air, displacing the water that holds them down. Designers say the gates will hold back most of the incoming tide up to two meters above the level of water in the lagoon. The gates are independent of one another and, when raised, can undulate slightly with wave motion. When the tide goes down and the sea and lagoon reach the same level, the gates fill with water and return to their places in the inlet bed.

London, Paris, and Brussels cost roughly fifteen billion dollars and took eight years. The Central Artery/Tunnel Project, otherwise known as the "Big Dig," will bury Interstate 93 beneath downtown Boston, Massachusetts. When it is completed in 2004, it is expected to have cost more than fourteen billion dollars—an astounding figure for an American public works project.

On the other end of the spectrum, and closer to the cost projected for the mobile gates, the Italian and Rome governments spent 1.75 billion dollars to refurbish the capital city, whose prominent buildings had been hidden behind scaffolding for years, for the 2000 Holy Year Jubilee—an event declared every twenty-five years since 1300 by the pope. In the United States a massive freeway expansion and reconstruction project in Utah's Salt Lake Valley cost 1.59 billion dollars. When it was started in 1997, it was believed to be one of the largest public works projects under way in the United States. It lasted four years and every square inch of concrete in the seventeen-mile-long (twenty-eight kilometer) freeway was ripped up and replaced, and dozens of bridges and interchanges were demolished and rebuilt.

With the mobile-gates construction, there is a catch: Each of the three entrances must be kept open to normal shipping into and out of the lagoon during the full eight years of construction. Any ship that wants to enter the Port of Venice must be able to do so with a minimal wait in special locks—locks like those in the Panama Canal—that the Consorzio has promised to build.

This was a concession the Consorzio made in the late 1990s to win the support of the Autorità Portuale di Venezia, or Venice Port Authority, which had opposed the gates for years because of the project's feared impact on shipping.

It is obvious the port officials carry a lot of weight in this economically challenged region. The port generates 1 billion dollars a year and handles one-third the traffic that the Port of New York does. The Port of Venice is bigger than the Port of Rio di Janeiro.

Stefano Della Sala, the Port of Venice's safety and environment manager, proudly ticks off these statistics. We are ensconced in his bright modern office deep in the bowels of a remodeled medieval building facing the Giudecca Canal just a few dozen feet and across a humpback bridge from the Zattere waterbus stop.

He is an intelligent young man who is also eager to talk about all the environmental work that is going on near Port Marghera, where much of the sediment that covers the lagoon bottom was tainted by decades of unfettered chemical and petroleum operations. But for now we talk of the gates, and he describes an interesting dichotomy: The Port Authority no longer opposes them. The Consorzio's promise to create a series of locks similar to ones in the Panama Canal to keep shipping traffic flowing during construction and when the gates are in operation removed that opposition. This means, in theory, shipping can enter or exit the port even when super-high tides keep the gates closed longer than just a few hours.

Then Della Sala, speaking as a Venetian and not as a Port Authority representative, throws the zinger. He—and, I find out later, even Port Authority president Claudio Boniciolli—questions whether the gates are the right solution for the lagoon's flooding problems.

"The people of the Consorzio say the gates will be obsolete in one hundred years; then we will need to find a different solution. There is something funny with this," Della Sala says. "It would be like putting a scaffold around this building because one day, years from now perhaps, we know that this building will need a restoration. Okay, if we will need new solutions beyond the gates one hundred years from now, let's wait until that day!" His is a typically Venetian comment—another variation of what I have heard all over the city, everywhere but at the Consorzio offices. President Boniciolli, also a Venetian, underscored his employee's remarks a few days later.

Of course the Port Authority does not oppose the gates since shipping will be unaffected by them, but that does not mean they should be built, *il presidente* says while looking out his large picture window with a sweeping view of the Giudecca, where the *fondamenta* just a few feet below his window is being raised to withstand high water up to nearly four feet (1.20 meters) above mean sea level.

"They must examine, with intellectual honesty, some other solutions," Boniciolli says. Then he sighs. "But I, as president of the Port Authority, cannot object. As a Venetian, I can. These gates will cost a lot of money. Also it will take a large bureaucracy to run this enormous machine [the mobile gates]." Boniciolli knows the Consorzio's task is enormous. "An engineer, a friend of mine, told me: 'It is quite simple, the problem, and quite difficult to find the solution.' Could you imagine what would happen if the high-tide alarm goes off and then the gates cannot rise?" he asks. "Or maybe just some of the gates come up, or some won't go down?" He shakes his head in disbelief, obviously horrified, in his role as president of the Port Authority, at the prospect.

Several months later I had another conversation with Della Sala in which he underscored the troubling position in which he and Boniciolli find themselves.

"The city must come first—always!" Della Sala exclaims. "If the gates are needed, let's do it tomorrow." But he worries that the gates as a solution represent "an old project that does not look at the future." Here his remarks echo what many others who worry about the gates' effectiveness are saying: The gates are not stepping-stones to more permanent, longer-range solutions. They are an end in and of themselves and cannot be built upon, or expanded, if they quickly become, as many critics predict, obsolete in the face of the dramatic sea-level rise that is expected over the next century. Indeed, if the project were launched "tomorrow," it would take ten years to design and build; then it could be used for a few years, and its impact on the lagoon and its fragile ecosystem could not be predicted. One critic says, "They would do to the lagoon what we do not know."

CHAPTER TWELVE ~

The Great Debate

Talk of restoring the lagoon to its original
morphology is at best naive and at worst misleading. What is original, in the first place?
—PROFESSOR ANDREA RINALDO

Now it is many months after my discussions
with impassioned Venetians who in all sin-
cerity question the need for the mobile
gates, and equally impassioned gates advocates. This feeling, based on both emotion
and thoughtful reflection, is counterbal-
anced by mounds of material that, une-
motionally and scientifically, discuss how
the mobile gates would be built and put into
place in the midst of two high tides and two
low tides per day, moving under normal
conditions at seven meters per second, a
speed much faster than a human's ability to
walk. Consorzio engineers say these gates
would be designed and constructed to func-
tion, with proper maintenance, for one
hundred years.

The *New Civil Engineer* article is straightforward. It dispassionately describes the engineering solutions to placing the gates, and the author seems convinced that the gates would run as smoothly in the reality of the wild and woolly Adriatic as they would in a laboratory experiment under controlled conditions:

> In all, 18 different caisson types are needed to house mechanical and electronic plant, and anchor the gates and abut the islands. . . . Meanwhile, fabrication of the gates will call on ship-building technology. They are designed in steel, with a welded reinforced sheet metal skin supported on traverse frames with compound beams. It is planned to build the gates within the lagoon at Marghera, a district dominated by heavy industry including ship yards. Though the barrage has a 100-year design life, it is envisaged [that] gates will be replaced for maintenance on a five-year cycle. . . . Preliminary placement [of gates into caissons] will be to within 300mm accuracy.

While reading in that article a discussion about the expected maintenance plan that includes replacing individual gates every five years, I remembered a conversation I had in early 2000 with Consorzio spokeswoman Monica Ambrosini. The use of the equivalent of 1.80 billion dollars of Italian taxpayers' lire over the next ten years to build the gates—plus 113.5 million dollars to design them—is just the beginning, she says. After the structures are finally in place, it will cost 9 million dollars to maintain the gates each year—as those dollars were valued in the year 2000. The Consorzio did not factor in inflation.

By the mid-1990s, pressure from the European Union and from environmentalists and gate opponents had been building against the Consorzio's gates plan and against its monopoly status. Yielding to this opposition, the national Italian government's interministerial committee for the safeguarding of Venice in 1995 ordered the Venice Magistrato alle Acque to conduct an environmental impact study (or, in its Italian acronym, VIA) to determine how the mobile gates would affect the city and the lagoon. It was inconceivable that this step, common elsewhere in the developed Western world during the decade of the 1990s, took so long in Italy. The project is staggering in the immensity of its conception, but during the twelve years of its development, neither the Consorzio nor its supervising Magistrato had been asked to initiate such a study.

The Water Authority retained a group—an international panel put together under the direction of scientists at MIT to coordinate VIA development and to certify its results.

The following year, 1996, Italian Prime Minister Lamberto Dini took things a step farther. With the backing of the minister responsible for the then-combined Ministries of Environment and Public Works, Dini ordered that an international group of independent experts, to be known as the College of Experts, or *Collegio di Esperti*, review the project's feasibility. Its membership also was coordinated by MIT, an institution that Maria Teresa Brotto, a Consorzio engineer and assistant to the general manager, heralds as one of the most prestigious institutions worldwide that can be called on to review such work. It is clear that the Consorzio wants blessings for its project from some of the world's most distinguished scientists; its press office repeatedly stresses the magic of the MIT name in citing reports by the two panels.

Amid the ever-shifting arena that makes up Italy's political fabric, a new prime minister, Romano Prodi, replaced Dini. Prodi divided the environment/public works portfolio into separate ministries—an act that was to lead to another drama two years later when the environment minister came out against the gates, in contrast to the public works minister, who oversaw the activities of the Venetian Magistrato alle Acque and the Consorzio. The environment minister became the only ministerial committee member opposing the gates.

The VIA looked at three options: (1) doing nothing; (2) only raising the city's and outlying islands' *fondamente* to protect the city from floods up to 1.20 meters above mean sea level, and reinforcing the Adriatic sides of the barrier islands; and (3) building the mobile gates. The conclusion was that damage to the lagoon, the city, and its inhabitants would be "extensive" with options (1) and (2), and "marginal" if the gates were built.

If the gates were not built, the VIA concluded, the lagoon would continue to lose sediment, and the island shores would "suffer a marked increase in the extent of erosion." The increase in lagoon water level would mean that the level of salt in lagoon water would approach that of the sea, and would "contribute to reduced oxygenation of the water on the Lagoon floor, a greater dilution of the contaminants coming from the drainage basin and a greater vivification [the spawning of increased plant growth] of the Lagoon."

More water, of course, would cause more flooding, the report concludes, "further exposing the human population to contact with the polluted water, with potentially negative consequences." This section states that without the gates, "Venice's priceless historical and monumental heritage would be increasingly threatened and damaged."

The most significant conclusion of the environmental report, at least in the eyes of gates supporters, is that gates costing approximately two billion dollars would be far more cost-effective than dealing with the economic cost of increased levels of more frequent flooding. This would be especially true if global warming raises mean sea level a projected average of twenty centimeters or more over the next one hundred years—the midpoint in three sea-level-rise scenarios considered in the VIA.

(By the end of 2000, scientists were anticipating that data to be released early in 2001 by the Intergovernmental Panel on Climate Change would increase that midpoint number to a possible forty-seven centimeters, a range considered unlikely just a few years earlier. The new number projections were borne out when the data were issued.)

In October 2000 an article titled "Blocking the Tide" appeared in the U.S. trade magazine *Civil Engineering*. It was written by the four scientists from the original MIT-sponsored group hired by the Magistrato alle Acque to manage and review the study, and it described their conclusions concerning their supervision and review of the VIA work:

The panel concluded that under constraints imposed by existing laws the only viable solution to the problem of flooding consisted in the proposed movable gates. It also found that the project had benefited from excellent engineering and thorough conceptualization. The "diffuse interventions" [raising pavements in the city and around the islands, etc.] were not by themselves seen as capable of solving the flooding problem—and some, the panel warned, might prove damaging to the environment. . . . The panel believed that the project in question was justified under present conditions and fur-

234 ~ Venice Against the Sea

thermore that the city could not afford to "wait and see" whether the sea level would continue to rise and flooding would worsen.

This assessment can be compared to the more detailed later study by the Collegio di Esperti that was supervised by the Public Works Ministry. The Consorzio points to the reports of experts from both panels as positive ones. While the Collegio's report is positive in an overall sense, it does raise some concerns about the gates and their impact on the lagoon that are not discussed by others. Despite these concerns, however, in June 1998 the Collegio presented this bottom line: "The mobile gates system does adequately address the problems of the present while it leaves the options open for the future."

This report lays out several conclusions, beginning with the statement: "The lagoon environment has been degraded, and Venice faces problems of economic restructuring, declining population and the dominance of tourism. High water in the lagoon is one of the major factors that makes the solution of these problems more difficult."

The report then acknowledges that flooding frequency and the level of exceptional high waters is likely to increase over the next fifty to one hundred years, and that the VIA scenarios "provide a sound basis for planning."

Then the Collegio's report begins to take on a more cautionary tone. The gates system "is flexible and robust and will be effective for protecting against high water under a wide range of sea-level-rise scenarios. However, the project requires some improvements, especially to prevent resonance and unnecessary leakage between gate elements."

The warnings continue: "The EIS is comprehensive but

unevenly detailed. Some parts of the study are rather weak, and some impacts are not studied in sufficient detail." With an increasing number of closures as sea level rises over subsequent decades, the reviewers warn, "severe conflict . . . may emerge between the protection of the lagoon, the protection of Venice, and the port activities within the lagoon."

In this section of their report, the Collegio scientists had written that chlorine and zinc from the gates protection systems would be released into the seawater. "It is estimated that up to 12 tons [of zinc] could be thus released yearly over the three inlets." The experts recommended that if the gates are built, zinc levels should be monitored in the lagoon's mussel farms "in view of the strong concentration power of mollusks for this element."

The Collegio's report draws some important conclusions. For example, it addresses the city's other problems—economic restructuring, declining population, and dominance of tourism—and says high water in the lagoon "is one of the major factors that makes the solution of these problems more difficult." Also, the report says clearly: "The need to protect Venice, and other urban centers, after the 1966 flood was based on conditions which have not improved in the last thirty years. On the contrary, the need is reinforced by the risk of sea-level rise induced by climate change."

The College of Experts warned that after 2050, if sea level does rise fifty centimeters or higher than it was in 1998, a whole new environmental study may be necessary.

Thus the College of Experts raises the specter that within a single lifetime, perhaps only five decades, a new generation of scientific, political, historical, and commercial interests may have to make even more difficult decisions about the lagoon's future as a commercial and historical center.

So, the mobile-gates project got a boost from a seemingly independent group that reported to the Public Works Ministry and not to the Consorzio. But delays, spawned by an unsettled national political environment—after all, Venice's problems with water were a national rather than a local issue—still plagued the Consorzio's desire to have its corporate life guaranteed for years to come.

Opponents to the gates remind dispassionate observers that the state-created, and handsomely remunerated, Consorzio Venezia Nuova was tasked with coming up with a flooding solution, designing that solution, and then *building* that solution. The Consorzio's supervising agency, the Magistrato alle Acque, then paid for the environmental impact assessment. In the end, that assessment supported the Consorzio's position that the mobile gates were the only solution to potential sea-level rise. *Then* the Magistrato used MIT scientists to review the VIA work. The Public Works Ministry, which supervises the Magistrato, followed by hiring more consultants, also organized through MIT, to comprise the College of Experts, or Collegio, which further blessed the work—albeit with some caveats.

Andrea Rinaldo, a Venetian by birth and a University of Padua hydrologist, dismisses allegations by gates opponents that somehow all these respectable scientists would reach conclusions other than valid ones—no matter who pays the consulting fees. Rinaldo participated in the first Magistrato-retained panel organized through MIT and coauthored the 2000 *Civil Engineering* defense of his group's work.

Nonscientists as well as Venetians I talked with remain skeptical of what they simply see as a cozy relationship, and wonder about the two panels' independence from each other and from gates-proponents' deep pockets. For whatever reason, political or otherwise, a succession of prime ministers has put off making a decision about whether to kill the gates project or let it proceed. Local and international news media have not been kind to the construction conglomerate-turned-monopoly of the Consorzio, despite its work to reinforce the barrier islands and raise the edges of the major islands within the lagoon to 4-foot (1.20 meters) above mean sea level. Such work is certainly necessary for Venice's survival, but it is also lucrative. Construction of the gates promises to create thousands more new jobs and pump up the Venetian economy and the for-profit Consorzio.

Some observers may not disagree that the lagoon needs an engineering solution to protect it from the rising Adriatic, but many did not like the idea of the Consorzio doing the work. One of those is Padua hydrologist Rinaldo, who, as we have seen, supports the gates. But during an interview early in 2000 he said he hoped the construction job goes to a firm other than the Consorzio. This opinion puts him in a tough position. He not only served on the scientific panel that reviewed the VIA, but high-ranking Consorzio engineer Maria Teresa Brotto is his sister-in-law.

Concern about the Consorzio's monopoly status is high in Italy and among officials of the European Union, of which Italy is a member. After all, the Consorzio Venezia Nuova was created at a time (1983) when prime ministers and politicians regularly dispatched lucrative government contracts to friends and supporters.

For the record, the Consorzio's monopoly status for gates

construction has changed. It is no longer legal for such a state-created creature to exist as a monopoly. But as Venice mayor Paolo Costa pointed out during a November 2000 interview, the Consorzio has "accumulated such a large competence" in the issue of the gates that no one can really compete against it for the contract to build the structure.

"It may not have a legal monopoly, but it has a technical monopoly." Costa says the Consorzio has a contract to design the gates and will do so if the government decides to proceed. But the loss of its monopoly status forbids the Consorzio from bidding as an organization for the contract to actually build the structures.

In fact, the European Union Commission ruled in February 2001—ironically at the urging of Gianni Mattioli, Italy's *ministro per le politiche comunitarie*, or the minister responsible for communicating with the European Union (EU)—that if the gates are put out to bid, at least 40 percent of the work must go to construction companies from other EU countries, such as Germany or the Netherlands.

"But there is nothing to stop the individual construction companies that make up the Consorzio from independently bidding for [the remaining 60 percent of] that work," the mayor says, indicating their "technical monopoly" will be difficult for other potential bidders to overcome.

Starting in 1992, many cozy relationships between big business and government were revealed under the glare of the so-called *Tangentopoli* (bribesville) investigations, giving that nickname to Milan, where the *Mani Pulite* (Operation Clean Hands) investigations began and where many leading politicians, civil servants, and business executives were arrested.

Daily revelations by the news media of the arrests and imprisonments fueled cynicism in an already skeptical Italian populace that long had guessed that such sweetheart deals abounded throughout the twentieth century. One British newspaper, *The European*, in November 1998, promoted this theme by publishing an article entitled "Going Under: The Protection Racket That's Sinking Venice." The thrust of the article was that Venice was more in danger from the Consorzio's desire to perpetuate itself by building and then operating the mobile gates than from the rising waters.

Suspicion continues to swirl around the organization. This is despite nearly ten years of *Mani Pulite* investigations that have never uncovered any shady deal making involving the Consorzio.

"When the *Tangentopoli* investigations were taking place, we weren't even questioned," *The European* quotes Consorzio communications director Gian Paolo Maretto. "This shows that there was nothing illegal happening." To which the journalists add their own opinion: "Or perhaps it shows that investigators were told to look elsewhere or did not look hard enough."

In the middle of all this, the Ministry of the Environment threw a major obstacle into the Consorzio's path during late 1998. By that time the ministry was long separated from the Public Works Ministry and run by Green Party members and sympathizers. The Public Works Ministry had come out in support of the gates following the College of Experts' favorable assessment.

The environment minister, Green Party member Edoardo Ronchi—backed by the minister for cultural affairs (who had been urged on by local superintendents responsible for Venice's

architectural, environmental, and archaeological heritage)—
said he would not support the gates. His remarks came after his
staff issued a four-hundred-page report critical of the gates
program.

The report was written in part by Andreina Zitelli, a Venetian and a member of the ministry's National Committee
of Environmental Evaluation. I spoke with Zitelli and Italian
senator Giorgio Sartor during a November 11, 2000, dinner
at the American Academy of Rome, where, during a lengthy
conversation, she said her committee's report stressed that not
enough research had been done to justify the mobile-gates
project. She believes that the VIA fell short because it did not
deal adequately with the gates' ramifications for the lagoon's
future. Zitelli pointed out that the mid-1990s VIA had focused on gates as a prime solution even though gates were not
mentioned in the early 1980s special laws for Venice. The
other interventions—such as raising the city's pavements, narrowing lagoon inlets, and filling in a portion of the *canale dei
petroli* inlet at Malamocco—had been mentioned in the special
laws. But the Consorzio and its overseers relegated those projects to secondary importance while promoting the more controversial—and more lucrative—gates.

In fairness to the Consorzio, the Environment Ministry's
report did not exclude the possibility that a temporary closure
system might eventually be necessary if predictions of extreme
sea-level rise due to global warming are confirmed. The report
simply stated that the mobile gates, or an improved version,
"could be reconsidered once basic work to re-establish the general health of the lagoon and the city has been undertaken and
its effects on their vulnerability to flooding taken into account."

In other words, the ministry wants the government to hold
off on a mobile-gates decision until everything else can be

done in the lagoon, including completion of works to fortify the city and neighboring islands to withstand the 1.20-meter-high tides and to narrow the lagoon entrances along the Adriatic to reduce water intake. Floodwaters draining into the lagoon from the mainland rivers also have to be dealt with. Then the gates, or other, longer-term technologies that might be developed in the meantime, could be considered.

This evaluation was obviously a blow to the Consorzio. The environment minister sits on the powerful interministerial committee, led by the prime minister and charged with evaluating the need for the gates. While Ronchi's *no* vote was in the minority, he issued an all-important decree urging that all those steps be taken before gates were considered. Everyone else on that committee, except for the then mayor of Venice, Massimo Cacciari, had remained in favor of building the gates. The decree effectively stopped the gates decision, but the document was challenged in regional court. By the summer of 2000, that court rejected the ministry's decree, not on the merits of its arguments that the gates await all other interventions but because of technical problems associated with the decree's wording.

That gave the Consorzio new hope that it could proceed with the Executive Project and begin creating final gate designs. Consorzio spokeswoman Monica Ambrosini excitedly told me during the summer of 2000 about the court's ruling, saying that the environment minister's evaluation had been overturned. Not quite. The environment minister's decree was ruled invalid, and the government ministry immediately began work to appeal the regional court's action.

"The Ministry of the Environment will appeal," Zitelli said emphatically. "It is the *duty* of the administration to appeal." Or, she added, to submit a new decree.

Without a decree, she and her colleagues believe, the project is frozen. She also believes that if a decree is not issued, it will become necessary to undertake a new VIA.

By the end of 2000, it became clear to all that no one could proceed with the gates project without a decree that met all legal challenges. The Environment Ministry was hard at work designing a new decree that one Italian senator, Green Party member Giorgio Sartor, predicted would be "tougher, much tougher" than Environment Minister Ronchi's first effort.

"The technical problems will be eliminated, and it will require that the other lagoon safeguards be accomplished," said Sartor, who represents Venice, Mestre, Marghera, and much of the Veneto Region in parliament.

Through 1999 and into 2000 the drama was being played out elsewhere as well. Late in 1999, Venice mayor Cacciari, who along with his city council had long shared the Environment Ministry's skepticism about the gates and had driven much of the demand for an environmental study, resigned two years early. He wanted to run in the April 2000 elections for the office of regional president.

A few weeks later, on January 12, 2000, he dropped his bombshell in the middle of a city council meeting that erupted in pandemonium, declaring that it was time for the mobile-gates project to advance to the Executive Project phase. According to a January newsletter from the Venice in Peril Fund, a private British fund-raising group dedicated to restoring Venice's art treasures and buildings: "This *volte-face* caused [an] uproar in the City Council and complicated even further an already difficult choice of candidates for the municipal elections, also due on 16th April."

Under Italian law when a mayor resigns, no interim mayor is appointed. The office stays vacant until the next election, which was called for April 2000 to coincide with the regional elections. Stepping in to run for that job—along with an anti-gates Green opponent and a Center-Right opponent—was Paolo Costa. A former head of the University of Venice, an economist, and, more important, a former national minister of public works in the mid-1990s, Costa had been asked to serve on the Collegio di Esperti but was replaced when he advanced in the mid-1990s to head the ministry.

He was one of the first supporters of the mobile-gates project, and he was never wavered from that position—although in early 2001, the mayor supported the notion that longer-term studies needed to be conducted before a final decision could be made about the gates.

Following a runoff, the elections gave Costa a clear victory. Ironically, Center-Left candidate Cacciari lost the regional election as most of Italy's regional governments shifted from the Left to the Center-Right, and faded from view.

Meanwhile disagreements among the various government ministers continued to fester. A "working group of experts" or Planning Committee (not to be confused with the Collegio di Esperti)—drawn from technocrats in the Ministries of Public Works, the Environment, and Cultural Heritage and the City of Venice and other related bodies—was assigned to reassess the entire mobile-gates proposal. It studied the accuracy of long-term predictions of sea levels, rates of subsidence, and tidal movements. The Venice in Peril Fund newsletter reported that the report, apparently given to Cacciari two days before he resigned, "evidently showed [that] disagreements were more pronounced than ever." The report was due to be presented to the cabinet-level interministerial committee, but its delivery was delayed until after the April elections.

When it was finally submitted during the summer of 2000, Sartor and Zitelli told me, it was obvious that the technical experts' original report had been rewritten by people in the Water Authority office, the Consorzio's overseers who report to the national Public Works Ministry. The Planning Committee members could not abide by the changes inserted into the document that supported the Consorzio's gates position and refused to sign off on it. It was then kicked up to the committee of ministers, whose president at year's end was Prime Minister Giuliano Amato. And there it sat as 2000 drew to a close.

That politically volatile summer of 2000 affected many aspects of Italy's governing bodies. Prime Minister Massimo D'Alema, a Center-Leftist and gates supporter, did not get the mandate he wanted from the regional elections, where many of the regional presidencies went to the Center-Right.

This presaged his fall from power as Center-Rightists began pushing for early 2001 national elections. To end that threat, and to give his Center-Left coalition time to rebuild its strength with the voters, D'Alema resigned in April 2000. In stepped Amato, representing Italy's fifty-eighth government in the fifty-five years since the end of World War II.

Amato, also reputedly a gates supporter but who privately, according to Senator Sartor, has said he would never move to advance the gates, reshuffled his cabinet. That meant anti-gates Environment Minister Edo Ronchi was pulled out of that job and offered a position handling Italy's relations with the EU. Ronchi refused the post and, like Cacciari, dropped from sight.

But still the prime minister, despite his professed leanings in favor of the project, remained publicly silent. Amato had bigger fish in his skillet and was fighting for survival as a viable candidate in national elections set for May 2001. Former prime minister and Center-Rightist Silvio Berlusconi re-emerged as a major threat.

As 2000 ended, Amato increasingly saw the slimness of his chances to be the Center-Left candidate, and was able to save his office for his coalition, at least until early 2001, by offering popular Rome mayor Francesco Rutelli—a former Communist and Green with a relatively skeleton-free closet—as his coalition's candidate and heir apparent to run against Berlusconi.

In the middle of all this, the gates project was shoved onto a shelf in the desperate prime minister's office. He held the Environment Ministry's four-hundred-page negative report, which had been lovingly crafted by ever-passionate environmentalist and Venetian Andreina Zitelli and a staff of ten ministry experts who toiled "day and night for months to produce this document. It is complete, documented with more than a thousand footnotes, and perfect," as she told me during our lengthy American Academy dinner in Rome.

"It has never been challenged," she said. "The Consorzio, obviously, does not like it, but they have not challenged its results."

Work at the Consorzio, meanwhile, turned frenetic through the last half of 2000. There were new dragons to slay, and one, in the form of a tall, angular, sharp-nosed archaeologist with a Midwestern U.S. twang, started getting attention as his conclusions that the mobile gates are a waste of time and money received media attention in Europe and the United States. Colgate University archaeology professor Albert Ammerman maintains that sea level is rising to the point that the gates, if approved and finished by the Consorzio's preferred target of 2010, would be deployed so frequently during the high-water winter months that the lagoon would not have time to properly flush out and recover. He, along with Italians involved in the environmental group Italia Nostra, are convinced the gates will become a multibillion-dollar environmental disaster, and that their effectiveness would be so short term that the two-billion-dollar-plus price tag is not worth it.

"The city can very perfectly survive a rare event [of exceptionally high water]," believes Ammerman, who has lived in Venice for most of each year since 1985. He points out that such events have affected the city throughout its history. "There is enough time over the next five to ten years, while the other interventions are being built, for scientists to come up with a longer-term solution than these gates."

Ammerman and his supporters believe that the 1996 environmental impact studies "are seriously flawed" and must be repeated. Reasons for this are many, he says. For example, the original study, supported by the international group of experts, used incredibly low numbers for the projected rise of sea level over the next one hundred years—numbers that begin as low as 1.7 inches (4.4 centimeters) and as high as 19.6 inches (fifty centimeters). These experts indicated that they considered such a high number to be most unlikely. However, recent revelations about the impact of global warming on sea levels by 2100 now make the higher number more likely.

Also, Ammerman says, the Consorzio and its scientists never addressed the "seasonality" problem. Advocates look at the average number of projected gate closings over a full calendar year and have concluded that the devices would not be raised often enough to cause much ecological damage. Consorzio spokeswoman Ambrosini maintained, as late as November 2000, that the closings on days when the water reached 3.28 feet (one meter) above sea level would average only seven a year. Most observers, including Ammerman, believe that number would be much greater—as often as twenty-four times during each winter month, he says.

Independent numbers from the Venice Port Authority, which is concerned about the impact any closing would have on shipping into and out of the Venice lagoon, projected that for the 3.28-foot-(one-meter) above-sea-level scenario, the gates in 1996 would have been raised forty-three times—numbers taking into effect twenty-one closures because the water actually did go above 3.28 feet. Because of uncertainties in the forecasting system, they also included twenty-two "false" closures that would have taken place because the water levels ended up not being as high as forecast hours before a tidal event.

In an article for *Science*, a prestigious American journal, Ammerman predicts: "If one takes into account variability in the number of extreme high tides from one year to the next and also includes false alarms, this means that a given bad year may experience as many as 150 gate closings . . . day after day and week after week during this 4-month period." The Consorzio says that number is grossly overblown, and it sticks by its seven-times-a-year estimate.

Ammerman divides his time between Rome and Venice and his Hamilton, New York, home. He is media savvy and has been shown in several television documentaries on Venice rowing his *topo*, a small Venetian-style boat, through the city's canals. He has been filmed pointing out high-water marks on the Grand Canal's buildings, and rowing into flooded entry-ways awash during nearly every high-water incident.

In their efforts to date early historical activities in the area, he and geology professor Charles McClennen, also of Colgate, pioneered techniques for taking core samples from the lagoon's sediments. The pair first came to the attention of Italians involved in the struggle to save Venice in July 1999 when they, along with Maurizia De Min of Venice's Superintendency of Architecture, published in the June 1999 issue of *Antiquity* an article suggesting that early inhabitants of the lagoon ferried in soil to build up their islands to stay ahead of rising tides.

In a series of interviews with the international news media, lead author Ammerman went far beyond his role as an archaeologist and jumped into the middle of the political fray over the mobile gates, telling reporters that the multibillion-dollar mobile-gates project was doomed to failure. In the *Antiquity* article, the authors took to task noted Italian scientists who for decades have studied the lagoon and its rates of sinking as well as the rising of Adriatic water. In response, these Italians—most of whom are involved with Italy's National Research Council—criticized Ammerman's reliance on archaeological techniques. Such techniques, involving studies and carbon dating of materials found in various lagoon layers, they maintain, are less precise than their decades-long hydrological measurements of changes in relative sea level.

Ammerman's article suggests that the new dating techniques used on deep-lagoon fibers found in core samples show them at depths that in the misty past of millennia ago were once dry land. From this, the scientists concluded that until C.E. 400, relative sea level rose about three inches (7.6 centimeters) per century. Then the rate increased significantly to about five inches (12.7 centimeters) per century, and, in this century, has accelerated because of industrial development and global warming.

Then on August 25, 2000, Ammerman and McClennen came up with another bombshell in the form of the article in *Science*. In a subsequent statement the scientists said that they had been requested by *Science* editors to produce a "review of the current situation for the international scientific community." In it the pair wrote that because of global warming, the mobile gates, if built, would have to be raised with increasing frequency—not just the few hours every so often that the Consorzio predicts.

"During the time the gates are in use, the lagoon will be completely cut off from the sea," the article says. "Open circulation with the sea is essential to the life of the lagoon; after any one closing, it will take several tidal cycles to flush out the pollutants that accumulate from various sources and to restore the lagoon's equilibrium."

Ammerman and his colleague believe that the sea-level-rise scenarios considered by the Consorzio and supported by the College of Experts and other scientists are too low:

The impact studies conducted by the different agencies all used the same three scenarios for the rise in RSL [relative sea level] by the year 2100, the projected life of the gates. Because of a lack of knowledge at the time about the long-term trend in RSL for Venice, the low and middle scenarios (a rise of 4.4 cm and 16.8 cm, respectively) were based on attempts to

separate effects of earth subsidence from effects of the behavior of the Adriatic Sea. The only scenario to include a
consideration of global warming was the high one (53.4 cm),
which was treated as an extreme or unlikely case in the impact
studies.

The scenarios were based on a tide-gauge record at Venice
that spans only 26 years (1970–1996), and this constitutes the
fundamental weakness of the evaluation process. In light of
the high level of statistical noise in tide-gauge data, it is widely
held that one needs measurement over at least 40 years to
establish a reliable trend. The problem is that Venice's 100-
year tide-gauge record has been split into three pieces because
of the pumping [between 1929 and 1971] of ground water at
Porto Marghera. Neither the 1897–1929 nor the 1971–1996
piece is long enough in terms of oceanographic science for a
sound projection of change in RSL [relative sea level] at Venice over the next 100 years.

The article pointed out that the new low scenario for sea-
level rise by 2100, by their calculations, must be raised to 11.8
inches (30 centimeters). Ammerman bases this on his and
McClennen's archaeological work at six sites throughout the
lagoon that show the progression of rise they believe took place
between c.e. 400 and 1900.

> If we start with the average, long-term rise in RSL as a bas-
> eline (13 cm per century), add a safety margin (4 cm per
> century) and make a *minimal* allowance for global warming (13
> cm over the next 100 years), a value of 30 cm is obtained for
> new low projection of the rise in RSL. The worst-case sce-
> nario (high estimate) would be on the order of 100 cm.

That upper end of a 39-inch (100-centimeter) rise is close
to the 37-inch (ninety-five-centimeter) rise projected in 1997

by the Intergovernmental Panel on Climate Change. As 2000 was drawing to a close, the professor and his adherents were eagerly awaiting new IPCC data that Ammerman predicted could double his 11.8-inch (thirty-centimeter) projection to 23.4 inches (sixty centimeters).

"If this happens, it will blow the Consorzio out of the water," he said during a telephone conversation from his home in Venice in early October 2000. According such a scenario, he says, there is no way the Consorzio can justify building the gates because they would have to be up day after day, tide cycle after tide cycle—something Ammerman believes the lagoon cannot sustain.

The IPCC's projection, hinted at in a premature release in the late fall of 2000 of its scheduled early 2001 report, was not quite double. In its proposed summary for the 2001 report that was being circulated to scientists worldwide for review, the IPCC projected a sea-level rise between 5.5 and 31.5 inches (fourteen and eighty centimeters). That is a much lower range than its earlier reports issued in 1995 and 1997. But, while the range is narrower, the IPCC scientists did say in the proposed 2001 summary that the midpoint scenario would be 18.5 inches (forty-seven centimeters), higher than the early 11.8-inch (thirty-centimeter) projection, but lower than the 23.4 inches (sixty centimeters) Ammerman feared.

In the draft summary the IPCC scientists report that the upper range of global warming over the next one hundred years could be even higher than they estimated in 1995. At most, average global temperature could rise 11 degrees Fahrenheit (6 degrees Celsius) from where it was in 1990. In its 1995 analysis the worst-case scenario was a 6.3-degree Fahrenheit (3.5 degrees Celsius) temperature rise over the next century.

By comparison, a *New York Times* report on the IPCC's draft summary pointed out that average temperatures in 2000 are only nine degrees Fahrenheit (five degrees Celsius) warmer than they were at the end of the last ice age. In other words, it took ten thousand years for Earth's average temperature to increase by nine degrees (five degrees Celsius), and that average could rise eleven degrees Fahrenheit (six degrees Celsius) in just the next century.

By the end of 2000 the Consorzio refused to recognize media reports concerning the startling global-warming information in the IPCC's draft summary. It preferred to wait until that summary and the accompanying report had been reviewed, finalized, and published in early 2001. Consorzio spokeswoman Monica Ambrosini said, in November 2000: "The Consorzio will use only official data. We prefer to wait until the final report is published." When asked whether her organization would do a new environmental impact statement based on the anticipated IPCC revised numbers, she was noncommittal. "If we do a new VIA, we will consider the new numbers, but only if they are official."

From several conversations with Professor Ammerman throughout 2000—both at his home in Hamilton, New York, and in Venice and Rome—it has become clear that the scientist believes, as do many of his Venetian friends, that the Consorzio is only after the money involved in the massive lagoon construction projects, and in perpetuating itself over the nearly ten years it would take to design the Executive Project and actually build the gates. It is equally clear that the Consorzio resents the professor's interference and the attention his comments are getting in the world's press. Following publication of the *Science* article, he was the focus of a profile in the August 29, 2000, issue of *The New York Times*, and was sought out by Italian, French, and British journalists for interviews.

When I called the Consorzio to ask about its official reaction to Ammerman's and McClennen's postulates, its public relations department was swift in faxing a burning riposte, headlined "Two Americans Very Much Involved in Venice 'Business.'" Acid dripped from nearly every Consorzio word, awkwardly translated into English from text that is probably much better phrased in Italian. In the following quote, the Consorzio pointedly used "Mr." in referring to the two Ph.D.s. Italians, a polite people, generally go overboard in labeling just about anyone in a professional setting, including newspaper journalists, *"Dott."*—the Italian abbreviation of *Dottore* (doctor).

"Mr. Ammerman and Mr. McClennen, most probably very well qualified archaeologist and geologist, but, for sure more interested to the political and commercial implications of the matters related to the project for the flood defense of Venice, are back again to show them up."

Starting with "They succeed through articles of very low scientific value," the press office reaction challenged the professors' grasp of the facts of the progression of the MOSE project, pointing out, for example, that the professors stated in the *Science* article that MOSE was put forward in 1991, when it was really proffered in 1990. "Just in case the two professors are interested to know it, they can call the Consorzio Venezia Nuova Press Office," the statement continued.

The news release then speculated that in their article Ammerman and McClennen were "less concerned with the validity of scientific data than they [were] with attempting to persuade the Italian government to withdraw the concession granted to Italian construction companies engaged in the protection of Venice."

The remarkable reaction ended: "It is worthwhile to know that the two American authors don't suggest any alternative solution for the protection of Venice; they are only worried to obtain an international competition with other Companies and other researchers. As the eternal Toto [a popular Italian movie comedian] used to say: 'There's the rub.' "

The fireworks continued. After Ammerman got a copy of the Consorzio's release from *The New York Times*, he wrote a response challenging many of the organization's assertions, calling the Consorzio's statement a press office "exercise in damage control." He addressed each point in the statement and then concluded by saying why he and his coauthor had not suggested alternatives to the gates project:

The aim in writing the article was not to propose an alternative solution to [the gates]. It is our view that fresh ideas on the problem of flooding in Venice will come forward in the context of a new international competition. The purpose of the article in *Science* . . . was to review the current situation. It may be useful to reiterate here our basic position: 1) in light of what is known today, the environmental impact studies that have been done so far are seriously flawed; 2) there is, in consequence, a need for the environmental impact assessments to be redone; 3) the new evaluations should be undertaken by those without conflicts of interest; 4) it is essential to take the long view—both in looking back and in looking forward—in trying to save Venice.

Then, Ammerman took a direct shot at the organization.

Such a press release tends to raise fundamental questions about the seriousness and integrity of the Consorzio Venezia Nuova (in Italian, what would be called its *"attendabilità"*). Is such an organization really up to the difficult task of saving Venice?

Then came another article—in the October 2000 issue of *Civil Engineering*—this one written by members of the panel of experts hired by the Consorzio supervising agency, the Venice Magistrato alle Acque, to review the mid-1990s environmental study. These four took potshots at Ammerman and Mc-Clennen without mentioning their names. They faulted the pair for using archaeological versus hydrological data, concluding that their "information [was] nothing new."

"It is unfortunate that recent articles published in prominent American publications have disseminated misleading information about, and suggested an impractical solution to, the problem of flooding in Venice," the four scientists wrote. "The EIS [environmental impact study] and the design for the mobile gates take into account every aspect of predicted sea rise." They ended their article by pointing to the years of study that led to the stabilization and slight pulling back of the Leaning Tower of Pisa, which was reopened to the public in 2000. "Venice deserves no less," they concluded.

It is interesting that the four scientists in the *Civil Engineering* article referred in passing to an 11.8-inch (thirty-centimeter) rise in sea level expected over the next one hundred years. In their original report they had downplayed the likelihood of a rise that high, offering a possible rise of 7.8 inches (twenty centimeters) as part of a series of scenarios. Ammerman and his colleagues had prophesied a thirty-centimeter rise in their 2000 *Science* article, and in the interim the four reviewers in the *Civil Engineering* piece seem to have embraced the archaeologist's number.

Why does the American professor tilt at the Consorzio's giant entrenched windmill? Consorzio employees hint darkly that gates opponents must be driving his statements, but they grow strangely silent when an observer makes a similar speculation that the Consorzio must be behind the defenses raised by its so-called "independent" consultants.

Ammerman responds to the Consorzio's charge he is being driven by anti-gates interests, saying, simply: "It would be [irresponsible] to not say something. We [he and McClennen] went to give a little window of light. We want to see the interests of the city preserved, and those interests would be served by taking the longer view [beyond the gates]. Maybe it would be more important to renew the 'vision of Venice.' " By that Ammerman says he means the creation of a process whereby Venetians and the Italian government could find out what Venice should be for Venetians and the rest of the world, and then work on safeguards that match that vision. "It needs to be thrown into the arena," he says.

Basically, he says, the recent history of Venice and its region is a history of failed engineering: the creation of the industrial zone of Porto Marghera within sight of a sublime historic center that goes back one thousand years; and the Valjont dam, completed in 1959 in an unstable area near Belluno. In 1963, a landslide filled the reservoir and pushed mud and debris over the dam, burying Valjont and four smaller villages and killing more than 2,000 people.

"Those are strikes one and two" for Venice and the region, he says. "The gates could easily be strike three."

Emotions over the gates are certainly high. In late 2000 this atmosphere combined with the government's preoccupation with political survival to delay a decision about their construction, one way or the other.

The delays, of course, were met with satisfaction by the groups fighting the gates. They feel that if the decision is put off long enough, compelling evidence of much-higher-than-expected-sea-level rise will force a reevaluation of what is needed to protect the lagoon. Such a group is Italia Nostra, the Ralph Nader/Sierra Club–type organization that seeks to stop the project and, instead, save the lagoon through cultural means, rather than using technical solutions to save industry and tourism.

A 1998 article by Lidia Fersuoch, widely circulated by Italia Nostra as a document detailing its position regarding the gates, is entitled "Saving Venice and its Lagoon: Environmental and Morphological Rescue or Technology-driven Artificialization?"

"[T]he survival of Venice depends on cultural rather than technological decisions," Fersuoch writes. She says the lagoon has been seen over the last thirty years as an "undeveloped asset, an un-urbanized, outlying area of a great historic city, somewhere that can be exploited, built up and altered in response to contingent needs." For centuries, she says, the city and the lagoon survived in "osmotic" equilibrium. During the nineteenth century other interests prevailed, and human intervention upset the hydrogeological balance of the lagoon.

Instead of mobile gates Italia Nostra proposes that the

depths be reduced at the lagoon's three entrances and along the *canale dei petroli*, going so far as to suggest, "[W]e ought in any case have the courage to declare the Port as incompatible with a proper approach to the management of the lagoon." The group wants to see the jetties at the lagoon entrances redesigned to slow the speed of tides flowing inward, to restore land that had been filled in over the years to serve industrial needs, and to reopen fish farms to free-flowing tides, giving the incoming water more room to spread out, thereby easing the pressure of high water on the city.

There are more demands: Ban drilling for natural gas off the Venetian coast that could cause further subsidence of the soils under the lagoon; ban oil tankers from entering the port; shut down oil refineries at Marghera. . . . The list goes on.

As I read Ms. Fersuoch's report, I think of the incorrigible, unflappable Professor Gherardo Ortalli, whom I interviewed one morning in his office at the University of Venice where he teaches medieval history. Ortalli understands reality and what "fighting the good fight" is all about: It is not always about winning.

"I don't think we will win the battle for Venice," he says as he walks me to my waterbus stop along the Grand Canal. "The town doesn't exist anymore. But I hope I will save my soul fighting the good fight. I have lost many friends who believe in and sustain the gates." His voice trails off, he shakes my hand, turns abruptly, and strides back to his office, filled with students waiting to take their oral exams.

Hard on the heels of bitter exchanges during the late summer and fall of 2000, the government in early October released its proposed budget, with more attention to vote-getting tax cuts. Money for design or construction of the gates was not included. After all, the regional court ruling against the environment minister's decree was waiting to be appealed, and the project, for the time being, was frozen.

The Center-Left government of Giuliano Amato was desperate to hold on to power as new elections threatened to replace the Center-Left with the Center-Right leader Silvio Berlusconi as prime minister. Amato promised Italians tax cuts and benefits worth some 41 trillion lire (18 billion dollars). The government pledged to cut 13 trillion lire by the end of 2000 and 28 trillion lire in taxes during 2001. The attempt was futile. Berlusconi became prime minister in the May 2001 election.

The Economist introduced its story about the proposal this way: "It is the most generous budget for a very long time, says the government; a cheap electoral ploy, sneers the opposition. In any event, Italy's taxpayers, for the most part, seem pleased." If parliament were to approve the cuts and the benefits improvements—cheaper medicines, more generous child benefits—the average Italian family would be around four hundred dollars better off. In fact, no sooner had the Amato government made its tax-cut promises in late September than a survey showed that Italy's consumer confidence index had risen during October. Financial experts had expected a decline.

CHAPTER THIRTEEN ~

Will Venice Survive?

Venice is like a person trying to run forward [by] looking backwards: "[Look at] how good we were; how great we were!" Venice is trapped between a huge past and no future.

—PROFESSOR ANDREA RINALDO

It rained across northern and central Italy most of November 6, 2000. I watched the somber, wet countryside swirl past the train window during my nearly five-hour train ride from Rome to Venice, stepping off the high-speed Eurostar in Venice's Santa Lucia *stazione* as moisture slanted down between the panels of the giant station roof. In front of the station, where the Grand Canal is sheltered by Venice's delightful, romantic, and sadly crumbling buildings, I climbed aboard the number 51 *vaporetto* for the twenty-minute ride along the Giudecca Canal and across St. Mark's Basin to my Lido hotel. Over the next five days in Venice I would need to wrap up final interviews, and, checking the tide charts prior to my trip, I did not expect to see significantly high water. The full moon would not appear until November 11, when I would be in Rome. For this night, November 6, the astronomical calendar informed me that the tide would peak around eight-thirty in the evening at a mere 12 inches (thirty-one centimeters) above relative sea level. That is well under the 27.5-inch (seventy-centimeter) mark when St. Mark's Square just in front of the basilica begins filling with water.

Reality in the form of a blast of salty lagoon water hit me full force in the face just as the waterbus turned into the exposed, wide-open Giudecca from the protected Canale Scomenzera, which parallels Venice's Tronchetto ship landing. Tasting the not-unpleasant tinge of salt, but with my clothes and luggage dripping, I scurried backward into the aft compartment doorway, where I stayed for the rest of the rough-and-tumble journey. I peered up through the legs of drenched souls who continued to brave the trip on the *vaporetto's* deck. These must be true Venetians, I thought, hardy souls who know that getting wet on occasion is a normal part of living in this city. A small boy, about eight and wrapped in oilskins and rubber boots, delighted in holding on to a handle welded to the cabin's outer wall and taking the full force of each breaking wave head-on, greeting each blast with a squeal of delight. From my drier position, I could see the lagoon's water beginning to pour over the city's pavements at places where work crews had not yet raised them to withstand four-foot-high tides.

A few hours later, from the deck of the lagoon's larger people ferry, the *Concordia*, I would witness the seventh highest *acqua alta* episode of the past 105 years as it washed over 93 percent of the historic city. By 9 P.M., the water would top out at an astounding 4.7 feet (1.44 meters) above relative sea level, floating the *passarelle* that city workers had hopelessly set into place hours earlier. This uprooting of the raised-walkway system put scrambling Venetians and tourists alike thigh deep in the water along the city's streets and *fondamente*.

If I, at five feet eight, had been unfortunate enough to be standing directly in front of St. Mark's Basilica at the storm tide's height, the water would have reached above my hips. (In 1966 it would have come just below my armpits.)

The Venetians, like the little boy on the *vaporetto*, were prepared. In addition to the boots they usually carry, some also pressed into service large plastic garbage bags tightly tape-wrapped around their legs. Visitors, who generally have no idea what is happening, are, like me, forced to make do with soaked legs and defenseless walking shoes. Those with deep enough pockets to stay in the luxury hotels are usually handed boots as they exit the glittering lobbies. Even that would not have worked this evening, though; the tops of those calf-high boots would have been submerged in the area around St. Mark's Square. Even the Lido was not spared. To get to the *Concordia*'s heaving deck so I could observe this phenomenon firsthand, I had to wade through ankle-deep water in the Piazzetta Santa Maria Elisabetta. Stunned Lido residents on their way to the St. Mark's landing waited apprehensively for crews to throw down makeshift walkways—an experience they usually do not have to endure on that much higher, and better-defended, barrier island.

As I rode the *Concordia* to the landing near St. Mark's Square, I watched as the ferry's commander struggled to make landfall to pick up several hundred passengers stranded on the dock and surrounded by high water—from the deep St. Mark's Basin before them and the submerged city pavements behind. It took the commander, fighting the high waves and winds, three tries to make the pier. One man, a Venetian who works in the historic center and was going home to the Lido via the *Concordia*'s return trip, muttered darkly as he finally struggled through the crowd and took his position next to me on deck.

"I have not seen it so bad for a long, long time," said this *acqua alta* veteran. "If this wind and rain continue through the night and the next tide comes in tomorrow morning behind such a force, it will be a disaster—worse than 1966."

It did not happen that way. I kept my window open through the night, listening to the drumming rain. The wind stopped about ten o'clock, the rain about two o'clock in the morning. Daylight dawned with a few scattered clouds that tried but failed to hide a blue sky. Venetians and tourists were able to walk the damp streets, and shop owners spent the morning mopping out their ground-level stores. They knew the drill. They had removed merchandise from the floors the night before, setting it above the water's reach.

That morning I walked across St. Mark's Square, where intermittent pools of water were slowly disappearing down the drains. As the last few gallons vanished through stone slots set in the bumpy, irregular piazza, an outdoor orchestra struck up a rollicking show tune, corn sellers surrounded by hundreds of pigeons appeared on the drying pavement, and the city began a new day.

"It is amazing that the whole city is anywhere near normal the day after, but it is," Venice resident and photographer Sarah Quill, an English woman, told me a few days later.

Her observation was most appropriate. In the years since the 1966 flood, most residents have abandoned the ground floors of buildings and moved either upstairs or to the mainland, and ground-floor shop owners place steel barriers in doorways to block high water. Electrical and telephone boxes are now near ceiling height in ground-floor rooms, well above the highest possible water. If a 6.3-foot (1.94-meter) flood hit the city today, it would be slightly more dramatic than the 1.44-meter event I witnessed, but nothing like what happened in 1966, when the city went dark and was isolated for days on end.

In the days following the 1.44-meter *acqua granda*, I pieced together details of what had actually happened meteorologically. I learned that water at that level occurs on average only once every six years. High water at 3.6 feet to four feet (1.10–1.20 meters), which I had witnessed on April 5, 2000, usually occurs two or three times a year, and once every two or three years it hits the 4.2-foot (1.30-meter) level. (Venice's biggest-ever-recorded flood of November 4–5, 1966, at 1.94 meters, had occurred thirty-four years and two days before my November 6, 2000, adventure.)

City officials and technicians in the Venice Center for Tidal Forecasts were caught by surprise by the magnitude of the November 2000 storm. The astronomical high-tide level had long ago been calculated at only twelve inches (thirty-one centimeters) above relative sea level. With no storm and regular weather, water would not even have come up in the city's lowest spot, St. Mark's Square. But the unexpected storm heaped millions of tons of water, which represented an additional 3.7 feet (1.13 meters), on top of that relatively low high tide. Then sirocco winds from the south, clocked at sixty miles an hour, pushed the additional water up the Adriatic and through the lagoon's Lido entrance. From there the water smashed against Venice's historic center and, as in 1966, the sirocco gales held it there.

Venice mayor Paolo Costa's assistant, Guido Moltedo, told me the next day that the surprise was so complete that if the mobile gates had been in place, they would probably have been raised too late to stop the highest water. And had they been raised, I learned later, they would have had little effect on the nineteen-foot-high waves recorded at the Lido mouth or the twenty-five-foot-high waves recorded in the Adriatic, a half mile away.

Another factor would have made the gates useless for this particular storm: The water during this highly individualistic event was, because of the wind, much higher in the lagoon than it was in the Adriatic. If the gates had been raised, they would have prevented the water from flowing back into the much lower sea. At 3:40 that afternoon, about the time I was wetly making my way across the lagoon from the train station to the Lido, forecasters expected a 3.6-foot (1.10-meter) tide to hit at 8:30 P.M. At the time of that forecast, the water was 33.8 inches (86 centimeters) above relative sea level at the tidal gauge located at the Church of Santa Maria della Salute, across from St. Mark's Square, 26.7 inches (68 centimeters) at the Lido entrance, and only 24 inches (62 centimeters) a half mile out to sea, where Italy maintains a tidal research station.

The water through the afternoon and evening continued to rise, but levels in the lagoon were between four and eight inches (ten and twenty centimeters) higher than at the Lido and a half mile beyond, in the Adriatic. Forty-five minutes before the 4.7-foot (1.44-meter) peak that hit at nine o'clock, water at the Salute was at 1.42, at the Lido entrance 1.31, and at the research station on the sea, 1.14 meters.

This information undercuts the mayor's call in the newspapers the following day when he demanded that the national government make a decision about the gates. WE NEED THE

MOSE—YOU HAVE TO DECIDE, rang the headline in the Venice newspaper, *Il Gazzettino*. His implication was that the gates would have prevented this event. The reality of the situation was the opposite: The gates would have made it worse. One critic, speaking in Rome five days later, said the November 6, 2000, *acqua alta* was "the best evidence why the gates should not be built."

As usually happens in Venice, the high water of November 6, 2000, will be forgotten. Merchandise was protected. No one died in the city. The water, as usual, went down. During the height of the massive storm, newspapers reported that seven people were killed in related flooding elsewhere across Europe.

Venice bends.

For more than one thousand years, it has sat on the mud of a lagoon that is bathed twice daily by the waters of the Adriatic. It is held softly in that mud by the hundreds of thousands of fingers of petrified tree trunks, upon which craftsmen centuries ago laid stone barriers against the elements. But no matter how much stone was heaped on over the past millennia, the buildings hold fast.

Even when there is an earthquake nearby—like the 1977 quake near Friuli, fewer than one hundred miles to the north, in which one thousand people died—Venice barely seems to notice. A longtime Venice resident described the experience this way: "Here, it was certainly unpleasant, but we rocked a bit and swayed and perhaps settled somewhat. But nothing collapsed. This is a city built in the mud, and it is flexible. It rebounds."

Venice will probably rebound for decades. Many view the

mobile gates as a short-term solution. Continual delays in their construction, rising opposition to them within Italy, a growing awareness of global warming worldwide, and a concern for environmental issues that was not present when the Consorzio Venezia Nuova was created in the early 1980s—all combine to put the gates' future in jeopardy.

"We are at the stage of unequal equilibrium," says venerable Italian scientist Roberto Frassetto, a member of the team that came up with the gates concept in the early 1970s. "One slight push will take us ahead, or it will stop everything."

A prominent Italian senator, Giorgio Sartor, who happens to be the Veneto's lawmaker, wants to stop the gates project. With his Green Party colleagues, he has launched a major campaign to remove control of the safeguarding of the lagoon from the Consorzio. They want the massive undertaking placed in the public hands of the Planning Office—*ufficio di piano*—of technical experts from the various regional, city, and national agencies and ministries.

During an interview in Rome in mid-November 2000, Sartor waxed philosophic: "This range of the lagoon's individuality—for example, the November 6 [2000] *acqua alta* was very individual and unlike any other storm before it—cannot be reduced to one simple engineering answer like the gates."

The Planning Office, he believes, would launch a major effort over the next five to ten years to come up with long-range proposals—perhaps even what some refer to as "the Dutch solution," or a series of dikes around portions of the lagoon, similar in concept to dikes in the Netherlands. Supporters describe the concept in this way: The lagoon would be separated from the Adriatic by dikes, broken up by a series of "locks" that would allow a controlled exchange of water between the lagoon and the sea. In this scenario Porto Marghera would be cleansed of pollutants; the historical city would get a long-awaited, traditional sewage system that would carry urban sewage to treatment plants on the mainland. This almost unbelievable concept, Sartor hopes, would be constructed within the next quarter century, as seas fueled by global warming rise dramatically.

Sartor says it is important, whatever the solution, that this *ufficio di piano* come up with and direct the interventions to safeguard Venice—not the for-profit, privately owned Consorzio.

His and his colleagues' plan in late 2000 was to tie their support of any future governing coalition to the Venice question. He says he proposed to Prime Minister Amato that over the four months between November 2000 and February 2001, Amato decree that the Planning Office receive funds from the special laws for Venice and take over the planning for lagoon interventions. All this was on hold by mid-2001 in the wake of Berlusconi's victory.

Sartor also asked Amato to emphasize interventions other than the gates—reducing the depth of the *canale dei petroli* entrance at Malamocco, reopening the cordoned-off fish farms to the ebb and flow of the tides—and building a loading-unloading station for oil tankers that would be tied by a pipeline to Marghera—proposals all on hold since the elections.

The oil tanker issue is a particularly troublesome one for environmentalists. In early December 2000, a 37,000-ton tanker from Malta ran into shallow sandbanks during low tide in the Canale Malamocco. The ship was not damaged, but Center-Left environmental minister Willer Bordon—a former mayor of Muggia, located near the port city of Trieste—directed that all single-hull tankers carrying dangerous or polluting materials would be banned from the lagoon beginning in 2001. The Coast Guard followed up on Bordon's directive, issuing the single-hull decree on February 22, 2001. (For the record, the Maltese ship, *Sea Bravery II*, has a double hull.)

Also, Sartor wanted it ultimately agreed that Venice will share its petroleum-hub responsibilities with Ravenna to the south and Trieste to the northeast. This, he says, will "spread out" the danger that Venice faces from spills in its current role as petroleum hub for the northern Adriatic.

If the government did this by February, Sartor says it would be difficult for a successor government, even one of the Center-Right, to reverse it and "go backward." All was on hold by mid-2001.

Amato, before he left office in May 2001, did not approve the gates or the Executive Project. To move forward, the government will have no choice but to redo the environmental impact study. This, Sartor says, will open the door to coming up with solutions more long term than the mobile gates, solutions that will last a century rather than just a few decades.

Engineers and scientists have their pet ideas about saving Venice. They offer technical solutions and, given the nature of the professions involved, different people usually come up with conflicting ideas. Those operating in the field of precision science, such as hydrologists, usually resent social scientists, such as archaeologists, for interfering. Their methods are not scientific enough, the hydrologists say.

Italian politicians, in turn, tend not to want to go out on long limbs for such a costly and massive undertaking that—in the face of weather and global-warming trends—may not work. They, like their colleagues in the United States and elsewhere, generally only worry about the next election, not the next decade. The concept in Italy of slashing taxes and improving benefits for citizens just before an election tends to win votes; building controversial mobile gates for Venice does not necessarily win votes.

So, short of a major flooding disaster in Venice equal to or greater than the *acqua granda* of November 1966, the decision to build or not to build mobile gates languished throughout much of 2001. It simply remains too expensive and too controversial within Italy and without to come to an easy resolution soon without a major flooding event to propel politicians forward. Berlusconi talks instead of a bridge linking the toe of Italy to Sicily and of improving highways.

The less controversial work on the city's infrastructure, along with the reinforcement of the barrier islands, improvements on Piazza San Marco's drainage system, and other lagoon improvements, is likely to progress. This is work that should have been routine for decades and, if the Venetian Republic's original defenders were still in charge, such improvements would have been commonplace. Now that the city's former economic greatness is nothing but a fondly remembered dream, its problems have lost their urgency in a world eager to move forward.

But Venice is facing a reality—a reality that dozens of other coastal cities are facing worldwide: The seas are warming and sea level is rising. The Intergovernmental Panel on Climate Change, which represents the views and findings of hundreds of scientists, says such a rise is inevitable. And, it says, even if greenhouse gases were brought under control tomorrow, it would still take centuries to reverse the impact that twentieth-century industrialization has had on the planet.

The IPCC's reports make clear one reality: What scientists

and engineers are offering in their efforts to save the dream Venice hopes to recapture are at best short-term solutions for the city and its dwindling number of inhabitants.

Long-range solutions, such as the "Dutch solution," are seldom discussed in the heated debate over the mobile gates. This lack of farther-reaching discussion concerns one Venice watcher who studied the lagoon and the potential impacts the various solutions would have on it, and then wrote a remarkable treatise on the subject.

Meghna Chakrabarti, who in 2000–2001 was in Harvard University's graduate program of Environmental Science and Risk Management, produced the report as part of completing her honors B.S. in environmental engineering at Oregon State University in 1998. She raises some interesting issues.

She points out that solutions such as the gates are single-function in nature. They stress only flood control. Meanwhile as we have seen, Venice is a city beset with numerous problems: a declining, aging population; too many tourists; too much industrial pollution. By focusing on the gates for more than thirty years, from the early 1970s to 2001, such "limited thinking snuffed out the possibility for quantum leaps in the revitalization of Venice," Chakrabarti believes.

Engineering solutions certainly are necessary, as the four environmental-assessment reviewers stressed in their *Civil Engineering* article supporting the gates, but she encourages decision makers to go several steps farther.

Once built, she writes, the gates would not solve the sea-rise problem; they would merely prolong Venice's ultimate demise. Instead the city must consider "enduring solutions,"

solutions arrived at in the context of the city and its people— not just technical ones.

"[T]he true salvation of Venice is in the return of her people, and a redevelopment of *residential* will to rescue Venice. Saving the city calls for nothing short of complete urban renewal." Get Venetians back into Venice, she is saying. And when they reclaim ownership of their city from the tourists and global interests that now hold it, Chakrabarti believes that the Venetians will see to it that it is cared for. If this means making it more livable by controlling tourism, so be it.

In e-mail communications during the fall of 2000, she amplified this theme: "Irritating Anglo-European (and now, American) arrogance" fosters the belief that "Italians are an old society, old and past its prime," she says, adding that such thinking misses the point entirely. Chakrabarti says we should be asking instead: "Can *we*—the rest of the world—be trusted to save the city when it can only truly be saved by her own residents? The real point is that saving Venice is not an Italian issue, but a Venetian one. Whether or not a fragmented national government can organize itself is not important. What is important is whether or not the Venetians have the will to live. If they do, then *any* long-term plan is potentially successful."

EPILOGUE ~

Just before this book was scheduled to go to the printer, the *Italy Daily* headline grabbed my attention. "Rome OKs Venetian Dyke Plan." It sat over the page-one story, written by the English-language paper's managing editor, Christopher Emsden, chronicling a December 6, 2001, announcement from Italy's capital. The news—repeated the morning of December 7 in newspapers all across Italy—caught most mobile-gates supporters and opponents equally by surprise.

After twelve years of high-pitched wrangling and debate, the Center-Right government of Silvio Berlusconi said yes to the controversial plan, now estimated to cost 3 billion euros ($2.67 billion), to put submerged gates at the three mouths of the Venetian lagoon—gates that designers promise will rise from beneath the waves on command to block storm-driven tides that frequently surge up the Adriatic Sea.

The announcement came just nine months after the *Comitatone*—created by Berlusconi's Center-Left predecessors to safeguard the lagoon—had told state-created construction giant Consorzio Venezia Nuovo that it could not proceed with the Executive Project to design the gates. The May 2001 elections had decisively shifted power in Italy from Left to Right—a shift the Consorzio desperately needed to build one of the most ambitious projects in modern European history.

Gates opponents and members of the environment-oriented Green Party—which has no influence or seat of power in the new conservative government—were as dismayed by the December 6 announcement as proponents were thrilled.

Associated Press writer Peter Mayer quoted Green Party official Luana Zanella: "It is deeply perplexing that so many resources are concentrated in a project questioned by the scientific community." Mayer then quoted Gaetano Benedetto, an official of the World Wildlife Fund's (WWF) Italian branch: "Today the city's destiny rests on a pretentious, costly, and environmentally harmful technological gamble."

Benedetto's reaction could hardly be unexpected. In March 2001, the WWF had held a conference in the Sala del Piovego of the Doges' Palace—the room where Venetians traditionally laid out the body of a newly departed doge—on the subject of "Venice and Its Future." During the session, the Consorzio was openly attacked.

Mobile-gates supporters and officials in the new Center-Right government matched the opponents' rhetoric in intensity.

Italy Daily quoted Giancarlo Galan, president of the Veneto Region and member of Berlusconi's Forza Italia (Go Italy!) party, as saying: "December 6 will be a historic day for Venice. The whole world will applaud, and only makers of galoshes will be sad." Galan, who said he believed MOSE was necessary to make Venice "a place where it is possible to live," then made a remarkable prediction. He said the gates would be in operation by 2009.

That would be a major feat indeed, even if all the money to build the project were immediately available and MOSE moved forward with no further challenges—both unlikely prospects. The Consorzio has long said it would take two to three years to complete the final design phase known as the Executive Project, and up to ten years to actually build the gates.

Venice mayor Paolo Costa, who believes Venice's problems are tied to subsidence and not global warming, wasted little time following the announcement to attack gates critic and archaeologist Albert Ammerman. "I can assume he knows everything about the past, but not about global warming," Costa was quoted by Veneto-based consultant Dominic Standish in an *Italy Daily* op-ed piece on December 10.

At this point, it is important to note that the Italian government, throughout the more than thirty-five years since the *aqua granda* of 1966, has made many dramatic announcements about solving Venice's high-water problem, and regularly promised billions of lire to get the job done. As we have seen, great quantities of appropriated money either disappeared or were hijacked for projects or problems elsewhere. The 3 billion euros for the mobile gates are not in Italy's 2002 national budget, and no one is really clear where that money will come from—particularly in light of the Berlusconi government's promises to launch an ambitious country-long highway-improvement program, and to build a massive bridge across the Straits of Messina, connecting the toe of Italy's boot to Sicily.

One astute, long-time observer of the Italian way of doing things told me a few days after the announcement: "The new government is eager to announce it is changing the world and is a 'can do' outfit. Consequently they wanted to put an end to the endless MOSE debate, as they do also with the Messina bridge project. And since they are optimism mongers, they want to say

yes to both! Unfortunately, there is not an abundance of money.
And as you know, [in Italy] there are lots of announcements and
little actual progress. I would be skeptical of the announcement."

Keeping that admonition in mind, the government's December 6, 2001, decision was not, as many believed, a blanket
approval for the gates, but approval of a step-by-step process
toward creating the 79 steel flaps. The prime minister's cabinet
essentially voted to go ahead with the Executive Project. Once
that is completed in two years or so, government ministers will
decide whether to proceed with actual construction. Court
challenges will inevitably erupt to delay the process even further. And as any close observer of the Italian scene knows,
there could easily be a new government sitting in Rome two
years from now. Certainly, several governments could come
and go before the first MOSE flap is ever fabricated.

But as *Italy Daily*'s Emsden reported in his newspaper's December 7 edition, Berlusconi's environment minister, Altero
Matteoli, sitting in the same chair occupied by the man who
just months earlier had refused to support the MOSE project,
vowed that the gates approval included a commitment to respect "all environmental guarantees."

Aides to the minister later said that Matteoli had insisted
on corollary measures, "such as banning oil tankers from the
lagoon"—a dramatic step long called for by the Green Party
and cultural/environmental group Italia Nostra—"and building
a new offshore platform connected to refineries by an underwater pipeline," *Italy Daily* reported.

In addition, regional President Galan indicated that Insula's
work on raising *fondamente* and dredging canals in the historic
center's interior would continue. The Consorzio remains involved in a 24-million-dollar project to renovate the underground drainage system in St. Mark's Square, with an eye

toward significantly reducing the impact of high-tide floods that enter the heavy tourist area almost daily throughout the winter. Whether this project involving Venice's prime visitor destination will begin soon and be free from criticism is anyone's guess.

And portions of the city are being prepped for a major makeover. In 2002 crews are scheduled to begin demolishing decrepit warehouses and storage terminals in Venice's rundown sections. Spanish architect Enrico Miralles Moya has been selected to redesign the area with buildings that local officials hope will lure back former residents who have abandoned the crumbling city.

A lot has happened since I last sat in Costa's office in early November 2000. There, the left-leaning mayor, generally at political odds with his right-leaning prime minister, predicted that then-Prime Minister Amato would likely deflect the gates decision—Costa referred to it as a *patata bollente*, literally, a "boiling potato," or the Italian equivalent of "hot potato"— onto a successor. Amato did just that and, seven months after the May 2001 elections, Berlusconi apparently grabbed the blistering tuber and was holding on.

During an interview with CNN.com Europe correspondent Craig Francis—published on December 7, 2000—about Venice's plans for its rejuvenation, Costa echoed sentiments expressed to me in one form or another by nearly all the people I talked with during two years of working on this story—people who, no matter what side they are on regarding the Consorzio and the gates, all love Venice and worry over either its fate or its future.

"We risk disappearing due to excess love," Costa told Francis. "All those who are using Venice for their own interests must make a contribution to preserve the myth."

ACKNOWLEDGMENTS ~

As with any project of this magnitude, help from many different directions made it possible. For thanks, I begin with my son Todd Keahey, of Casa Grande, Arizona, who accompanied me to Rome and Venice on my final information-gathering trip in November 2000, and raised many important issues during my interviews with key players. With me, he experienced the historic 1.44-meter *acqua alta* and saw as I did just what Venice can increasingly expect to face over the next century as global warming pushes sea levels to new heights.

I thank everyone who took the time to speak with me: the scientists from a variety of disciplines, the historians, arts preservationists, engineers, ordinary Venetians, and non-Italians. While many disagree about the solutions for Venice's woes, all hold it as an ideal and lament its loss of residents and identity as a "real" city. I heard over and over again from these lovers of everything Venetian how the city must find its soul in order to survive. Once the soul is found, they believe, the technical solutions will become known.

I particularly thank Meghna Chakrabarti, whom I never met face-to-face, but with whom I had an e-mail correspondence that broadened my perspective and taught me to look at Venice beyond the technical solutions proposed for the city's survival. And I thank Stefano Della Sala of the Venice Port Authority for putting me in touch with her, and for hosting my son and me at a lunch in Venice at which I finally began to grasp the depth of the problems the city is facing in finding solutions to keep it alive.

Closer to home, I must express gratitude to friends without whom this would have been a much more difficult undertaking. First, I thank Bill Slaughter of Salt Lake City, a historian and archivist who read my very rough first draft and made critical suggestions that I took to heart and incorporated in this book, including some painful cuts he suggested. It is better because of what he did, on very short notice. His humor and joy in everyday life sustained me through stressful insecure months.

Second, I thank Ann Larsen and Paul Larsen, who, on numerous weekends throughout 2000, turned their central Utah home over to me—a home intentionally without telephone or television— where I could work undisturbed away from the usual weekend pressures and to-do lists at my abode in Salt Lake City. Theirs is a place of comfort, silence, and solitude, where I could relax by walking through green fields, observe artists at work, and gaze with delight each night at a sky full of stars—something I could never see in my brightly lit home city. Their generosity made this project much easier.

I also thank my good friend Jacob Korg of the University of Washington, Seattle, whose ongoing encouragement helped sustain me.

Once again, I thank my thoughtful partner, Connie Disney, who continued to throw her full support and faith into this project, as she has done so many times in the past. She continues to put up with the clutter that surrounds a project of this magnitude and with my absences during long weeks in Italy and numerous weekends in central Utah, and she always keeps the love and encouragement flowing.

SELECTED BIBLIOGRAPHY ~

Agenzia ANSA. *Venice 1966–1996: 30 Years of Protection as Covered by the Press*. Rome: ANSA Dossier, 1997.

Ammerman, A. J., C. E. McClennen, M. De Min, and R. Housley. "Sea-Level Change and the Archaeology of Early Venice." *Antiquity* 73 (1999): 303–12.

Ammerman, Albert J., and Charles E. McClennen. "Saving Venice." *Science*, Aug. 25, 2000.

Broad, William J. "That Sinking Feeling: Digging into Venice's History Casts Pall on Plan to Save City." *The New York Times*, Aug. 29, 2000.

Brown, Patricia Fortini. "The Self Definition of the Venetian Republic." In *City States in Classical Antiquity and Medieval Italy*, edited by A. Molho et al. 511–27. Ann Arbor: University of Michigan Press, 1991.

Caniato, Giovanni. "Venetian Boats: A Heritage to Be Preserved." *Ligabue Magazine* 15, no. 28 (1996).

Carbognin, Laura, and Giovanni Cecconi. *The Lagoon of Venice: Environment, Problems, Remedial Measures*. Prepared for Meeting on Environmental Sedimentology, Venice, Oct. 27–29, 1997.

Chakrabarti, Meghna. "Saving *La Serenissima*: A Case Study of Pollution, Its Effects on, and Remediation of Venice, Italy." Corvallis: Oregon State University, 1998.

Debray, Régis. *Against Venice*. Translated by Philip Wohlstetter. Berkeley, Calif.: North Atlantic Books, 1999.

The Economist. "Payback Time," Oct. 7, 2000.

Emsden, Christopher. "Rome OKs Venetian Dyke Plan." *Italy Daily*, Dec. 7, 2001.

Fay, Stephen, and Phillip Knightley. *The Death of Venice*. New York: Praeger Publishers, 1976.

Francis, Craig. "Venice to Have Modern Makeover." CNN.com Europe, Dec. 7, 2000.

Gambolati, Giuseppe, et al. "Coastal Evolution of the Upper Adriatic Sea due to Sea Level Rise and Natural and Anthropic Land Subsidence." *CENAS*. Amsterdam: Kluwer Academic Publishers, 1997.

Ghetti, Augusto, and Michel Batisse. "The Overall Protection of Venice and Its Lagoon." *Nature and Resources*, October–December 1983. Paris: UNESCO Publications, 1983.

Gilbert, Stuart, and Ray Horner. *The Thames Barrier*. London: Thomas Telford Ltd., 1992.

Grundy, Milton. Preface by John Julius Norwich. *Venice: An Anthology Guide*. Over Wallop, Hants., England: BAS Printers Ltd., 1998.

Harleman, Donald R. F., Rafael L. Bras, Andrea Rinaldo, and Paola Malanotte. "Blocking the Tide." *Civil Engineering*, Oct. 2000.

Heaney, Seamus. *Beowulf: A New Verse Translation*. New York: W. W. Norton & Company, 2000.

Huang, Shaopeng, Henry N. Pollack, and Po-Yu Shen. "Temperature Trends over the Past Five Centuries Reconstructed from Borehole Temperatures." *Nature*, Feb. 17, 2000.

International Herald Tribune. "Ice Records of Fur Traders Show Earth Is Warming," Sept. 8, 2000.

Kurlantzick, Joshua. "A Sea of Concerns as Bangkok Slowly Sinks." *Christian Science Monitor*, Sep. 15, 2000.

Macadam, Alta. Blue Guide. *Northern Italy: From the Alps to Bologna*. London: A. & C. Black Ltd., 1998.

Mayer, Peter W. "Italy OKs Venice Tide Barrier Plan." The Associated Press, Dec. 6, 2001.

McPhee, John. *The Control of Nature*. New York: Noonday Press (Farrar, Straus & Giroux), 1989.

Meccoli, Sandro. *La battaglia per Venezia*. Milan: Sugarco Edizioni, 1977.

Morris, Jan. *The Venetian Empire: A Sea Voyage*. London: Penguin Books Ltd., 1990.

———. *The World of Venice*. New York: Harcourt Brace & Company, 1995.

Morton, H. V. *A Traveller in Rome*. London: Methuen & Co. Ltd., 1957.

Muir, Edward. *Civic Ritual in Renaissance Venice*. Princeton, N.J.: Princeton University Press, 1981.

New Civil Engineer. "Time to Stem the Tide," July 25–Aug. 3, 2000.

Nicol, D. M. *Byzantium and Venice.* Cambridge, England: Cambridge University Press, 1988.

Norwich, John Julius. *A History of Venice.* New York: Vintage Books (Random House, Inc.), 1989.

Officer, Charles, and Jake Page. *Earth and You: Tales of the Environment.* Portsmouth, N.H.: Peter E. Randall, Publisher, 2000.

Quill, Sarah. With an introduction by Alan Windsor. *Ruskin's Venice: The Stones Revisited.* Aldershot, Hants., England: Ashgate Publishing, 2000.

Recer, Paul. "Study of Freeze-Thaw Records Heats Up Global Warming Debate." *The Salt Lake Tribune,* Sept. 8, 2000.

Revkin, Andrew C. "Scientists Now Acknowledge Role of Humans in Climate Change." *The New York Times,* Oct. 26, 2000.

Robinson, Charles A., Jr. *Ancient History.* New York: Macmillan Company, 1967.

Ruskin, John. Edited by J. G. Links. *The Stones of Venice.* New York: Da Capo Press, 1960.

Salti, Stefania, and Renata Venturini. Translated by Steven Cooper. *The Life of Galla Placidia.* Ravenna: Edizioni Stear, 1999.

Sediari, Michela. "Rereading the Ancient Sources on Venice." Abstract, presented October 5, 2001, at Colgate University, Hamilton, N.Y.

Standish, Dominic. "Environmentalists Can't Save Venice." *Italy Daily,* Dec. 10, 2001.

Stevens, William K. "Researchers Find Ocean Temperature Rising, Even in the Depths." *The New York Times,* Mar. 24, 2000.

Suplee, Curt. "Unraveling Riddles of Global Warming." *The Washington Post.* Feb. 24, 2002.

Watson, Robert T., Marufu C. Zinyowera, and Richard H. Moss, eds. *Climate Change 1995: Impacts, Adaptations and Mitigation of Climate Change: Scientific-Technical Analyses:* Cambridge, England: Cambridge University Press, 1996.

———. "The Regional Impacts of Climate Change: An Assessment of Vulnerability." Summary for policymakers; published for the Intergovernmental Panel on Climate Change, Nov. 1997.

Wright, Rupert, and Chris Endean. "Going Under: The Protection Racket That's Sinking Venice." *The European,* Nov. 23–29, 1998.

Zorzi, Alvise. *Venice: The Golden Age, 697–1797.* New York: Abbeville Press, 1980.

INDEX ~